ACCLAIM FOR
GOOD FROM FAR, FAR FROM GOOD

"Chula's adventurous story resonates with all of us who live life to the fullest."

— **RICHARD COHN,** author, *Journey of Love*, publisher, Beyond Words Publishing

"A fascinating read. Chula Harrison has a lot of love and spirit to give and share."

— **ANN RAYSON,** University of Hawai'i associate professor of English (ret.)

"'Don't people write their memoirs when they are about to make *(die)?' This was my response to Chula when she told me about her book. After reading it, I like to think of her memoir as only Part One. This is her story of growing up in Hawai'i during the good times after World War II. Of course, one would expect her story to be racy and naughty, with some of the names changed to protect their families. However, this is also a story of her intriguing life and family, with its ups and downs. Cleverly woven throughout are her lessons in life and her keen observations about self-realization, acceptance and forgiveness. Personal relationships are laid bare— not with the thought of hurting anyone, but perhaps as a nidus for self-help. This is not just about her but more importantly, her way of reaching out to touch and help others. Oprah, are you there?"*

— **DR. ARTHUR KAMISUGI,** Honolulu orthodontist, sailor and fisherman

Other books by Chula:

Cucumber Seeds Don't Sprout Radishes
Joy Can Be Your Favorite Song

GOOD FROM FAR, FAR FROM GOOD

A LOVE STORY FROM HAWAI'I

GOOD FROM FAR, FAR FROM GOOD

A LOVE STORY FROM HAWAI'I

BY CHULA

LEGACY ISLE
PUBLISHING

ISBN 978-1-935690-46-7

Library of Congress Control Number: 2013950584

Design and production
Kristin Lipman

Cover background photo: Thinkstock

Legacy Isle Publishing
1000 Bishop St., Suite 806
Honolulu, HI 96813
www.legacyislepublishing.net
info@legacyislepublishing.net

Printed in the United States

TO MY BELOVED ROBERT,

*tirelessly patient and giving to everyone
—especially to me—
who I feel blessed to love forty-three years later*

"YOU'RE BIG, BUT ARE YOU HUNG?" Not terribly romantic, but those were the first words I spoke to my beloved. Bawdy, gauche and certainly not the refined twenty-six-year-old I wish I could claim to have been. At six feet, five inches, barrel-chested, with bulging biceps, Robert threw back his head and laughed, and said, "Not particularly." I retorted, "Too bad," and walked away. That's how he remembers it forty years later, but, then, neither of us has a brilliant memory.

This night in 1970 I was champagne-fueled and had crashed his 'Iolani School faculty party in Kāhala (where I had recently lived with my first husband), with a similarly imbibing friend, Cynnie-Belle, from whom I had heard about this Adonis, this gentle giant who was raising his two young sons. I continued burbling to his colleagues, most of them English lit teachers like him, until I felt compelled to lean over with a bit more sarcasm. "That's a lovely tank top," I giggled to him, checking out his maroon velour shirt. The sweat slid down his handsome dark-skinned face, neck and tree-trunk arms as he toiled over the barbecue, chuckling before his circle tightened around him again.

When next I saw him he had changed his shirt, and somehow I knew my teasing had hit its mark. Not long after our first meeting, Robert had his ex-in-law come to stay. Michael Hernstadt was a cute, funny guy from Aspen who had been married to Robert's ex-wife's sister, and he'd remained a presence in Robert's life for many reasons. Michael's son was the same age as his cousin Rob, Robert's eldest, who was at this point nine years old, and he played together with Todd, who was six, the second of Robert's two adorable sons. Michael lived the high life, burning thousands of dollars flitting to and from his huge property in Aspen, on drink, drugs and women. But his sense of humor had a machine-gun delivery, and he got a kick out of his wayward and wild lifestyle, which contrasted with Robert's steadfast, solid, wholesome one. Never having worked, he delighted in shocking Robert and everyone around him. So when I was called by Cynnie-Belle, (cousin to my ex-husband) soon after that first night, to see if I'd go out with Michael, of course I said yes, as I'd heard enough about Michael to know I'd laugh a lot, and that I'd certainly see Robert again. C.B. was single, had had her eye on Robert for months, but, when that didn't pan out, she told me to have a go at this amazing guy. Meanwhile, Michael needed a date.

Out for an amusing night of drinks and dinner, we returned to Robert's three-bedroom house in the tony neighborhood of Kāhala. Michael immediately launched into Robert ("Bigfoot," he called him, because his feet are size thirteen), who was grading papers in his living room while the three boys were asleep, cracking wise about the pool table next to us piled high with clean laundry. Glancing about this attractive house, with its sweet courtyard, high ceilings and small pool in the back, I sat chuckling and slyly checking out this erudite gentleman Robert, who enchanted me. These two men were poles apart, but, having just left my first husband (whom I'd actually not yet divorced) in Lexington, Kentucky, I was in the mood for silliness, flirtations and maybe even, well, not sex, but certainly a fun make-out session.

I was mother to my own son, Robin, a precious towheaded munchkin, who was not quite two. His father, Stephen Johnston, was a darling, spoiled playboy who had been friends of my handsome, funny older brother Jimmy. Stephen had an endearing sense of humor and a huge trust fund, and we had lived the past three years in Lexington, close to some of his charming family and many old friends. This was our second marriage to each other; our first had been short-lived, in Kāhala, a block from the beach. Stephen had never worked, but he was so generous and charismatic, I failed to see that as a warning sign. He'd played golf, partied and I fell right into the delirium. Who wouldn't want to be adored by a good-looking guy from a wonderful family? His sister, elegant, beautiful and head of the Junior

League, indulged her younger brother; she was insightful and clever, and I loved being with her and her family. Their older brother was as courtly and sweet as anyone I'd ever known, and enterprising as well, and I was immediately close to his lovely wife and their children.

I had a job with Hawaiian Airlines in 1965, a flight attendant for only nine months, but, when Stephen courted me with fancy restaurants, *lei* and fun, I fell fast and hard. It was a bit of a struggle to keep flying when we had such late nights, and the morning I woke up on Maui at the hotel for flight attendants, hungover at 5 a.m., scrambling for my uniform, I began to think I couldn't achieve the sense of decorum one needed to bring back a plane full of passengers to O'ahu. My white blouse, which peeked out of my aqua jacket and skirt, was supposed to be complemented by legs sheathed in stockings (Stockings. In Hawai'i. I'd never worn stockings before.) and an aqua beret. Nowhere to be found were the heels completing this uniform, and they had to be replaced by my slippers. Pink slippers. Oh, well, hopefully I wouldn't run into any of the higher-ups on this flight.

Prior to this unprofessionalism, when asked by a passenger on a twilight flight between O'ahu and Kona, "What is the name of that, miss?" as she pointed at lights out the window. I peered out and answered, "Kaho'olawe, um, you know, their harbor." Briskly walking away, I realized it was simply the light on the wing. There were no islands at this point, but she probably didn't know that.

These mishaps were prefaced by a feeling opposite to what you'd expect from your stewardess (as we were called in those days): fear of flying. Not radical, white-knuckle fear, but a steady feeling that "I'm not loving this flight," and, "Wonder how it'd be if we were in crisis," and how I'd probably race to be the first one off the plane at impact, yelling, "Follow me!"—which wasn't in our training manual.

Anyway, it seemed an opportune time to gracefully exit Hawaiian Airlines, before I got fired, really embarrassed myself or put passengers in jeopardy, and when Stephen asked to marry me, I was thrilled. My Aunty Barbie—Barbie Cox Anthony (the wealthiest woman in the country), my godmother—offered to pay for our beautiful wedding at the Pacific Club. Thus, our fanciful life raced on toward near decadence in our pretty rented home, with neither of us working and bills that overflowed the dresser. I began to see that, though Stephen had endless cash flow, he ignored paying bills he could easily afford. So I swept them all into the top drawer and on we swirled, he playing golf at Wai'alae Country Club (where the Hawaiian Open, now the Sony Open, was held annually) while I played tennis there.

Though very much in love, I realized he was Peter Pan, beguilingly charming, but not any more responsible than a child. We had wonderful evenings with his siblings, with Waikīkī entertainers such as Don Ho and Kui Lee, who became our friends, because we frequented the clubs, and with my brother Jimmy, who adored Stephen as well. And though I had days full of tennis, lunches and beaches, I saw the cracks widening in our marriage after only a year or so. Stephen tried talking me out of a divorce, but I suspected he had been unfaithful. He had recently gotten a part-time "job" as a liquor distributor, which got him out and into bars even more, and I confronted him with my suspicions, which he denied. So, after one appointment with a psychologist for which he didn't show, we divorced, and he began dating in the next ten minutes, which rather confirmed my accusations. This actually hurt me deeply, so I decided not to bear witness and went back to Australia, where I had lived for a year in Adelaide not long before.

CHAPTER TWO

After graduating from Punahou School in Honolulu in 1962, I went to the University of Arizona. In those days, kids didn't jaunt off to the Mainland to check out colleges, and I'd only been to the Mainland twice before. I picked Arizona because it was known as a party school, and, though I was bright enough, I was no scholar. I saw myself performing as I did in high school, studying enough to get by and having fun. When I arrived in Tucson, I was dismayed by the bleakness of the surrounding desert, and the fact I had to trudge across campus to classes that didn't excite me. I made friends with a character from the Virgin Islands and a Southern belle. An odd trio, we nevertheless hung out together when we realized we'd rushed ourselves out of the sorority scene. It all felt too cliquey to me, and anyway, I'd been having a fling with a senior from Punahou, whose bed I seldom left.

When semester break required students to leave, or, if staying on campus required all to follow dorm rules, we three did neither and partied nonstop. After break, we were called in to face the school board, as apparently someone had reported us (what had happened to the school's party reputation?), and we were easily dispatched. I went home, got a job at a television station as a receptionist (my first job) for six months and saved money to travel Europe with a Punahou pal. My father helped me buy a car in Germany, which I halved with my friend, and off we went. I thought this was much more of an education for me than returning to college after one semester.

Arriving in Barcelona, giddy with the freedom of doing as we pleased, we immediately filled our boda bags with cheap wine and met two California dudes. When they learned we had a car to pick up in Mainz, Germany in a week, they offered to fetch it for us. Delighted, we settled into exploring the city and cafés until they returned. The next new friends we made were stunned we were trusting enough to give ownership papers to almost-strangers, and predicted we could kiss the Opel goodbye. But back they came, and we all took off for Portugal, the south of France, Venice, Austria and Switzerland with them (one of which had become my lover; I laughed at his quick wit constantly), and a group of five or six other attractive Australians and Americans. We lived close to the pages of *Europe on 5 Dollars a Day*.

Eventually we rented a house in Mallorca and a month of hilarity ensued, with three cute American girls and three of the funniest men I'd ever met from Australia. Innocent as our partying was in those days, we consumed our staple of wine and beer with such ferocity that my lover had to depart, his yellowed eyes indicating severe jaundice. If the drinking wasn't enough, someone introduced marijuana into the mix. I'd never heard of it, but when Peter from Adelaide climbed through my window at 2 a.m., stoned, I, of course, had to learn to smoke cigarettes so I could smoke pot. Perfectly logical to a nineteen-year-old in the early '60s.

We debated going to the nearby isle of Ibiza when our month was up in Mallorca, but decided instead to pop in to Pamplona for the running of the bulls, which we'd heard was coming up. Peter, who had now become my lover, my school chum and a few others piled into our Opel as well. The night before the big event found us in a bar, practicing our meager Spanish and polishing our imbibing skills, when into the bar strode Teddy. I squealed with surprise to see my Punahou classmate in an obscure bar in Pamplona, and we promptly had him join us to get caught up. Handsome and wealthy, Teddy smiled at our wild stories and recounted his tale of building a yacht in Mallorca with his uncle right before we lived there.

Peter and Ted got on well, everyone was in high gear and the din was tremendous, so much so that we didn't understand what was happening when fists began to fly. "Owww, he bit me bloody ear off!" yelled Peter, clutching his head. Chaos reigned, and I lurched into Peter to see if it was true. As blood oozed through his fingers, I looked up to see Ted's uncle charging into the bar. Right then the high-pitched *eeya, eeya* of a police siren wailed, and Ted's uncle hugged me briefly

while I summed up what had happened, and he insisted that we get
the hell out, because you were considered guilty until proven innocent in Spain.

I grabbed Peter and we fled. Quickly leaving the mayhem, we
quizzed Peter as to who'd bitten him. He showed us the gore where his
ear had been and only a sliver remained. Being drunk enough not to
see this as particularly alarming, now that we were safely away, Ted
asked us where we were staying. Peter's lovely face remained as un-
ruffled as mine when we admitted we had no clue where our pensione
was, and Ted gallantly offered to let us bunk in with him at the Hotel
Tres Reyes.

Peter mentioned casually that Ted "Wasn't getting it on with his
bird," and I laughed with Teddy, saying, of course not, the three of us
were pals and grateful to be in this elegant hotel. Though buzzed, I
soon realized that Ted was a horny dog, and actually did try his tricks
as I fell into a coma, with Peter propped up on pillows next to the bed.
I kicked him away and we all slept like the dead until Peter woke up
moaning. His bite was infected, and we needed to find him a
doctor.

"Bitten off by a Spaniard, you say?" asked the doctor. "Where is
the ear? I will sew it back on if you find it." Peals of laughter assured
him that, no, it was on the floor of a bar, and so he stitched up Peter's
wound.

Feasting on a hardy breakfast revived us enough to stumble off
to the festivities. Everywhere swarmed white-shirted men with red
scarves or bandanas, and we were excited to be among them. Peter
staggered into his seat and we perched as the screaming crowds
packed into the arena, just before the line of men galloped in ahead
of the bull. Riveted, we felt our adrenaline pump as well, as we witnessed an enraged bull stomping, goring or tossing men as if they
were rag dolls. Primal, thrilling, dangerous, we felt one with the mob,
having just been through a similar sort of primitive scene the night
before.

Soon after Pamplona, Peter returned to Australia with his mates and my cohort and I kept trucking, on a shoestring. Germany, Norway, Sweden and London (where we sat in with the House of Lords, because Ma had an old friend who was a lord) captivated us, as did all of Europe, the food, people, languages, cultures. At some point, we somehow ventured into Morroco. Once there, we followed a trickle of water in a dirt lane to the rough home of a gracious family that invited us in for tea. Dressing me up in their scarves and burka had us giggling and, though we never learned enough in any language (except French, which we'd studied at Punahou) to truly engage, we seemed to interact well enough with hand gestures if they didn't speak English.

After nine months of Europe we parted and I returned home via Tehran, Bangkok and Hong Kong, with only a bit of excitement in Iran. Arriving alone at night only began to trouble me as I walked through the empty airport knowing I had not booked anything for the night. Why, I cannot fathom now, but perhaps it simply wasn't important at twenty years old, feeling that I was a seasoned traveler. I had been chatting on the plane in my fractured French to my seatmate, and he approached me now, asking if I needed help. Turned out that Mr. Meshkat had his driver outside and was happy to take me to my hotel. As we drove I had to admit I hadn't booked anything. "Oh," he enthused, "you could stay at my hotel." He had extra rooms, he added, and lived there himself.

When we pulled up and he escorted me to my room, fatigue enveloped me and I told him I was grateful, said little more and locked my door. Awakened sometime later by the door opening and Mr. Meshkat asking if I needed anything, I mumbled no, please leave me to sleep. Was I quite sure, he persisted, sidling up to my bed. Realizing how naïve I had been, I insisted vehemently that I was fine, please go.

Next morning Mr. Meshkat wanted to drive me around the dusty streets of Tehran and insisted I accompany him to meet the shah. We stopped in a bazaar so I could shop for some of the pretty brass pots I'd seen everywhere, and he actually announced he wanted to marry me, and asked what I thought about marriage. Startled, I tried not to crack up laughing, for, as bizarre as the proposal was, he was serious.

I somehow politely changed the subject as we drove to lunch with the shah, then thought to ask the time. When he told me, I gasped. My flight was in a few hours.

I said that we needed to hustle to the airport immediately, that I could not miss my flight. He casually announced it was fine, I could always take the next one, and only then did I realize the severity of the situation. It turned out the next flight was not until the next week, and I screeched at him to get me to the airport that minute. As we pulled up, he remarked that my plane, he was quite sure, had already left. I leapt out and ran to the counter, where it was confirmed that, yes, my plane was taxiing down the runway. I raced out the door and ran down the tarmac, yelling and waving, my armload of brass pots clanking noisily. Somehow the pilot pulled up at the pitiful sight of a desperate American screaming as if she had just escaped the clutches of a strange Iranian suitor, which is precisely how I felt.

Upon returning home I quickly became employed again so I could leave for Adelaide to see Peter in the next six months or so. I had also met his outrageously adorable and funny sister Jane briefly, while she draped herself on a balcony, flirting drunkenly with several Spanish youths. She was as pretty as Peter was handsome and I could hardly wait to laugh with them again. I booked passage on a ship from Honolulu to Sydney, and would fly on to Adelaide after a few days with friends. But after a boozy farewell party onboard the ship, I tearfully hugged my pals goodbye and began throwing my lei down to them as I gripped the railing. For some reason I was suddenly anxious at my weeklong journey alone on the ship, and I sought out a steward to see if it was too late to disembark. Of course, it was, I knew as Honolulu Harbor slipped away.

I woke up happier the next morning, and soon met a lovely fellow traveler, who was delightful, amorous company for the entire voyage. Sydney was a stunning and sophisticated city, the little I saw of it, and I launched into my next year without a backward thought the moment I arrived at Peter and Jane's family home in Adelaide. Their parents were typically proper, but Jane was so wickedly improper, we became the closest of friends. When she went off to model and Peter went to his father's accounting firm, I looked for an apartment and a job. Soon I was a dental assistant living in a big flat with three attractive roommates.

The social life of Peter and Jane was alluringly bawdy and wild. All their friends partied often and had brilliantly honed senses of humor. I soon spoke with their accents and copied their slang, and I felt I belonged in this milieu of contemporaries who spoke English as if it were an art. My friends at home seemed conventional and their dialogue tame compared to the fanciful conversations here. I fell in love with everyone there, as well as with Peter, but when he asked me to marry him I realized I wasn't that deeply in love and eventually made plans to go home.

CHAPTER THREE

LUCILLE, MY MOTHER, was born to Walter and Lucy Ackerman in Kohala on the Big Island. A descendant of King Kamehameha and a brief acquaintance of Queen Lili'uokalani, she was one of four sisters and three brothers and cousin to Richard Smart, who owned Parker Ranch. Her father, Walter, managed the Bank of Hawai'i and could afford to send his children to O'ahu by freighter to attend Punahou School, the largest private school in the country. They lived in the dorms and returned home for holidays until they graduated, and Lucille then went to the University of California at Berkeley for one year. Afterward, she worked until she met Clark Reynolds, who had just moved to Honolulu from Iowa, where he'd been raised by his mother and older sister. A brief courtship, while Clark became a realtor, led to marriage. He was of slight build, blue-eyed, with curly black hair and had a sarcastic sense of humor. Lu, one-quarter Hawaiian, was pretty, wise, forthright and lighthearted.

Their first child, Michael, was joined by Linda two years later, and Jimmy two years after that. The Big Island of Hawai'i had water wells raised up on stilts for use when droughts occurred, and Michael climbed up the stairs one afternoon when Clark and Lu had left the housekeeper in charge. My mother got the call, the worst news a mother can hear, saying she couldn't find Michael, and they raced home to find that he'd drowned in the well. Five years old, their adorable son. It was a tragedy; too devastating to accept that he was gone.

My father had ridden horses all his life, had become a polo player after moving to Hawai'i, so he decided he would play polo in Mexico City. It would cost considerably less there to maintain polo ponies and two children, and they needed to get away, a different scene. While Lu grieved, she got *hāpai* (pregnant) with me, so she was glad for the change as well. It was what they'd hoped for, and then, on the fourth day of the fourth month, of the forty-fourth year, along came Chula, Chiquita, Chulita, as the housekeepers called me (though I had actually been named Robin). We returned to Oʻahu when I was one and a half, and Clark bought himself a string of polo ponies, Ma fixed up the house in Nuʻuanu they'd bought and put Linda and Jimmy in school.

Eventually we moved to a beachfront property on Kalanianʻole, past Wailupe, to an open, four-bedroom house with maids' quarters. It was an idyllic childhood for me, playing on the beach and in the shallow, reef-studded ocean, as well as in the big koi pond. It spiced up our lives to have a tiny stable built next to the pond for two horses Dad brought home. Jimmy learned to stick and ball, the term used for practicing polo, which they played in Kapiʻolani Park, and he, Linda and I often rode on the beach with Clark. Our parents had glamorous friends, who they entertained often. I remember Jimmy Stewart and his family, as well as other celebrities and dear friends at these parties, and the oft-repeated phrase, "Children are to be seen and not heard," by which we abided on those evenings.

Mummy had wonderful friends. The three to whom she was closest were Aunty "Ole Lady" Wilcox and her cousin Aunty Mu (Muriel) Flanders, and Aunty Barbie. Ole lady, as she was called for acting like an old lady as a child, was one of the matriarchs of the Campbell Estate of Hawaiʻi, which owned enormous parcels of land all over the Islands. Aunty Mu was refined and elegant, while Aunty Ole Lady was a zany, charming character, and Aunty Barbie, smart, funny, imperious and athletic. Hanging out with these ladies enriched Lu's life immeasurably, though she remained the same down-to-earth, warm woman she'd always been. *Muʻumuʻu* was Lucille's usual garb, unless she was decked out in simple elegance with a fresh tiare in her short, curly hair for parties.

Daddy, on the other hand, usually dressed in slacks and monogrammed shirts. He purchased a house on the North Shore, or the "country," as we called it. We had been blessed to rent a friend's beach house at Malaekahana Bay for a few years, and that's where he bought a small, old house with three bedrooms, scarcely big enough for the recent addition to our family, Melissa. The three girls slept on bunk beds, and Jimmy had his own room.

We all bodysurfed the waves in front of our house, as well as galloped the beach on Dad's polo ponies, which he kept in the stables and paddock near our home. Ma would take us into the hills to pick guavas for sherbet and ginger to make lei, to go "fluming" (floating down raised irrigation tubes). We'd go skinny-dipping at night while she played her *'ukulele* on the beach. Then she would cook while we played the player piano and sang, and we'd clean up after dinner. Some evenings our parents would have cocktails with old friends who had country homes as well, traipsing between their homes on Malaekahana Bay.

I had Punahou pals to the country often, sometimes three or four at a time, and we'd sneak beers and cigarettes in our early teens at the tack house, where the bridles and saddles were kept, far enough away to be private, with a huge pasture for the horses. A stream bordered one side of the pasture, and the rest was fenced in. We were allowed to drive our Jeep around it, and all of us shrieked with laughter as we bounced along, learning to drive. I was a seasoned driver by the time I could finally get a license three or four years later. We all grew up together in this wholesome environment.

And yet, innocent as we were, I seemed to be more *kolohe* (mischievous) than the others. More daring, a thrill seeker, I would jump off the highest cliff at Waimea Falls, swim through underwater rock tunnels. I'd know when the guys were staying at a nearby beach house, and we'd sneak out after the flicks at the Kahuku Theater. They'd escort us into the hills above, where I'd ridden horses with Ma and Dad, and we'd start up tractors and other Army vehicles kept there, charging around in the dark with glee.

My first real boyfriend, at fourteen, lived on the North Shore and was known to surf and drive all sorts of vehicles in the hills. No rocket scientist, he went to siphon gas out of a tractor one night and lit a match to see how much gasoline was left. The explosion burned his chest and legs badly enough to send him to Kahuku Hospital. The allure was too strong; I felt compelled to push our Volks out of our yard, down the sandy driveway, before starting the engine and driving to the hospital at night.

Sneaking into this country hospital was a cakewalk, and I'd climb into bed with him, careful not to bump the sterilized cage over his torso and legs. Making out here seemed more titillating than ever before, and, when he finally healed a few weeks later, we made love on the beach. Ma asked me one day if I had anything to confess, as she was concerned about something. My mind raced, because I'd done so many things lately, I couldn't decide, should I tell her about the military vehicles in the hills, the smoking in the tack house or perhaps start with the most innocuous? She smiled, said no, that wasn't it, and as I babbled, her eyes widened. Finally, she laughed when I got to the Volks-pushing down the driveway in order to drive to the hospital, and I recounted the whole story.

The romance was short-lived. A few months later I discovered he had another girlfriend he'd been going with even before knowing me. I was crushed to realize what a bad boy he was and cried a whole day. I might have been a wild child, but he was more than wild, he was dishonest. Ma hugged me tenderly when she circled my neck with a pikake lei to assuage my bruised heart.

Fortunately I had other, even more amazing beach houses where I was welcomed in my childhood. Patsy Wilcox was my closest friend from the womb, as our mothers were dearest friends. Aunty Ole Lady was adored by all and my mom and I were often invited to Hanalei, Kaua'i, one of the most beautiful beaches in the world. Patsy's parents' marriage was like a merger, as her dad, Albert Wilcox's family, owned much of Hanalei for years, as well as land on the south shore of Kaua'i. Albert would inherit a huge home at the end of Hanalei Road, surrounded by acres of manicured lawn, fish ponds, pine and coconut trees, with sweeping mountain and ocean views. The lush emerald and mauve mountains threaded by waterfalls flanked all vistas behind as well as framing ethereal Hanalei Bay. Patsy was raised in the small beach house opposite the "Big House" where we would stay. Her brother, Gaylord, was in Jimmy's class at Punahou, and so my brother, as well as other pals of Gaylord's, joined us in our teen years.

We water-skied in the summer and surfed in the winter, when the otherwise turquoise, *malia* (placid) bay churned with waves. Patsy was one of the most beautiful athletes around; she could snow ski, dance, play tennis, all with grace and flawless timing. Waterskiing with her at Hanalei instilled my desire to learn to surf with her as well. I had been on the Punahou swim team and, after three years, I'd swam fast enough to make the state's fifty-yard freestyle record. I was strong, but never as agile and graceful as Patsy. Yet that didn't stop me from jumping the wake on one ski behind Gaylord's boat, dropping my ski and scrambling up on his pal's shoulders. Such excitement culminated in furtive make-out sessions nightly with my ski pal after bonfires on the beach.

Hiking Kalalau range, the same mountains bordering Hanalei, was a stunning adventure, with verdant cliffs plunging to the ocean below, and my lust for thrills was quenched between Hanalei, Kauaʻi and Malaekahana, Oʻahu. I did not take these blessings for granted, as Mummy often intoned how lucky we were to have such beauty, such a rich and healthy life. She would talk about God, and He was a spiritual presence in my life, unsullied by religion. I was aware of these gifts, and I had a conscience, but you wouldn't know it for the next escapade in my teens.

I had a boyfriend in the eleventh and twelfth grades, and we had hung out with the gang in previous years on the North Shore. "Mount Rushmore" (I called him for his sarcastic, deadpan humor) I saw daily at Punahou; we were "going steady." Around this time, I was turned on to motorcycles. Malaekahana was the perfect setting for dirt biking, and a striking, powerful friend of Aunty Barbie's and my parents came roaring into our yard and asked if I wanted to go for a ride. I jumped on the back of his bike. Where I had galloped horses and illicitly rode army tractors, I now charged up on a dirt bike. Hanging onto Danson's muscular back as we sped up "Red Hill," flying past guava bushes and ironwood trees, I realized I loved speed; I was hooked. Danson returned again to pack me into the mountains, to race across the Kahuku golf course nearby.

Soon this harmless fun took on a shadier tone. With my *lolo* Punahou mate as our connection, since Danson was his mentor, it was arranged that I would meet this married man twice my age for a drink in Waikīkī. I knew it was naughty, but, why not? I thought. I wasn't used to going into bars at sixteen, much less with this scoundrel, but meet him I did. After a glass of wine, he told me he had a secret cabin in the hills above Waikīkī, and he'd just love to take me there. It wasn't difficult to seduce me, so off we went. It was quite a different sort of sex act with him. I had no idea about all the nooks and crannies of my body, but I was aroused. We had a few of these liaisons before I pulled away. I'm not certain if it was conscience, him being married, and a well-known hound dog in Honolulu, but I'd had enough. At this point, lolo was going with Patsy, and our wholesome life hanging out with the gang appealed more to me.

Without a backward thought, I plunged back into Punahou life, the football games, canteens, parties, tennis team (after the swim team), occasional studies and eventually graduation. I had been fortunate to be included on a few trips to the Mainland, not a common occurrence in the early '60s (and certainly not college-scoping trips for anyone I knew). Aunty Ole Lady and Patsy took me skiing in Tahoe, and another time Lolo and Rushmore joined us at Disneyland. The distant future of college was now upon me, and, as I mentioned, I went off to the University of Arizona in 1962.

CHAPTER FOUR

"Chula, it's Cynnie-Belle, and I've got a date for you this afternoon." I had just moved home from Lexington, where I'd separated to divorce Stephen again, and I'd woken up with a hangover. "Not up for that, sorry, C.B., but I partied too much last night." "But you have to! I've just made the biggest sale in real estate history in Hawai'i, you know, the Kaiser Estate in Portlock, and we're going out with the new owners!" "Really? Who are they?" I asked. "The Goldmans, these two brothers, and I get the cute one." I laughed. "Alfred's the cutest, so you get Monte, as I'm the realtor. Seriously, this is huge, they're buying it for ten million dollars!" she snapped. "Take aspirin and I'll pick you up at two. We'll have a swim in the pool, a few beers and maybe dinner."

We laughed as we drove out to the east end of O'ahu to Hawai'i Kai and Koko Head, down past the expensive beach homes to the end of Portlock Road. Naturally C.B. was excited at the prospect of her huge commission and dates with the new owners. At the gate she punched in a number, which felt very VIP to me, and the heavy gate swung open. Two guys welcomed us, and they both seemed cute, with big grins, one blond and curly-haired and the other, Monte, dark-haired. They cracked jokes from the moment we arrived, welcoming us onto the sprawling estate. The brothers seemed down to earth, their fortune made by their dad, who invented the shopping cart.

They laughed at how it was just a one-bedroom house, not big enough for both, and pointed across the pool and yard to the servants' quarters, which was being renovated for the other brother. We sipped beers as we lounged in the pool, gazing out at the hugest ocean view I'd seen from a private home. When the subject of dinner came up, I was buzzed, said I really didn't think so, as I didn't know how long my mom would watch Robin, plus my hair was dirty. I was handed the phone to call and ask Ma, then Monte offered to wash my hair.

I found this hilarious, so I traipsed after him into the shower with my bikini intact and, as he shampooed away, he looked up and said hello to his mother. I giggled through suds as I was introduced, as if this was the most normal scene in the world, but the door was open to this pool shower, so why not meet Mrs. Goldman now? Then off we went to Waikīkī for dinner, had more badly needed drinks and, en route home, they stopped to buy the *Honolulu Star-Bulletin*. Wow, seeing the headlines blazing across the front page with their picture was a stunner; this sale was by far the biggest in the late 1960s in Hawai'i. It seemed just as exciting for them to see it, and they did not pretend otherwise.

We continued to celebrate when we saw them on the next several dates, with tennis on their court, swims in their pool, drinks at their outdoor bar, parties oceanside or dinners out. We always double-dated and they kept Cynnie-Belle and me in stitches. *Pakalolo* (marijuana) was easily available in Hawai'i along with smoking cigarettes the past few years, it was also Mai Tais and pot.

The first reality check for me that perhaps I was being negligent was the sobering afternoon at home at Ma's, when I was catching up on my ironing. My two-year-old, Robin, played nearby. I announced to him I was going into my bedroom to get more clothes and he was not to touch the iron. I was firm as I looked at this adorable little gremlin, his big blue eyes locked into mine, and I hustled into the next room. Then, a scream pierced my heart, and I ran. Robin had grabbed for the iron and it had fallen onto his hand. I yanked it off, cried out in fright and took my child into my arms as he sobbed. Racing him off to the hospital was heartbreaking. We were met by an excellent plastic surgeon soon after the first doctor medicated him. The top of his hand was badly burned, and skin was taken from his *'okole* (bottom) for a graft. I comforted him, cuddled him, snuggled him, as I always had, and repeated how sorry I was to leave the iron where he could reach it.

I had longed to get hāpai, and having a baby was actually my real motivation for marrying Stephen the second time. Having Robin at twenty-five years old was the most wonderful event of my life. I knew Stephen wanted a child. I was still in love with him when we separated, but doubted much had changed. I was realistic. He wouldn't go to counseling in our first marriage, and when I made an appointment to see a psychologist, he didn't show up. I realized then, as the therapist said, that being married to him would have lots of ups, but also lots of downs.

Stephen built the Rusty Nail, the name of his restaurant in Lexington, Kentucky, and most of his family and friends were excited for him. He'd never had a real job, certainly never worked in a restaurant, and I wasn't enthused that his only real experience was dining in them. But life was such fun in Kentucky with his wonderful Aunt Rosie and all her grown kids, I let myself believe in this.

Rosie was a character out of a Southern novel. She was sister to Stephen's mother, who had died in her early twenties. Helen, beautiful, blonde and smart was married to Stephen's dad, Duke Johnston, whose father had started the Chemical Bank. He was neither a bright nor a funny man, in fact, he was rather corny, but he'd inherited lots of money, and all three of his kids had trust funds. When Stephen's mother died, he was a child, and Rosie helped raise him. Rosie herself had four children, three husbands and a full life as a top golfer, mother and grandmother.

Stephen and I lived with her for a month in Lexington when we moved there after our second marriage. Her small, charming house was crowded with family photos and knickknacks, which one of her housekeepers, Emerson, kept clean. Rosie would jump up when she saw me, asking, "Are you hungry, honey? Let me make you some fried tomatoes, or would you like a ham sandwich, darlin', or how about a bowl of fresh soup I've got on the stove?" When I'd laugh and say I just had breakfast two hours ago, she would sit back, chuckling around the cigarette that eternally dangled from her lower lip, the ash extending out an inch, and we'd chat.

Rosie was not beautiful, but she was the funniest woman I'd ever known, and she'd recount stories in her husky voice, her favorite pas-

time outside of cooking for her family. "Jesus," she'd start, lowering
her voice, "all hell broke loose here this mornin', I got to tell you. I'm
having that small dinner party tomorrow night, honey, you remember,
and damned if Emerson doesn't choose just that moment he's carrying the whole tray of silver he's going to polish, to have one of his fits,
he's epileptic, you know, and he just throws that big ole tray up and
every piece of silver goes flying," she gestures with both hands, "just
every which way!" I cackled as I reached, palm up, to catch her ash, as
I often did. "His body's jerking and jumping around, and I quick try to
put something in his mouth so that he won't bite off the end of that big
pink tongue he's got, Jesus, I just hope he doesn't have one of those
while I've got a houseful!" I was cracking up with her at this point, as
she leaned over, both arms on plump, spread knees, her nightie tucked
between them.

"Oh shit," she said, getting to her feet, "I meant to turn on that
game, you know darlin', the basketball game, and look at me still in
my nightie." She turned on the telly, sat back down, legs apart, and
lit another cigarette. Rosie smoked all day and into the night, but she
never took a drink, never had, saying somebody's got to stay sober in
the family. All four of her adult kids drank heavily, though I never saw
them drunk, and she always had hilarious anecdotes about Mary, Buddy, Cissy and Helen, their spouses and their children. "Mary's smart
enough, just like me, really. Helen's a smart-ass, everyone knows she
is, but she's so damned mean nobody will stand up to her. Cissy always
finds a man who's not good for her, don't you know, but now finally
she's got herself that Carrington, and I hope to God she doesn't screw
up. That damn Buddy, I can't believe it, he never got 'round to paying
his taxes and now that som'bitch is going to jail! If they'd only stop
drinking they might have some damn sense, but look at me, smoking
like I do."

Stephen and I loved her kids almost as much as we loved Rosie.
They were all raconteurs, a family out of an eccentric Southern novel.
We would be invited often to the Idlehour Country Club for martinis
and dinner, served by black tuxedoed waiters. We'd sit there smok-

ing and drinking and, soon after moving there, they asked me who my family was. I wasn't sure what they meant. They wouldn't know Clark and Lucille, how could they? But I surmised they wondered about my background, my lineage, so I told them the alluring bits, that my daddy played polo, Mummy was a descendant of King Kamehameha and my godmother was Aunty Barbie Anthony, which I knew would get them. "Barbie Cox Anthony?" they asked, and they henceforth saw the expensive dresses from her wardrobe that I wore, delighted to enhance my sparse closet. "That one of Barbie's?" they'd ask, as obviously it was a different cut from my skimpy miniskirts, and we'd laugh.

Much of their lives was centered around horses and horse races, at Keeneland and, of course, the Kentucky Derby where I felt I was breathing rarified air as I trotted along behind Stephen and Buddy while they checked out the horses and decided which one to bet on. I never quite understood the whole betting thing, I'm not a gambler, but it was fun watching the spectacle and all the money won and lost on horses. Derby day was anticipated by all, and it would begin with an elaborate breakfast at Rosie's or at her youngest, Helen, and her mellow husband Bob's, then we'd board an air-conditioned bus with Emerson serving us mint juleps (which we'd already sampled at breakfast) in silver cups with a sprig of mint.

The hour or so drive to Louisville (pronounced "Loo-a-ville" by everyone there) was raucous, and then we'd file up to the family box, the most prestigious seats on the track. Back and forth they'd all go to their bookies, or down below to check out the horses they were betting on. I loved smoking, drinking and laughing with the family while checking out the fashionistas' hats parading by, their outfits and jewelry. Then, the moment before the race, talk subsided, then bang! The horses bolted from their stalls with jockeys astride them in brilliant plumage, and careened around the track. Everyone leapt up yelling, fists pumping, as the race neared the finish line, then there were cheers and shouts, with quiet demeanor among the losers.

The family was too dignified to talk about money, but Stephen would ferret out who had won and what kind of cash they'd collected.

Once the derby winner's owners had a box next to us, and it was a rush to be a part of their excitement, their glamour, their talk about "sires," jockeys, etc. Overserved, stimulated, we'd climb on the bus back to Lexington. Emerson would be clapped on the back, greeted heartily (they all were fond of their "help") when he served us juleps the minute we boarded.

When the Rusty Nail opened it was a hit. Serving primarily steak and lobster, it was frequented by Stephen's family and friends, and Stephen the beaming host greeted them all, cigar in hand and wearing a blue blazer. He was a sweet man and truly loved, and his voice became as accented as the local Southerners. But, as the months wore on, he came home later and later, and I knew he was drinking heavily. It was fun for me to dine there occasionally, but I was a mother by then, waking up early as most mothers do, looking after Robin (though I'd had the luxury of Talitha, a nanny, the first few months after giving birth). Stephen was a wonderful father, as I knew he'd be, but he wasn't a wonderful husband any longer, coming in at two or three in the morning. When I found tiny slips of paper with phone numbers, I knew I had to leave. It was sad, certainly. This was Robin's dad. I understood these other women weren't anything I should take personally. Nor was the very brief dalliance I then had with a lovely young guy who lived near the Idlehour and helped me lick my wounds.

So I packed Robin up, wept my goodbyes to Stephen and Rosie, and we flew home to Hawai'i. I missed Rosie the most and thought of her the whole way home. How she had been such a hotshot golfer as a girl and loved watching all sports on the telly, knowing each player's name and background. How she adored gossiping with that husky voice in her chair, the telly blaring with Billy Graham, her cigarette dropping ashes everywhere. How I'd asked her recently about her husbands: Which one was the one she'd loved the most? When was the last time she'd made love? Did she put a little something more into it, knowing it was the last time? How she'd roared along with my cackling, repeating the story to her kids the next time we dined at the Idlehour.

CHAPTER FIVE

"HI ROBERT, IT'S CHULA," I said when he answered the phone. "I heard you're an A-tennis player and wonder if you'd like to play with me in a tournament coming up next week?"

Dating Monte those few months, when he came and went back and forth to the Mainland was frivolity, but it was much more intriguing to seek out Robert, the schoolteacher stud. So, in 1970, I devised a plan, after seeing him a second time with his ex-brother-in-law, Michael Hernstadt. "Oh," he replied, "that sounds good, I'm happy to be your partner, but only if you'll have dinner with me afterward." I dandled the phone on my knee, pretending to check my calendar, then answered, yes, I was free.

About four days later I called Robert to tell him I was sorry, the tournament had been cancelled, and he said, as I'd known he would, "Well, that's unfortunate, but hopefully you'll still have dinner with me." I waltzed into Ma's room to tell her I was going out with Robert, and asked if she could stay with Robin. She was happy for me, having listened to me prattle on about his courtly ways, his dulcet voice and craggy good looks, his sons, his job and home. So when Robert came to pick me up a few nights later, Ma opened the door first with a wrench in her hand and, after hello, she handed him the tool, asking if he'd mind fixing something out by her tiny pool. Robert and I burst out laughing at Ma's forthright gesture the minute she met my date, and he followed her out, chuckling.

We drove past Hawai'i Kai, Koko Head, Makapu'u Beach, lava rock, indigo ocean and crashing waves, to Buzz's Restaurant in Lanikai, a forty-minute drive to the northeastern end of O'ahu. As I slurped my Mai Tai, I immediately told Robert I had something to confess, and told him about the fictitious tennis tournament. He cracked up with me and the night rolled on. Admittedly, the Mai Tais imparted a rosy glow to our date, as well as the open-air restaurant and the tang of the nearby ocean, but I was beguiled with Robert's full lips and kind blue eyes, which focused their full attention on me. We talked about our sons and why we'd divorced, especially why Robert had custody of Rob and Todd. (If I'd known I would fall in love with a man named Robert, whose son was named Rob as well, I wouldn't have named my son Robin!) The boys' mother had gotten hāpai with Rob when she was only eighteen, and Robert was still in college at the University of Colorado. Todd was born three years later.

Robert's beloved mother was dying in Boston, where he was born, and they moved back to help, to be with her during the end of her life. When Gertrude died, Robert moved his family to Providence. Robert enrolled part time in Brown University, as well as teaching full time at a private school and coaching three sports. In 1966, the summer of his second year at Brown, at six foot, five inches and 260 pounds of muscle, he played in the Steelers' preseason program, though he declined their contract offer to play full time. He knew football wasn't a career for him, and he went on to graduate from Brown with a master's.

When their marriage unraveled, Robert applied to schools in Hawai'i. He needed a fresh start, needed to get away from his father and the brutally cold winters. Hartwell Harrison was a brilliant surgeon at Harvard, was loved and revered by everyone. He was on the team of three men who performed the first kidney transplant in the world, but Robert did not feel close to him, nor did he feel he'd made the effort to be a good father to Robert's three siblings. The oldest, Johnny, had been in therapy for years and finally got into AA; his younger sister, Nina, drank little but perhaps shouldn't have drunk at all; and his youngest brother, Jeffrey, was loud, spoiled and definitely an alcoholic (who hadn't owned up to it yet).

Now that his cherished mother was gone, he took his two sons to Hawai'i, starting anew on an island with a new job. He'd applied to Punahou and 'Iolani, but was not impressed with the womanizing headmaster at Punahou (those of us who went to school there weren't either), so he chose 'Iolani School. It was a private boys' school, and soon Robert was immersed in his new life in a home he bought in Kāhala, with Rob and Todd, who were able to attend 'Iolani for free. Their mother came out not long after and lived briefly in their home, only to feel it a confirmation of her choice to leave.

Robert began dating, and ladies lined up to meet and adore him, for, certainly, in those days, it was exceptional for a man to have custody of his boys. And he was unique, with his handsome face, powerful chest and arms, he was someone people turned to stare at (though, curiously, I'd never been drawn to a hunk myself). But his most interesting features were his gentle nature and his humility. His obvious love for his boys was apparent in his inclusion of neighborhood pals wherever he went with Rob and Todd, a kid magnet as well as a chick magnet.

Rapt on our first date, we laughed often and, after a huge salad and steak, three Mai Tais and at least that many gin and tonics for him, we drove off, never considering the alcohol consumption a problem, since Robert, built like an oak tree, could handle his booze. But we hadn't gone ten minutes, before we got to the Pali (the mountain tunnel route between the south and north of the island), when I told him I had to go *shi shi* (urinate), could he please pull over to the side of the road. He chuckled, did as I asked and I hopped out and peed nearby. I had never done this before and later I knew it must've been a sort of test—would he be put off with the real me? We went on, chatting, laughing, and the frisson between us was tangible. When we drew close to the Kāhala neighborhood on our right, he asked if we should go right or left, on to Niu Valley, to my mom's. Naturally, I answered right, without a qualm.

We quietly returned to his home, which I had seen twice, once when I crashed his 'Iolani party, and the second time when I came with Michael Hernstadt. This time we were alone, except for his two sons who were asleep and the sitter gone. We made tender, urgent love, and I knew, no question, I was besotted. When I found out years later that Robert had thought I was a bit easy for making love on our first date, I howled with laughter and asked what that made him. Why wasn't he "easy" as well? He had the decency to admit with chagrin that this was so. "I knew we were desperate to make love, so why pretend?" I asked. "And why ask if we should go right or left, so I would have to choose to be the easy one?" In fact, why had he chosen to drive back the opposite way, through the Pali, through downtown, with his home coming up first and Ma's house afterward?

Robert and I had our next date alone, then we included our three sons in the following one. I felt as easy and in love with them as I did with him. Robert was endearing with Robin, and it went smoothly. We saw each other this way almost every night, and I knew he was committed to our relationship over the next many months. Rob and Todd and Robin were bright, funny boys, and it was as natural as rain for me. Also, Robert's friends overlapped mine, so our social lives were fluid, mellow. If we were going to the drive-in, I giggled when the boys' extra pals hid under a blanket in the back until we got in. If Robert was cooking from his gourmet book, *101 Ways to Cook Hamburger*, I helped, while Robin played with Rob and Todd, either in the tiny pool or at the pool table (after throwing the mound of clean laundry on the couch). If we went the two blocks to Kāhala Beach to play football with the neighborhood kids, we'd all go. Though occasionally Robert would catch my eye, raise an eyebrow and, after bringing Robin home for a nap, we'd take a "nap" of our own, having asked Rob at ten years to look after Todd, a seven-year-old.

We could not get enough of each other, and I constantly hugged Robert, jumped up with my legs around his waist or punched his arm for punctuation when he teased me. Robert played his guitar whenever he was free to, sang in his dulcet voice and, as others observed, he sang like a songbird. Whenever he came to Ma's house, he sang to her as well, "Take Me Home," "Four Strong Winds," "Rocky Mountain High," "Peaceful Easy Feeling," "Sloop John B," and Ma's favorite and mine, "You've Got a Friend." When his pure voice soared, "You just call out my name and you know wherever I am, I'll come running to see you again," I liquefied, sure he meant it just for me.

We finally did play tennis occasionally, but, though he was incredibly patient, he was so much better than I, I lost interest in singles and we only played doubles. We'd take the boys to the beach to body-surf every weekend. Ma thought he hung the moon, and he got a kick out of her. It was inevitable that Robin and I move in with him. This was quite different from when I dated Stephen and spent the night out with him occasionally, only to return one day to see my suitcases outside Ma's door with a note saying it was time for me to move out. I simply laughed then, and, of course, soon after I did move in with Stephen. Now Ma was happy for me. I was going to be the mother of three little boys and, as she said, "Get married soon; why would he need a cow if he can get the milk free?" I saw her point, but wasn't worried about him marrying me, since we'd been dating almost a year and were the real deal.

Becoming mistress of a bachelor home was not gradual. The clean laundry no longer remained on the pool table in the living room, it got folded by Rob or Todd as one of their chores. Hamburger for dinner was only one of my menus: shoyu chicken, chicken sautéed with veggies, beef stew, shepherd's pie, big green salads, etc. And I'd make four breakfasts every morning before school of scrambled eggs, bacon and toast, French bread, hot cereal, etc., while also making their lunches, all lined up according to age. Robin was still home with me, because he was not yet three, but I was able to take him to Mrs. Sakamoto, who had other gremlins in her home nearby, whenever I needed to.

Other chores were asked of the boys, and I soon saw Robert's only flaw. I would ask Todd if he would rake the courtyard and, soon after, I'd look out to see Robert sweating and raking and Todd standing holding a plastic bag. "I thought I asked Todd to rake?" I'd say, and Robert would answer, "He is, I'm just helping." I'd point out that that was a chore Todd could do alone, and the whole point was to get them to help, to be responsible. Or Todd would come and ask if he could get a new swimsuit and I'd answer he had several and really didn't need more. Then, later that day, he'd come in beaming, wearing a new suit. I'd approach Robert quietly and explain that this undermined my decisions, and that he needed to look at why he felt compelled to "help" in ways that ultimately weren't helpful, as any therapist would agree.

But life was rich and full for all of us, except perhaps Todd, occasionally. I constantly hugged him as I did the others, snuggled him, kissed his damp neck, but, of course, he'd have so much wished to have his own mother, not Robin's, and, furthermore, he could have done without Robin. "I think I'm alerthic to Robin," he lisped. And "I want my real mommy," which hurt me and yet I so understood. Rob was independent, seemingly carefree, though this perception was challenged a decade or so later.

CHAPTER SIX

NOT ONLY WAS MA CRAZY about this dear man, my soul mate, but Linda, four years older than I, was as well. In her second marriage with Peter, she had grown weary of his lampshade humor when he drank too much, which was fairly often. Linda married the first time around when she was only twenty-two and got hāpai with Kelly, to an olive-skinned contractor with curly black hair and a roving eye. Their marriage was over almost as soon as it began. I felt sad I'd seen him with other girls and finally told Linda this, which was all she needed to confirm her doubts. Soon after they divorced, he drowned while working on the job, checking the pilings under a house he was building.

Linda had not seemed as happy as I growing up, and her life now wasn't easy. Pretty, blonde, blue-eyed and slender, she worked as a legal secretary while her adorable Kelly was little, before marrying Peter and giving birth to Chris several years later. Kelly was a scrumptious child who I taught to swim while looking after her occasionally.

Melissa too, did not seem as lighthearted as I was, but when she was in her early teens we all realized why she brooded. "I'm gay," she announced to Ma, who, with her usual forthrightness, said, "Well, it won't be easy for you, but I love you and hope I can make it easier for you." She wasn't entirely shocked, because her youngest daughter had exhibited obvious tomboy behavior her whole life, more pronounced by far than Linda or me. Melissa went away to school in Arizona soon after coming out, then moved to Alaska, only returning home occasionally.

Jimmy, born two years before I was, was closer to Dad than our mother. Apparently, after Michael's death, when Jimmy was only a baby and I not yet born, Daddy had made it clear that he was in charge of this son. He would raise Jimmy as he wished, thus, Jimmy was initiated into the world of polo, the good life and young girls. Daddy had been unfaithful to my mother for years, and when he decided to go to Tahiti to build a hotel, Jimmy had full rein to seek out lovely young women.

I was unaware of his philandering until I came home unexpectedly one afternoon to what I thought was an empty house, and instead found Clark with a dark-skinned girl not much older than I. I cried with my pal Jackie and my cousin Wendy, as I was only about fourteen and still naively thought marriage meant loyalty. Ma divorced Dad a few years later, with Aunty Barbie's love, support and financial help. It turned out that, though Dad made a good living, he spent way more than he earned, and he'd even put up Ma's small inheritance as collateral for a loan he never paid back, leaving her almost broke. So Barbie actually bought her the small three-bedroom house with a tiny pool, and encouraged her to work for Mummy's old friend, Francis Brown, as his secretary in his and his wife's beautiful home next to the Wai'alae Golf Course, part time and not too demanding.

You needn't be a brilliant psychiatrist to understand why I had a fling with a married man when I did, or to see why Jimmy, who was urged to join his father in Bora Bora, had dalliances with lovely Tahitian girls, one of whom he married when she was still in her teens, after he graduated from Cornell. And, many years later, it gradually became clear why Melissa was as confused as she was.

"So Ronnie Hirahara said he's going to tear that old house down on Kalanian'aole," Jimmy said on the phone. "I told him to wait, as I thought I knew someone who'd like to have it. Thought you and Linda might have it moved out to Malaekahana for yourselves." "Really!? That would be amazing! Hell, yeah, we want it!" I replied.

Jimmy had an A-frame house on the point of the western end of Malaekahana Bay, and I had often felt wistful that he continued to enjoy the country life we'd all had in our childhood. He had divorced Norma, his sweet Tahitian wife and mother of his three sons, Michael, Mark and Mathew, and married Stephanie (Robert and I witnessed their wedding by a justice of the peace), a beauty he'd met hot-walking polo ponies. With her dark-blue eyes, dark hair and olive skin, she soon began hot-walking my brother. Jimmy reminded me of Stephen, my first husband, buying his new wife gorgeous clothes, jewelry and a lovely old home near the ocean on the south shore. Later, as a result of Jimmy's brilliant business acumen, he leased land on the North Shore and built a house with a big deck overlooking the pastures, horses and ocean.

So, although Robert and I had a fun, happy lifestyle, which was augmented by Robert's trust fund from his deceased mother's family, we'd been content to spend free time at the beach, his rugby games, our tennis doubles, the boys' soccer or softball games and occasionally nights out for dinner or a movie. It hadn't occurred to me we'd ever be in a position to have a country house, too! It was terribly exciting. Linda and I agreed to hire a moving company and go in together to pay for it, as well as hooking up plumbing and electricity.

It was decided we could use the Campbell Estate land between the tiny stream on the property (that my pals narrowly missed falling into while learning how to drive), and the polo field that Dad and Jimmy had put in a year or so before. Dad had been living with Estelle, a young Tahitian he'd shacked up with for many years, on the point of the bay, right on the ocean.

I had adored Estelle since I'd met her in Bora Bora when visiting Dad after going to Europe. Clark had been living in one of the grass-roofed huts he'd built at his hotel, and I hadn't seen him since I'd been there a few years before. That first trip I'd met Emile, a handsome Tahitian fellow on the plane down to Tahiti, and we had a romp for a week on the undiscovered island of Bora Bora, scooting around on his Vespa, making love on the beach under the coconut trees, eating fabulous Tahitian food with his family. The second time I went I called Dad ahead of time, to be reassured he would be alone, not with another of his babes.

It was one thing to have his current mistress, but another for me to have to deal with a woman in his home daily. And, of course, though he said he'd be alone, there was Estelle, younger than I and living with Dad. But I instantly liked her, with her long black hair, twinkly Chinese eyes and ready laugh. In fact, we got on famously the first night when we went to dinner at the only other hotel on the island, Hotel Bora Bora, which was much bigger than Daddy's Hotel Nui Nui. Estelle and I danced to the swingy band, till she drove me home on the back of her Vespa, the two of us giggling the night away. It must've been a breath of fresh air for Estelle, since Dad, though he liked a dirty joke or story, had a perennial frown, and he was even known as the guy with the upside-down smile. From then on she was "stepmommy," which we giggled over every time.

I'd come to love Estelle now that they lived in Hawai'i and we would be neighbors during summers or on weekends. And I adored Stephanie, Jimmy's wife, who had a naughty sense of humor when my brother wasn't around. So it was that Linda and I excitedly sat in the pasture one summer morning waiting for the movers. As they bumped down the sand driveway, the four sections of the house teetered pre-cariously on the trailers, while Linda and I giggled. But amusement turned to surprise when we realized we weren't certain which part of the house was which, as we'd only seen it once, and then in one piece. Now we muttered that perhaps we should have put red, blue, yellow and green dots on each, to match them up.

When I asked which section was going where, it became appar-ent the living room, which was most open, would be facing backward; instead of looking out at the pastures and polo field, we'd be looking through the ironwood trees to the tiny stream. So I requested that they turn it around, realizing they'd have to unload each section be-fore picking it up the other way around. "Nah, no problem," the guys answered when I wondered aloud why they hadn't brought up this subject beforehand. "Las' week we pull up and the guy wen' say, 'Hey, brah! That's not my house!'" Linda and I cracked up imagining whose house was taken by mistake and wondered just how efficient these movers were.

We had a carpenter put it back together and, though a bit uneven,

Queen Lili'uokalani (center) and Ma (holding doll), 1916

Ma, Chula, Linda and Jimmy, 1948

Clark and Lu Reynolds, Linda, Jimmy and Chula, 1951

Chula, Jimmy, Linda, Melissa and Jim Kennedy at Kapi'olani Park, 1952

Chula and pal in front of Niu home, 1952

Lucille Reynolds, 1952

Clark Reynolds, 1952

Jimmy Reynolds, 1954

Clark Reynolds at Mālaekahana, 1957

Robert playing college football, Washington and Lee University, 1958

Hawaiian Airlines stewardesses (Chula, second from left), 1965

we had a house. Robert had the summer off and worked nine hour days until he got the pipes laid and the plumbing installed. A plumber finished it, and an electrician checked out the connections. After cleaning it, we bought bunk beds from an Army surplus and furniture from Goodwill. It was old and tacky, but we loved it, and we stayed weeks at a time. Our black Labrador, Mau Mau (given to me by Aunty Barbie, who never had fewer than two or three Labs) ran wild, and the boys bodysurfed, fished for tilapia in the stream or played in the sand on the polo field.

Right away we knew we had to invest in used dirt bikes (Robert still rode a huge motorcycle daily) and we all went to Lanikai to pick out three of them. The biggest was a 150 HP for me, then a 75 HP and a 50 HP for the boys. This was a thrill for all of us, to jump the hills in the pastures, and I packed Robin, now three, in front of me. The boys brought out their pals to stay with us if we weren't sharing the house with Linda, Peter, Kelly and her little brother, Christopher. We were laid back because they couldn't ruin anything in the house, and we even let them draw on the walls of their dorm-like bedroom. Doing my yoga in there much later, I looked more carefully at what was written: "shit," "fock," "damn" and other naughty words, and I wished I'd had this much freedom as a kid.

Life changed immeasurably when summer ended with Robert back at school, taking the boys with him. Because he taught English literature as well as history, he had loads of papers to correct every night, and I was busy cooking, cleaning, driving and organizing our lives— being a mom. Robert had endless energy, played sports every day, either tennis or rugby, and often had tournaments on the weekends. He never seemed to tire and was unfailingly sweet and helpful, though I sure got tired. Eventually, after our spring break in the country, when soccer games for the boys were *pau* (done) and summer loomed, Robert suggested we go to Boston to meet Hartwell and Sis, his adored second wife. He called his dad with the plan, but surprisingly was told they'd love to meet Chula, so why not bring her back with our three sons after we were married?

I had wondered when Robert would get around to asking me. I'd hinted at it, of course, so I was amused. When I still hadn't been asked by late May, and the plans were made again for Rob and Todd to go back to see their mother in California for a month, I made a plan of my own. When Robert took them to the airport the first week of June, I packed up Robin and went to the country house of a pal of mine, who'd already heard how wonderful it was living with Robert, but enough was enough. She laughed, saying I could stay as long as it took him to come to his senses. After our second night there on the North Shore, sure enough, Robert arrived, got down on his knee, and, with his blond hair blowing under the coconut trees and a sheen of sweat on his powerful body, we both laughed when I said yes almost before he got the words out.

Our wedding was August 1972, given by Aunty Ole Lady at her charming home on Kāhala Beach. Close friends and family made for an intimate service and reception. I hadn't invited Daddy, because Ma would have been uncomfortable, nor would he have fit in or cared, plus he'd never called Robert by name: It was always "your big jock." Robert's parents couldn't come, but his younger brother Jeffrey did, and I was stunned at how different the two brothers were. Jeffrey was normal size, not as handsome and self-absorbed. When I shared this with Robert he laughed, saying yes, Jeffrey had been spoiled rotten by his dad and it was too bad he was the only family member I'd met. We had been invited back to New England for Christmas though, and, in four months, I'd meet them all.

We were all excited to have a white Christmas (Robin especially, as he'd never seen snow), and we were embraced with great warmth and joy by "Granddaddy" and Sis at their home in Dedham, Massachusetts. It was actually Sis' house, which she was living in when they married several years before, and it was large and comfy, with a big hill behind it for sledding. I adored Sis on sight. She was truly down to earth, sweet and wise, with a delightful sense of humor. Granddaddy, from Virginia by birth, had a slight Southern accent, a big laugh and was endearing. He fixed me a martini at night and we all interacted as a close family, which I'd not had for years. Hartwell soon began calling me his "little Hawaiian princess," and when we played on the covered tennis court at the country club, Robert and I versus Sis and Hartwell, I felt like a princess. Sis was a beautiful athlete, and had amazing drop shots, though she wasn't good enough to carry Hartwell against his son on the court. Robert refrained from his hard shots, which was necessary against them, but it was good tennis and we laughed often.

Robin felt cherished by Sis and Hartwell as well. Meeting Robert's older brother John was surprising, as he seemed so insecure and unlike Robert. Nina was dear, small and as good an athlete as any of them, but she also seemed typically New England, in that she did not express her feelings easily. Yet they and their mates laughed readily with me, and we had an easy rapport. Though I'd never been to the East Coast before, I came to realize the majority of the people were more uptight than in Hawaiʻi. When I swept downstairs in my new purple, form-fitting outfit, with feathers at the wrists and neck, to meet his dear old friends, I felt I was meeting older, conservative people. We giggled in bed later that night about how proper they were compared to me and even to Robert.

His family and friends all called him Bobby, or Bob (that I'm sure was apt when he was younger and smaller, which I knew beforehand), but to me, "Robert" was manlier, more robust. What I didn't know before was how buttoned up all of his old friends were, though we got on fine, and I even provoked them more than necessary by my outspokenness. But more revealing were the stories his old pals recounted about Bobby. One pal began to chuckle as he described how Bobby had been given tickets to the Longwood Cricket Club for the national tennis tournament (outside of Boston) when they were seniors at Choate together. When he handed the tickets to the fellow in the booth, he said he had a few extras, and so please would he give them to some deserving couple who couldn't really afford them. Seated, Robert smiled at the couple that came in and sat next to them, asked if the tickets had been a good price, only to find out that they'd paid the highest fee.

Robert jumped up, strode out to confront the ticket taker, accusing him of cheating the couple and, as he gestured, he actually knocked the booth over with the man in it. Bug-eyed, the man lay captive as a weasel until Robert finished berating him and hove his bulk off the booth. Tears streaked his pal's face as he told this tale, and, of course, I cracked up, though Robert seemed a bit chagrined as he laughed.

I was amazed to hear how revered Hartwell was by all ages, realizing the magnitude of his feat, one of three men who performed the first kidney transplant in the world. And to observe the relationship between him and his second son. "I remember buying that old Chevy for you, Bobby, and you . . . " Hartwell began before being interrupted. "No, Dad, you never bought me a Chevy, that was Jeffrey. You never bought me any car. I bought a motorcycle at eighteen and each car after that I paid for." I saw firsthand Robert's fierce independence, how it was important he'd moved away from home. Far, far away.

Coming home, Robert exclaimed over and over, "I can't believe I'm coming home to Hawai'i! God, am I glad I moved here. I love my family and friends, but I'm so glad I left! And I wouldn't have met my little Chu Chu, right?"

For me the reality check was the undercurrent between us over his enabling our sons. I would walk into the kitchen to see Robert happily sweeping the floor or loading the dishwasher, and I'd ask why Robby or Todd wasn't doing this chore as I'd asked. He was so energetic and helpful every moment of his life, he just could not understand that he was enabling, so it continued and we argued over it. I came to realize that he'd walked on eggshells since gaining custody of Rob and Todd; it was rare in those days for the father to raise his children. So I could, in part, see why Robert was enabling them: he was grateful. He cherished them. As did I, and yet when Ma told me how "brave" his ex-wife was to give up her sons, I doubted that was the right adjective, eventually realizing she wasn't really maternal and up to the task.

The months stumbled on into summer, and I looked forward to going to our ramshackle house in the country. Robert signed up to teach 'Iolani summer school, half days, and would commute the hour and a half, each way, and that in itself was telling, if I'd heard it. But I was busy with our boys, surfing in the bay, buzzing around on dirt bikes in the pastures, hanging with my sister and her family, with Jimmy's family, and occasionally Estelle and Dad. When Robert came back out, the same conflict would arise when I'd say no, they could not have a soda, that's pure sugary crap, then out one of them would walk, swilling a can of soda. "I thought I said no more soda, Rob?" And he'd say, "Dad said I could!" I'd approach Robert later and ask why he'd buy soda when I'd been saying for months it was a rare treat, not for every day. It was hard for Robert to get this, since the garage fridge in our Pueo Street house in town had been stocked with soda for the kids before we met.

I'd strived to have us eating healthier, and we always sat down together for meals during the school year, but he hadn't gotten it. Perhaps the tension was mounting, but I had only been a mother for a few years and now I had three sons to raise, and probably I was too assertive with Robert, too strong a disciplinarian too soon. When his Uncle Carrington came to visit, Robert insisted to me he would not be allowed to drink in our home. Carrington was Hartwell's brother, a serious alcoholic, who could only go a few days without a drink, and soon he was drunk. Robert finally asked him to leave, which he did. In his gracious way, Robert always welcomed everyone into our home, some staying for months before I came, "B.C.," Before Chula, as it came to be known. When Michael Hernstadt would arrive out of the blue, would do lines of coke at night on the dining room table after the boys were alseep, I didn't mind; I'd tried it and thought it was great fun. But when he left all his paraphernalia on the table to greet the kids the next morning, I did mind. I'd repeated it would be best for Hernstadt to stay in a hotel from now on, since he could easily afford it, but Robert couldn't tell him this. No matter that our house only had three small bedrooms for the five us.

So we had a few problems, but certainly nothing we couldn't work out. I thought. So imagine my shock when Robert walked out at the end of summer. Just said he'd had it, this wasn't working, it was over.

I don't actually remember the details, it's a blur, but when Robin and I moved back into Ma's, she said, "I always thought the only thing wrong with Robert was that he was too perfect. What happened, is he the Holy Ghost or what?" I couldn't answer her.

I felt erased.

I called Robert and told him I needed at the very least an explanation, a reason he could walk away. Why were we pau? What was going on? He came over a day or so later and calmly said he just could not take it anymore. "Take what anymore?" I asked, but he had no answers. What had I done? I beseeched. But he was more evasive than he'd ever been, and my fury took over. I leapt up, snatched the glasses off his nose and smashed them against the wall. He gaped at me, picked them up and walked out. It felt like the tide had gone out, way out, like before a tsunami, leaving dry sand and rocks.

I kept breathing, kept being a mom, though it was excruciating when I had to try describing to Robin what was going on, where was Daddy-Bob, as he'd called him (to differentiate from Daddy-Stephen), where were his brothers?

Mummy was supportive, sweet, as were Linda and Stephanie. Linda's marriage wasn't good anyway, she had mentioned it was about pau recently; and Steph confided in me what a prick my brother could be, he needed to control her, was often rude to her. But my misery did not need company, I was too baffled, devastated. Robert and I talked about everything, minuscule or big. He was not this mild, reserved guy who couldn't share his feelings. He actually had kind of a wild hair up his ass, like I did; I'd seen it manifested more over the past year and had heard about it back in New England. How he'd been kicked out of Milton Academy after ninth grade, gone on to graduate from Choate, but later was expelled from Washington and Lee in Virginia before going into the Army for a year, then on to graduate from the University of Colorado. So I thought I knew him.

Imagine my despair when I heard he'd begun dating Connie.

We belonged to the Outrigger Canoe Club on the beach at Waikīkī, because I'd been a member with my family since I'd been a child, when it used to be located next to the Royal Hawaiian Hotel. Now it was at the other end, on the gold coast, on a good surf spot, and it offered canoe paddling and competition. I wasn't interested in paddling canoe, and Robert and I had played tennis doubles occasionally, so we'd been invited to play paddle tennis (smaller court, short-handled wood paddle instead of a racquet) and we'd met a whole other group of friends at the Pacific Club. I'd liked Connie, what I knew of her, but I was enraged when I heard the rumor, because she was pretty, very bosomy and sexy. I was consumed with jealousy. I almost stalked them, driving by Robert's Pueo Street house, and when I saw them walking into the house one day, I wept for days. Spewed to Patsy, Stephanie, Jackie.

What happened? The passion, that really got me, because we had such *passion*. Was he having this with her now? Lurid scenes of the two of them came unbidden to torment me. It was unbearable, so I chose to summon happier scenes: Robert playing his guitar and singing "Froggy went a-courting, he did ride, uh huh," to Robin and all of us singing along, "Up to Molly Mouse's door he did ride, asking Molly Mouse, won't you be my bride, uh huh . . ." Todd saying, "Chu Chu, can you not pick me up in your car right in front of school?" and me cracking up as I got what he meant. I had bought a car for $100 right before Robert began courting me, and it looked like what I'd paid. I couldn't tell one car from another, didn't care, and I don't know what this car was except cheap and old, and the ceiling upholstery hung down in ribbons, which I found hilarious. But the car drove fine, and I'd pick the boys up from school, and obviously Todd was embarrassed to have his friends see him getting into my car. And Robby laughingly telling his dad at dinner how I got so excited watching his softball game I kept cheering and running alongside him, from first to second base and past. How I had seen ducks swimming in the pond behind the Honolulu Concert Center, thought they were so cute I had to buy a couple of them to bring home to our pool. When I came in the three boys were in the tub together and I plopped the ducks in with them while they shrieked. They were in our pool afterward for months, until they began breeding, quacking, shitting everywhere. How I knew Robert and the boys loved dogs, so I'd asked Aunty Barbie about her breeder and she gave us a black Lab puppy, and . . . so were they missing me at Pueo Street, or did they have enough with each other and Mau Mau? I'd had this big family and poor little Robin had brothers he adored. Robin's last name was still Johnston, and though he was unaware he had a different last name from the rest of us, I now wondered if I would keep the name Harrison if we got divorced?

Jimmy was a helpful brother, pissed off at Robert and telling me he would make him pay some sort of support. He even got a lawyer, though I was embarrassed and didn't really want to think about it.

CHAPTER SEVEN

A FEW WEEKS LATER, Mummy, Aunty Barbie, Robin and I got invited to Hanalei by Aunty Ole Lady. My spirits rose thinking about my three favorite ladies. Plus Aunty Barbie treated us to the trip. Aunty Ole Lady greeted us wearing an expensive, beautiful silk shift that she'd hacked off at the knee, the better to offset the corduroy pants she wore underneath, and we all cackled at her trademark antic. She served us guava sherbet cubes she'd picked, blended and frozen in ice trays, and Robin smacked on several. Aunty Barbie rented a new Jeep and we charged down the white, hard-packed sand of Hanalei Bay and swam in the azure ocean. Departing a few days later, we drove past the Hanalei River bordered by acres of taro fields, the mountains as a backdrop, but the stunning scene failed to arouse my usual admiration. I'd had a few laughs, but I'd hoped for a respite from grief, and I realized you take grief with you. This formerly foreign feeling was a palpable ache in my chest, squeezing my heart, as I began accepting our marriage was over.

Returning home I decided I might be open to dating, and somehow I was asked to go horseback riding by a good friend of Jimmy's. He kept some horses on the North Shore near Malaekahana, which we rode one afternoon, with dinner afterward. We had a few dates, I don't remember any of it. And paralysis didn't make me a fun date. I then met a hang glider, don't know how or where, and we dated. But I knew I was simply going through the motions. Then one day I was at Linda's house with Robin playing in her pool with his cousin Chris, and Robert dropped by. I am vague about the details, but remember I was a wreck. We had a few beers, and talked sitting outside at the garden bar. I smoked, drank wine and alternated between watching every word I said and blurting out questions. Why? What...?

Our visit/date (?) was over without resolving anything, but the important thing was he had been going to a psychologist! He was working things out. He was looking within. It sounded like Connie wasn't in the picture. I was ecstatic, hopeful. Of course, I played a huge part in our separation, though I really didn't know what; I had repeatedly looked at my role in our marriage, my character, the unattractive traits. Such a relief to know perhaps it was more about his issues. How amazing he'd recognized this and was dealing with it.

Some nights later, in the middle of the night, as I lay sleeping, I was gently awakened to the big strong bear of a man sliding into my bed. His powerful arms encircled me, his lovely scent of Old Spice bringing tears to my eyes, and I instantly remembered he loved me. The honeyed tones comforted, "I'm sorry, so, so sorry, I don't know if I understand it yet, but I love you, I've always loved you, you are everything to me. I know I've hurt you, how much I must have hurt you, and I'm sorry. I think, I guess, I just didn't feel ready to be married. It wasn't conscious, but I just couldn't be, I don't know, controlled by anyone. And you were so strong, and I guess I felt it was too hard. Dr. Boyer has helped, saying that I need to speak up when I'm angry and say how I feel. I don't always agree with you, and that's okay, but we can talk about it and you're just so fucking strong!"

I giggled and we embraced, kissing, red-hot kisses. I remembered how we fit, my breasts snug under his big chest. I was on fire and clearly Robert was as well. We made love in a hurry so we could make love again, gently, murmuring to each other the whole time. Robert left after we decided we'd move back home, and I fell into a sweet slumber. In the morning Ma cautiously asked, "I have to say dear, I'm upset you seemed to have someone here last night. You were despondent for months, and now suddenly you have a man in your bed? How could you . . ."

"Ma!" I interrupted, "It was Robert! He came over to Linda's the other day when I was there and I didn't tell you, 'cause I didn't want to get too hopeful, and then last night he woke me up and, oh, Mummy, he really does love me and we're going to move back home today." That erased her frown and we both laughed, hard. "And he's getting therapy, on his own! How cool is that?"

It felt like home, and Robin and I settled right back in, like *'opihi* (tiny clam-like shellfish) on a rock. Slowly, I saw Robert expressing anger, becoming a bit more aware of his enabling. How interesting that such a lovely characteristic of his actually worked against him. Nobody was as helpful as he was, or kind, so he had trouble drawing the line. "Will it enable you if I do the dishes tonight?" he'd tease me. What about if I bring the kids home from school tomorrow, will that be enabling to you?" I giggled, because we both knew he brought them home some days, when he wasn't coaching football, since they were all three at 'Iolani School. And when he spoke about his dad, he truly vented: "You know, Chu, how he described the cars he'd bought Jeff, and at one point even lumped me in with that, I told him, no, damn it, you never bought me a car, I always paid for anything I got myself. I wanted to say it's too bad you're still unaware how you spoiled Jeffrey. How John went to that psychiatrist for years, never getting better, the guy was an asshole, and Nina, she scarcely knew you!" Letting out the anger from childhood.

The Pueo Street house no longer felt big enough for five of us, especially if there were to be six, as I had hoped. When I broached the subject, Robert was skittish, because he was conservative with money. Though always generous with me, like insisting I go clothes shopping, or buying me a newer car to replace the car Todd had been ashamed of, a house was another matter. I had no idea what his trust fund entailed and it became apparent how vague he was about money, that neither of us were financial wizards, but I pressed him to reveal that, yes, we could sell the small, old house and buy a bigger old house. I searched for weeks and found a lovely open, four-bedroom house on Aukai Avenue, with a tiny pool a block from Kāhala Beach. And really old, which made it charming. Robert balked, $120,000 was way too expensive.

A peculiar coincidence arose to alter our situation. Friends of ours, Kathy and Joe Muller, with their only child, Baba, needed to move from a nearby duplex to a house, and they loved the one we'd outgrown. Without paying a realtor commission, we all saved money, and they moved in while we bought the bigger house. We even helped them buy another black Labrador, which seemed fitting, since we took Mau Mau with us. This event cemented a fledgling friendship for life.

Robert was ultimately as happy as I was about our new old home, and I joked that I was the "idea" partner, so stick with me. My favorite song he played and sang for me had been "Follow Me," by John Denver: "Follow me where I go, what I do and who I know, take my hand and you will follow me," which I'd been only too happy to do. And the last line of the song is "Take my hand and I will follow you," an apt phrase for us.

I'd been learning sign language so I could work with the deaf (which I'd practice with the boys), but was not able to help in the school for long, as I had an extremely exciting event coming up. I was hāpai and Robert and I were over the moon. Initially, when I spoke of having a little girl, how much it meant to me, he'd replied, "Aren't three kids enough? And, anyway, how can we be sure it'd be a girl?" I teased if it weren't we'd flush it down the toilet, and yet, I craved a daughter in my life. We'd had that three-month separation and been a happy family for almost a year together when I got pregnant, so summer of '75 was the due date. It was fun being hāpai along with Stephanie. We were often together, eating and talking about the daughters we both wanted so badly. Steph was mother to Jimmy's three sons on the weekends and often all summer, so, though she was modeling and watched her weight, I ate like a truck driver. She had Sky four months before I was due. In June, after playing tennis with the Goldmans one afternoon, I was joyous to give birth within thirty minutes. (I'd had Robin after an hour and a half.)

Kilia was exactly what I'd described to Robert I wanted, a dark-skinned, green-eyed, plump little cherub. Years later, I realized she looked like the girls I'd drawn in my youth, the same profile (talk about creative visualization).

Robert and I were elated. She was the only one in the family related to everyone, and I caressed her constantly. We all went to the country for the summer when she was a week old, the forty pounds I'd gained disappearing before we got there. It was great timing for me, as Robert did the meals and chores, Linda wanted to hold her, as did thirteen-year-old Kelly, and five-year-old Robin would lift Kilia out of the crib to cuddle her. I nursed her on demand till the heat made it difficult. Steph and Jimmy were across the pasture much of the summer and Sky and the boys would join us on the beach often.

We laughed at everything that summer. If our Labrador, Mau Mau, charged through the house with our leg of lamb in his jaws from the kitchen counter, we cackled our heads off. If a rat ran through the living room, we chased it. If a window wouldn't open to the view, we'd push it out into the bushes. We sang as Robert played guitar, drank cheap champagne and played Password nights, while our three sons and their cousins Chris and Kelly cavorted outside. Once we noticed an old mattress had caught fire where it sat outside, and upon returning from the beach and seeing and smelling it, we giggled. Don't remember how that happened, but we had the freedom of nothing left to lose out here, why worry about this dilapidated house like we did in town? Jimmy wasn't keen on ever coming over, because their house was immaculate and he and Steph agreed on this, but Linda's and my family were kicked back out in the country.

Daddy only came as close to our house as his horses were, and, after seeing him playing polo with Jimmy and some of their pals in front of our open living room, Robert finally mentioned to Clark that maybe he'd like to ride. None of us had been riding lately and Robert had only ridden as a kid when he worked on a farm, so Dad was amenable and found a horse big enough. We all chortled, it looked like a Shetland pony under Robert, but he would stick and ball with Jimmy and Dad a few times, even played in one of their casual games. Dad actually called him by name, instead of "your big jock." But one afternoon, when Robert had his entire rugby team over for beers and a potluck, things changed a bit. The Samoans and Tongans got drunk and wild as well as the *haole* (white) boys, and, though Robert said many times to please close the gates between the beach and the pastures, one was left open that night.

"Where the hell's that big jock of yours!?" Dad yelled into our wide-open living room window the next morning, his face enraged as he sat astride a horse. "All my goddam horses are gone and it's his goddam fault leaving the gate open!" I was the only one up, Kilia in my arms, but soon Robert hustled out to placate the skinny bad wolf. He calmed him down way faster than I could have and promised they'd immediately go chase down the runaway polo ponies. It wasn't easy finding them, and we prayed none were on nearby Kamehameha Highway, but they were rounded up in time for the Sunday afternoon polo match, as Clark demanded.

Daddy had been playing polo for years, and as a child I watched them play at Kapiʻolani Park on the fringe of Waikīkī. The stables across the street (replaced by a large nursery, eventually), was a hive of activity, with horses in their stalls, muckrakers, hot-walkers, polo players. On weekends they would trot across the street to the park and canter around inside the wooden perimeter of the polo field to warm up before the game. Spectators sat on the hoods of their cars, chatting, cheering, hollering at any mishap. The thundering of hooves, the click of a mallet swing connecting with the ball, the shouting and swearing of the players made for lively entertainment. The heft of the horse and its speed charging across the field was danger enough, but, coupled with the players' aggressive pursuit of the ball, reining their mounts into a collision course with at least one other horse, often resulted in falls. The polo player would be lucky not to break a leg, arm or worse, and the mere jostling from careening horses would elicit a chorus of yelps from the audience. The agility required to swing a mallet while galloping full speed was impressive, and to aim and actually hit the ball without encumbrance from another horse, or even your own, was more so. And making a goal brought a great hue and cry, as horns would honk along with the cheers.

Clark broke limbs. I don't remember much of that, but he was as gutsy and foul-mouthed as any of them (Tuna Sampaio, Bob Mc-

Gregor, Charlie Pietsch, Fred Dailey), as much a staple of the ambience as the pungent odor of horse sweat and droppings. Players are rated on their prowess making goals, and Dad had a two-goal rating. Jimmy grew up hot-walking the horses between chukkers and after the game, to cool them down, and growing up with horses on both our south and North Shore homes gave him the skills of a fine horseman and eventually a polo player with a four-goal ranking.

It was a rich man's sport, and Jimmy began playing at Mōkule'ia on the North Shore bordering the ocean as a young man, and eventually could afford his own string of polo ponies. It became a toffee social event, decked-out fans driving to the country with coolers of champagne to sip with their picnics, to see and be seen. The players cut fine figures, with their white helmets, matching jerseys, white jodhpurs and boots, and Jimmy was even more handsome than Dad. Other younger *kāma'āina* (locals), such as Peter Baldwin, Ronnie Tongg, Al Lopaka, a Greenwell, infused a new vitality into the sport. They played visiting teams from Mexico, Chile, England (even General George Patton apparently played with them at some point), and I showed up at the game Prince Charles starred in, as well as the party afterward at the polo club, whenever that was. (It's tricky writing a memoir when you cannot rememba!) Of course, he was draped with lei afterward, maybe by a family friend who anticipated their imminent date.

CHAPTER EIGHT

MORE THAN A YEAR LATER, Robert and I needed to be alone
and farmed the boys out to their respective parents: Rob and Todd to
their mother in California, and Robin to Daddy-Stephen, traveling
on the plane by himself, which airlines permitted in those days, with
the stewardess looking after him. Kilia at just one and a half went to
close friends, the Gileses (who'd lost a daughter a few years prior);
Leslie was a nurse at Punahou, and needed to have a baby in her arms.
Robert and I exulted in a week in Aspen, seeing Hernstadt and other
pupule (crazy) friends of Robert's while I skied that beautiful resort.
(Bigfoot was unable to find ski boots big enough so worked out at the
gym instead.)

I had begun to jog with Robert (the first of anyone I knew at that
time), played tennis regularly with the *wāhine* (girls), and Robert
continued playing rugby (though it was a sport I couldn't have been
less enchanted with, except for football). I didn't understand the
game, and when I first married Robert I tried, but I realized he didn't
care if I did or if I made it to many of his games. He was the biggest
and strongest player on the team, and he loved every part of the game:
the strange scrum, the kicking for a goal and especially tackling. Socially it wasn't the first sport I'd choose him to play, either, as they'd
often swill down beers at Kapi'olani Park after they were pau. Once or
twice he'd forget to call when he was still there at 9 p.m., and the game
ended at 6 p.m. Worried, I screamed like a fishwife when he stumbled
home, nose bloody and sweat drying. He had so many minor injuries
over the years I finally threatened him, "If you get really hurt, down
for the count or even paralyzed, I'm not nursing you or helping you;
I'll be like that song and Ruby will take her love to town!" He'd laugh,
but I said I meant it.

But when he talked more seriously about wanting to play rugby in Australia in late 1977, I got excited, because, of course, I'd wanted to return there and he'd been keen on the idea even before we separated. Now that Kilia was two, it seemed timely to apply to schools in Oz. We'd live there for a year, take a leave of absence from 'Iolani. He looked at schools in Sydney, but I was voting for Adelaide, and he decided if he could get a job there, at Pultney Grammar, a boys' school, we'd go. We were thrilled when our friend Anne Abel-Smith pulled strings (her father was the largest cattle owner in Oz). She was well known in Adelaide, and he got the job. We rented our house in town, which paid for the airfare, left Mau Mau with a young guy in exchange for staying in the country house. Linda had divorced Peter, and she'd actually taken my advice and moved to Adelaide right before we did, with Kelly and Chris in tow.

Though they had vehemently opposed leaving Hawai'i and all their pals for Australia, the boys immediately got into their new mates and lifestyle. (I knew they would, as we'd gone back to Cape Cod the summer before to stay with Sis and Hartwell for a few weeks. They paid for the tickets, which Robert wanted to return, but I pointed out this was false pride; they could afford it way more than we could. So we'd found someone to rent our house for those weeks, starting a trend for us, and off we went, ignoring the boys' objections of missing out on the surf. When they realized how fabulous Sis' six-bedroom house was, on a hill overlooking the ocean, with a boathouse they could use as a fort, they were enthralled. Sis was a top sailor, and we sailed her boats, waterskied, played tennis daily on the clay tennis court. They made pals with all the old families' children and couldn't wait to return to Cataumet the next time.)

We'd rented the Adelaide house through friends before leaving for Australia, and the six of us moved right into our pretty, four-bedroom home with a tiny yard and scant furniture near their school. Robert and our sons settled into Pultney Grammar, the boys wearing cute little uniforms complete with caps and shoes, which they were not used to. Robert adored his teaching position, his colleagues, the students, the school. We all got a huge kick out of the accent and would parrot their sayings: "She'll be right mate," "Fair dinkum," "Fancy a root?" etc.

"You got new tits! Very sexy, dahling," Peter exclaimed as he wrapped me in a hug. I had breast implants done the year before, having always wanted more than the bumps I had. My own mother observed years before that it was curious I had "bee bites," since hers were bigger than mine. And my big brother would tease me mercilessly about being a carpenter's delight, a flat board. So I swept into Adelaide at thirty-one years old, ten years later, with cleavage. I had lived there single, we all had, and now it was like a new chapter out of a book, with all of us married with children. Craziness ensued as Robert had instant rapport with my old friends. "The yank tank," as they called him, hit it off of course, with his rugby mates. And nobody here was drinking any less than we had before. It wasn't enough that we partied during the week, but Sundays in Adelaide were known for long lunches at lovely estates and properties, starting about noon and taking us to dinner.

Jane was the only one missing. She'd married tall, handsome Ian, and they lived with their three kids on a huge, working property in Tasmania. She flew over for the one big party we had, and it would have been a wild enough reunion with her brother Peter and all the mates from Europe, as well as my old friends from ten years prior, if I hadn't just had my tubes tied two days before. I'd returned from the hospital the day before feeling great, except I hadn't been able to urinate, and now I was swilling champagne, as I'd done prior to leaving hospital, when Anne Abel-Smith brought in a bottle. So when Dr. McEvoy came up and asked how I was, I said, "Brilliant, but I need to do wees, as I haven't gone in two days." He patted my protruding belly and looked alarmed. "Chula, not to worry, she'll be right, but you need to come with me, a catheter will help, dahling." I remembered he was a urologist, turned out he lived a few blocks away, so at his house he inserted a catheter, saying how my bladder could have burst if I'd waited much longer. The release was urgent, and I tucked the other end of the catheter in my rose velour britches and returned to my party. Jane shrieked, "Getch your gear off, let's have a look," so it was known by all as my new fashion accoutrement.

Julie, with her delicious humor, was there, along with Janet with her sharp wit and naughty gay husband, Jeoffrey, who'd sired her son, and refined, lighthearted Annie Abel-Smith with a friend, also gay, so the ribald humor escalated the more we were on the "piss." Janet had us to many of her elegant but debauched Sunday lunches at her estate in the hills, and my sister Linda and I would shriek with laughter at Jeoffrey leaning into Robert, endearingly calling him a bitch. It was so acceptable to be gay in Oz in the late '70s, most of them were well out of the closet.

We went to the sheep-shed party in the Outback, after the shearing of the sheep with Annie, dancing, drinking, mingling with the locals and their colorful jargon: "G'dye mite, hah yuh doin'?" "Yeh, I'm as dry as a fuck with no foreplay." "Too right, dry as a dead dingo's donger." "Had a bit o' rain, mite." "'Bout as useful as lips on a chook."

Telltale signs we were partying too much were: Robert noticed at school one morning he had on one black shoe and one brown one; when I could scarcely get out of bed in the morning and Kilia trundled in naked and just peed on the floor next to our bed; Robin had nightmares running around the house at night with a rubber ducky in his mouth; when we came home late one night to see my ancient car with its roof caved in, as apparently Rob had been out with pals doing wheelies until it flipped; Todd broke his jaw ice skating, when we'd been away. The *coup de grâce* was when Robert was called in by Mr. McKinnon, the headmaster of Pultney. It seemed that, while the long queue of cars waited to enter the Oakbank Steeplechase in the country the past weekend, on the roof of a car pranced a lad who then proceeded to drop his drawers, pull a BA and was later identified as "the yank" by another student. Could that have been our son Rob? Mr. McKinnon asked, and Robert shamefully admitted it certainly could, for we'd gone to the same races and knew Rob was there with his mates.

Mr. McKinnon said the routine penalty for this sort of thing would be caning. Robert was stunned; this was so primitive. "I'm astonished you still cane the kids, and I'd urge you to rethink this penalty for any of the students, but wouldn't that be too easy for Rob? I mean, it'd hurt, but wouldn't it be wiser to make him come to school for four or five Saturdays and pick up litter around the school or something?" So we admonished Rob while trying not to giggle, and told him his punishment. Curiously, the upshot was that Pultney never used this sort of discipline again.

We definitely were carousing too much, we knew it, but it was de rigueur in Adelaide. Everyone we socialized with smoked and drank copiously, thus we didn't consider it a problem. We had busy days, we were all healthy and it was such fun. I played tennis a few days a week with my girlfriends on their private grass courts, and we'd chat and snack afterward, making it into an entire morning. I'd take Kilia to a daycare and pick her up before fetching her brothers from school.

I also got into modeling a bit, snagging a fun job at David Jones department store where they all shopped, actually dancing onstage while modeling clothes. Robert could scarcely contain his mirth when he popped in to watch, as I was not a dancer. I could if it was rocking out with a partner, though I wasn't able to follow a man's lead, as Robert discovered right away. He was a beautiful dancer and had often danced with his mother, but I didn't have the timing and was scarcely able to handle the choreographed songs from *Cabaret*, with several other ladies. I'd snort with laughter at myself, missing steps, but gamely danced on. I'd never have exploited myself at home, but you can reinvent yourself in another country.

We flew to Tasmania (an island as green as Ireland) during school break with Kilia and Robin, leaving Rob and Todd at home with a caretaker we'd had before. I was excited for Robert to meet urbane Ian, because I knew they'd hit it off. Jane met us at the airport, both of us giddy, and she fussed over Robin and Kilia, who was now three, telling them how fun it'd be for her three kids. Robert offered to drive and we scarcely drew a breath for the next half hour, when Jane noticed we had pulled over. "What're you doing, Robert?" she queried, using her patrician tone. "Well," he chuckled, "I've been trying to get your attention for five minutes, it seems we're out of gas." "Out of petrol?! Shit, Ian's going to be cranky," she shrieked. "He told me to fill up before we left, and I drove right by our gas pump!" We all cracked up, asking in unison, "You have a gas pump right on your property and you still forgot?" as Robert got out to hitch a ride to a gas station. Jane and I smoked cigarettes, chatted and laughed while Robin and Kilia ran around nearby till Robert returned in a lather forty minutes later.

Driving down their eucalyptus-lined driveway past acres of cattle and horses, we exclaimed over the beauty of the property and their lovely home a mile further on. It was an instant party, with lamb roasting in the oven, Ian and Jane serving us pints of beer and champagne, while Robin and her son explored the barn, and Kilia played with her daughters. We slipped into this bucolic, rustic lifestyle like we were home, and the barbecue they had for us out in the paddock the next night confirmed this sentiment. Jane and Ian's friends were as naughty as they were, told us stories about each other that had us in tears. And always we were regaled with rugby tales when they realized Robert was playing in Adelaide. Once again my Ozzie accent bloomed, the kids all did a great imitation, becoming raconteurs like their mates.

When their school year ended in late '78, it saddened me even more to say goodbye than the year I'd lived there prior to this one. Rob had to bid farewell to a girlfriend as well as all his mates, Todd and Robin were ambivalent about leaving and Kilia didn't remember much about home. Robert announced we'd be back—many times. Robert and the boys went back to 'Iolani in the middle of their school year as planned, Robert picking up where his replacement left off.

We came home to a dead lawn, which was no big deal, as our tenants had left the house in good shape. It wasn't their fault the grass had died, since we had no sprinklers. I announced to Robert how it was his fault, because he'd said it'd be too expensive to put them in, and that from now on I'd take charge of financial matters. I had a tiny trust fund and, because of his heftier one, we could afford to live in

Kāhala instead of on 'Iolani campus in a duplex. I realized it didn't matter who made the most money, had the bigger income, he wasn't inclined to run the household.

I knew I had to live healthier after our year of alcohol poisoning, so became more active, beginning a yoga class. Robert and I played tennis regularly, sometimes together in mixed doubles, and he continued rugby and going for a run, as I did. Rob and Todd played football, tennis and soon began playing indoor volleyball. Robin still played soccer and softball in the leagues, and we all noticed how much more competitive sports were here than in Oz, and how that had been a good respite. Kilia took up hula; she had the natural moves and grace and olive skin of a little Hawaiian hula girl. She was reunited with precious Sky, Jimmy and Stephanie's daughter, and Robin was also with Jimmy's three sons, Michael, Mark and Matthew.

We leapt back into our social life the next year with old friends and family. Linda had returned months before us from Adelaide and began dating Lee, a nice guy who was an executive at a television station. Jimmy and I began motorcycle adventures in the country, up in the hills. I thrived on the rush of charging up mountains, dirt biking behind my brother, eating his exhaust, trying to keep up.

Modeling became a part of my routine. Kathy Muller and I modeled in casual lunchtime fashion shows a few times weekly in restaurants around O'ahu. It was fun making a bit of cash, eating a free lunch and often being able to afford the cut rate of the dresses we modeled. (I was not a shopper, so this was right up my alley.) Kathy soon grew bored and decided she could make a lot more money if she started her own modeling agency, which was convenient, because I got occasional modeling jobs for television ads, etc. Kathy plunged into her new business, and she immediately signed Linda's beautiful daughter Kelly for a commercial, which went national. Kelly had decided before her senior year at Punahou that she would move out of her mother's home and find an apartment of her own. Nobody we knew had left home while still in high school, and Linda was aghast Kelly would be this independent. When she got a sizable check from her first foray into the modeling world, Kelly realized she would still go off to USC at the end of summer, but maybe to Hollywood after the first year.

Rob graduated as well and took himself off to Aspen, wanting to put off college for a year to work and play with William, Michael Hernstadt's son. A bit anxious about Rob hanging out with Michael as well, we nevertheless wept when Rob left, the first kid to go. I decided to get a real job, and began work at an employment agency now that Kilia was in kindergarten. The work didn't interest me, so when a job at the Honolulu Club, a new athletic club downtown, came along, I went for it for six months; I was to entice people to sign up for membership. In the meantime, my full-time work took its toll on our marriage. I could not seem to juggle this with mothering three children; I just didn't have Robert's stamina. I was feisty anyway, and now I became intense as well. By November we were arguing often, and Robert needed a break. Strangely, it worked fine to have his respite over at Ma's house for a few weeks.

We'd already had friends from Oz in our home, so it was an opportune time to have a brief split, and we resumed life as usual with better communication after Robert returned. I knew I could no longer party like we'd been doing, especially now that I was working. I needed to mellow out. I smoked pakalolo occasionally if we had it, which always made me laugh. And when cocaine emerged on the scene in Hawai'i, I was eager to partake. Robert was not interested in either drug, because he was afraid of being addicted. Cocaine was a dazzling rush, feeling like the top of my head flew off and I never turned it down when it was offered at parties. For the few years it was first prevalent, I had a blast, until I realized anything that took me up that high that quickly would also bring me down that fast. I no longer indulged.

For spring break of '81, Robert and I took off for a rugby tournament in California while Todd, Robin and Kilia stayed with close friends. We had only had a break that week in Aspen without children since Robert and I met, we needed to rekindle the passion, though I still wasn't keen on rugby. That summer, having rented our house for a month, Rob joined us at the Cape. Sis had bought a windsurfing board, and we all learned in her quiet Cataumet Bay to climb on the board, pull the sail out of the water and sail away before we had to come about. We felt blessed to have Sis and Hartwell in this amazing setting, so different from Hawai'i, with Robert's sister and brothers and their families around as well.

Afterward we continued to Lexington alone, leaving the kids with Robert's family for a week. Robert had never met Rosie, of course, and I was excited, though people found it peculiar that my current husband was going to visit my ex-husband's family. We were welcomed by an old friend and undertaker's daughter, who immediately told Robert he must come to her home to check out her recently deceased dad's wardrobe of jackets. They'd fit him perfectly, she said, so we went straight from the airport and Robert laughingly obliged. When we arrived at Rosie's, she got a huge kick out of Robert's new booty of several tweed jackets. "Well, I'll be damned! He's as big as a mountain, like you said, honey," she exclaimed, her lips clamped on a cigarette with an inch of ash, "but a whole lot handsomer than that old dad of Lucy's! Come on in, Robert, I'm just so glad to meet you." We hugged, sat the rest of the afternoon snacking on slices of salty Virginia ham and green fried tomatoes, and enjoyed belly laughs as we caught up.

Robert was amazed, touched when we went to the Idlehour Country Club that night with Rosie, only to find out it was a sit-down dinner party for Robert and me. To have all my dear old Kentucky friends, who were originally Stephen's family and friends, honoring us was so extraordinary I teared up before cackling the rest of the night. I remember nothing else while in Lexington, but Rosie's precious eccentric presence and that wonderful dinner party burned brightly in my heart. That was the last time I saw Rosie, but her charm will always be a part of me.

CHAPTER NINE

I HAD ALWAYS READ VORACIOUSLY and had read a few Edgar
Cayce books Ma had given me. It was compelling reading about reincarnation and other spiritual subjects, and gradually I read every sort
of metaphysical book I could find. I had also begun writing, though in
an entirely different genre. My first book was about a courtesan and
all her lovers, and I'd crack my friends up describing how aroused
I'd get on my typewriter for hours. "I'm getting so turned on," I'd
say, "that I have to turn off the typewriter and turn on my vibrator."
Michele retorted, "Why not just sit on the typewriter and hit that key,
you know, that zings across the page." We howled. "You kill me, Chu,
I'm assuming you write naked," Liz said, and Michele said, "How else
would she be?"

"Wait for me, Hotpants!" the note said, when I opened my drawer
for the vibrator. I giggled. I'd told Robert from the start that I used
his old vibrator. He had a metal massager to use on sore muscles, and
I'd kept it for spicier moments. I'd always had a high libido, which
pleased him, and never declined his requests for lovemaking. In fact,
I probably was more eager than he was, and was, fortunately for both
of us, trigger happy. Robert hadn't felt ambivalent about me using my
sex toy when he wasn't available, so it was strange that he'd hidden
it from me now, and I actually searched for it, then pounced on him
when he finally returned from school coaching football or volleyball,
asking what the hell and where was it? He laughed heartily, and, after
retrieving it, I reassured him that it never got in the way, right, so no
worries.

In fact, one of the most bizarre moments in my life was on a
scorchingly hot day in my bedroom as I typed a steamy, graphic scene,
so titillating I needed to take matters in hand. I closed the door and
lay down with the vibrator, when, just as I began the delicious buck-

ing and heaving of orgasm, my bedroom door opened! In walked Ma. I was so stunned, I jumped up and threw down the instrument, which proceeded to hum and bounce around my ankles as I burbled, "Hi, Ma! What's up?" She smiled benignly, asking how I was, as I stood there naked, pouring sweat, as if I was in the kitchen cooking and not in my bedroom, pleasuring myself. She followed me into the kitchen. I couldn't get away from the noisy evidence fast enough, yet couldn't reach down to turn it off without acknowledging it. We chatted inanely about what I was cooking for dinner, and after an interminably long charade on my part, she smiled sweetly and left.

Was Ma going "nitty notty" (the term she and Aunty Barbie used to joke about forgetting things)? But she still worked mornings for Aunty Barbie, as her private secretary, which was where she'd just come from. She would pop in on her way home, sharing anecdotes about Aunty Barbie and I'd recount tales of the kids, my minor problems, our social life, what book I was reading. I often dropped in on her if I was going by Niu Valley, and she might be gardening, swimming laps in her tiny pool naked or chatting on the phone with Aunty Barbie.

I called my sister to share the vibrator story so we could shriek with laughter together. Linda was not as close to Ma, not by a long shot. She'd always felt I'd been the favored daughter. It had come between us and she resented me, perhaps felt rejected by Ma. Now married to her third husband, Lee, she no longer seemed lonely. (I had begun to pull away from her while in Oz. Though she'd dated several men, they didn't last, and her being single meant a different social life from ours, hence I sensed a rivalry between us.)

I continued reading about metaphysics and writing books that would not be read. But it was easy to be distracted with a ski trip to Sun Valley with our pals Kathy and Joe. Todd, who'd not skied before, happily came for his graduation present that spring week, and I in my inimitably impatient way, gave him a half-hour lesson before telling him to follow me. By the next day, he joined me and Kathy's daughter Baba down the black runs, while Robert again struggled to find boots big enough to fit his size-thirteen feet. His body wasn't conducive to skiing anyway, and he didn't pursue the sport for long.

We were in the habit, ardurous as it was, of renting our house whether we were gone a week, a month or longer, which paid for our next trip to Oz that summer, while Robin went to Daddy Stephen and Kilia to camp. We immersed ourselves in the offbeat Australian culture with old friends, enthralled once again, and grateful to have time, as teachers do. Occasionally Robert felt troubled that he should do something more valuable, more meaningful in people's lives, and I'd point out how respected he was at 'Iolani, which was hugely apparent by all the feedback and adoration from students (who told us after leaving Iolani how they loved him) and other teachers. He loved what he did, they needed his candid, fun approach to learning and he obviously inspired everyone he taught. How many can say that? The pay was terrible, like all teachers, but, thank God, he had that trust fund from his mother.

One of the reasons he was such a wonderful teacher and related to his students so well was because he'd been "invited to leave" Milton Academy (their quaint expression for kicking him out) outside of Boston at the end of his ninth-grade year after being kolohe. He went on to Choate to graduate three years later. But, again, at Washington and Lee University in Virginia, he was summoned by the dean of students after ten football games. "You're doing great on the football field, Robert, but you're not doing shit in your classes. You need to go into the Army and grow up." Which he did for a year, before attending the University of Colorado. His offenses were no more than mine for getting kicked out of the University of Arizona, and I think having that wild hair up his 'okole certainly made him relate better, to be more broadminded and understanding as a teacher, and definitely made him a better counselor the few years he counseled at 'Iolani.

The lease on the land under our country shack had run out after twelve years, in 1982, so we no longer had the luxury of getting away for long periods, but we could camp nearby, under the ironwood trees next to the beach. My brother leased the whole point, his house and

Dad's shack included, and he let us camp whenever we wanted, on the cusp of Malaekahana and Kahuku. A glorious spot.

Our eldest, Rob, enrolled in Santa Barbara City College in pre-med, eventually getting a scholarship. He began raving to us that we would flip over Santa Barbara. It was gorgeous, rimmed by mountains and the ocean, with twenty-four volleyball courts, everyone played a great caliber of tennis, the homes were beautiful, with huge gardens and lawns. We knew we'd have to see for ourselves, but, meanwhile, I began a new job at Trade Publishing Co. selling ad space. It was fun but meaningless, and I didn't last long there either, and the next job, at an advertising agency, was worse. I realized I was out of my depth, this was not my milieu, and I actually got fired. I was glad to be out of there, but strangely felt like a failure. Kathy laughed at me, saying the jobs were just "not me."

I began training for volunteer work at a hospice. I also bought a windsurfing board. In those days, they were not light or sophisticated, but we'd drag it down the block from our house to the beach, and climb on. It took strength and balance, as the trade winds in Hawai'i were fierce compared to the protected Cataumet Bay on the Cape. Easy for the boys, but I struggled and kept at it, whizzing out, coming about, and sailing back in my purple bikini, the purple sail. Sometimes I took our dog, which meant I had to step around him, but it was a blast.

My thrill-junkie brother's leg had finally healed from being broken in about seven places in a polo accident, and now we had Jet Skis to add to our fun. His home was at the end of Kāhala Beach, where it turns into Black Point, a posh, tiny neighborhood where he kept his Jet Skis. We'd zoom out toward the surf break full throttle, and gun it when we'd hit each wave, getting air. Exhilirating to shoot high out of the water and slap back down, accelerating just enough to land smoothly, to turn and catch the wave.

If you fell, the Jet Ski would circle back, riderless, and you'd grab hold and climb on again. The danger was that the weight of it could crush you should it hit you. Sort of like dirt biking (motorcycling) the mountains: If you lost control, the bike could land on you, burning you badly. It always felt exciting to go off with my brother, like I was his buddy, courting danger. But there were quite contrary feelings when Jimmy had his accident on a motorcycle in the mountains some years later. Robert had come with us and we were in the Pūpūkea mountains on the North Shore, it was getting late and we were tiring.

We were charging down a ravine and I got stuck, could not go forward or back. Jimmy left his bike and came to help me, since he was the experienced rider here, and they were his bikes. Somehow he got it going but fell under it, screaming when his leg broke. I was terrified, because it looked as though his bone was protruding, and Robert flew back up the mountain for help. It was past twilight and Jimmy lay writhing in agony, while I tried ineffectually to be helpful. Finally, it was dark, really dark, and we heard the faint chop, chop of a helicopter's blades. It was difficult for them to find a level spot to land, but when they did, two or three firemen jumped out and rushed over. They lifted Jimmy into the helicopter and I relaxed when a curly-haired cutie said hello to me, realizing he was my first lover's brother. I think I climbed on behind another fireman, who rode me out on my motorcycle, and, when reunited with Robert, I wept. We visited Jimmy at Queen's Hospital that night and found out how bad it was; it was the same leg he had broken playing polo, he mumbled, they'd put a metal piece in his leg. He was in agony and wouldn't be playing polo for many months. Nor would we be dirt biking for a while.

I admitted to myself there were not many jobs that enticed me, much less that I was qualified for. We could afford for me not to work, therefore I kept writing, disciplined until I'd get rejected by publishers or I'd have to rewrite another draft. Thus I was free to join our family that summer in Santa Barbara for the first time, and it was everything Robby raved about and more. We'd become great friends with the Steeles, who lived initially in Hawai'i and had moved to Montecito, Santa Barbara, the most beautiful town I'd ever seen. Expansive woodsy properties with hills and gardens, often a horse or tennis court, and architecture out of a magazine, charming and understated.

I once again felt I breathed rarified air among these homes, as well as the lilac mountains in the background, and the ocean at the fore. An old Punahou friend and her family lived there, my cousin and her family, and we immediately dropped into this quiet, elegant neck of the woods, literally, like foreigners coming home, to the huge eucalyptus and oak trees, towering hedges and flowering shrubs. For many years to come.

In September we took in our first foster son. Adam's parents had died. His father, a pediatric psychiatrist, had just killed himself; they'd lived in Kāhala and somehow we knew he needed a home. He moved in and took Rob's empty bed. Adam was an unhappy camper of sixteen, but we loved on him as he grieved and gradually he came around months later and began to lighten up. He attended Kalani High School nearby, while Kilia was at Kāhala School (also public), and Todd and Robin were still at 'Iolani.

I had begun to write up interviews of several people in all walks of life on what they thought happiness was, and if they were happy, why. It was an interesting project, manifesting similar reasons and ways these individuals were happy. I began typing it into a book and, had I had the tenacity it took to follow through, it would have made a good study. Don't remember what came of it, probably laziness on my part and perhaps ennui when it came to the editing and harder work of selling it.

The hospice work trailed off in '83, but I became engrossed with Elizabeth Kubler-Ross, a renowned authority on death and dying. She was a diminutive but powerful woman, and I hung on her every word. Her workshops had us pounding out negative, scary feelings on a mattress with a bat. You began to understand how destructive these feelings were if they weren't released. And to understand that dying was neither frightening nor final, one of her most valuable teachings. After the Edgar Cayce books revealed his messages of life after life, I was open to knowing more about the entity "Ramtha" when it came on the scene in Hawai'i.

At first it was the tapes I listened to, an otherworldly voice that said it was Ramtha, coming through this woman, a vehicle through which to contact humanity from the other side. It was bizarre, but not difficult to comprehend or believe as I listened. Telling Robert about it drew blank looks and some eye rolling, with not much comment. When I went to an evening with Ramtha some months later, I was hooked. It all made sense to me, and when I talked about it those first months with Ma, who embraced the concept of reincarnation, she told me about the Theosophical Society. A small house in Mānoa housed all these books that I perused and felt comfortable, not freaky like other friends felt. Having been raised by Ma to love God, to appreciate the miracles of nature, I remained open to this new wisdom, this new way of thinking. Living in Hawai'i with the jade and indigo ocean and waves surrounding us, the lush green valleys, mauve mountains, jagged cliffs, the volcanoes and flowers, I felt enfolded by nature, created by God.

One day, as a freshman at Punahou, Ma got me and Melissa out of school spontaneously in the middle of the day, drove us to the airport, and we flew to the Big Island of Hawai'i, where she was from, to see Kīlauea Volcano erupting. All afternoon we saw molten lava firing skyward, fiery spurts blazing across the land, crimson against the darkening night. And she would go out of her way to show me a shower tree in full bloom, its brilliant yellow or pink petals lifting our hearts. Or when the ocean was malia, calm, with no wind, like a sheet of turquoise liquid silk to the horizon. I came to see this was how she fortified herself when her five-year-old Michael drowned, with nature's beauty and God's love. Her favorite expression over the years was, "My cup runneth over."

I began surfing the waves on a board again; it'd been years and I was rusty, but it was a new passion. Robin surfed whenever he could, studying only when he had to, as I had. He was a "grom," a little gremmie, his olive skin tanned, his hair white. Todd surfed, but he also played excellent tennis as well as volleyball, becoming skilled both at indoor and beach volleyball. He was a strapping, muscular lad, like his brother and dad, and I had to explain to Robin he'd never get as big as

Rob and Todd, as his Daddy-Stephen wasn't a big dude.

Kilia, a merry little sprite, played soccer, got good grades at school, and had Sky and her little pals over often to swim in our pool. I'd watch sometimes while cooking from the kitchen window, though Ki had swum like a porpoise since she was two, and stopped mid-chore one day when I heard her calling to Sky that she should swim over to her, where her brown little legs clamped onto the edge of the pool like an 'opihi, telling Sky she was having the "shakeys." I was stunned when I studied her and realized Kilia had her little tushie right over the waterspout. She was having an orgasm at the age of six! I couldn't wait to share this with her dad, and we both cracked up. I had only just stopped nibbling on her adorable body.

Kelly was making movies in Hollywood, and her glitzy life got more glamorous when she dated Charlie Sheen, the first of the movie stars in her life. When she brought him home, Jimmy and Steph had a family dinner party at their oceanfront home, and I think he was more impressed than we were, though he was a cutie in those days.

We no longer had our foster son Adam. He'd moved in with a friend a few months back, having gotten a job at the zoo, which became his career. Now we had another foster son, Owen, who Robert heard had gotten into fights and was scheduled to go to Juvenile Hall, so he announced to me the good news was Owen was not going to jail, the bad news was the judge sentenced him to our house. Owen was a sweet, soft-spoken, well-built lad and was easy to love for the next four months or so.

Todd graduated from 'Iolani and left for UCLA and we missed his quiet humor. Rob, in his second year at City College in Santa Barbara, worked part time as a stripper.

We were amused at his choice of work. It made sense when he explained he got paid well to strip for girls' parties, it was good exercise and he got a kick over girls drooling over his studly body. When I recounted this vignette to Kathy (who owned the Kathy Muller Talent Agency) one night at a party, she was indignant. "I can't believe you're letting him strip, Chu!" I stopped giggling to reply, "What do you

Hartwell and Sis Harrison, Boston, 1966

Robert, Rob and Todd in Providence, Rhode Island, 1967

Robert and his rugby mates, 1970-87

Robert at an 'Iolani football game, 1972

Chula and Robin dirt biking at Mālaekahana, 1973

Chula windsurfing at Kāhala, 1974

Kilia at the Mālaekahana shack, 1977

Chula, Kilia and Robert, Adelaide, Australia, 1978

Chula jet skiing, 1984

Robert at 'Iolani, 1984

Stephanie and Jimmy, 1985

Christmas, 1986

mean, 'let him,' Kath. He's twenty-one years old, for God's sake, and, anyway, why not?" "That's terrible, I don't undertand you." "Kath, I can't believe you're such a prude. Anyway, how is his making money off his bod any different from you, a flesh peddler?" Her eyes were slits as I turned, tapped Robert's arm (our routine) and signaled I was ready to leave. Robert roared over my description of my spat with Kathy as we hurried out. The next day at Kāhala Beach, Kathy and I made up and howled with laughter.

Sadly, Hartwell Harrison, Robert's father and esteemed surgeon from Harvard and Massachusettes General Hospital, lay dying. I was as down as Robert, yet intrigued that he was dying of cancer in the very organ he had been one of the three to originally transplant. Robert was grateful we'd been back to visit when he first got sick, and I marveled then that Granddaddy felt compelled to get dressed though bedridden and weak. A stiff upper lip, such a New England attitude. Robert went back for his funeral in January '84. A living legend was dead and mourned, back in Boston as well as here in our family, his grandchildren and little Hawaiian princess would miss him terribly.

CHAPTER TEN

MY BIRTH DATE WAS ON the fourth day of the fourth month of the forty-fourth year at 4 a.m. So I have my fortieth birthday in '84 (though on the invitation I omitted that I was also the fourth child and had four children of my own), and invited forty friends at 4:44 in the afternoon, just so the highlighted fours on the invitation kept lining up, a bit more fun. The party is at Kathy and Joe Muller's house, which used to be ours until we sold it to them. I am layered with pikake (my favorite) and ginger lei, with gardenias in my hair, and I feel loved.

A roast by a friend has everyone in stitches, teasing me about being into the "woo-woo," Ramtha, Edgar Cayce, Seth (from *The Nature of Personal Reality*), etc. Another old pal, in a smaller group, has to share how I goosed friends when coming up behind them, a gentle hand gesture up the 'okole, and that when it was done back to me by a pal, his hand up my miniskirt and me, oops, no panties, his fingers (three, he gestured), just like you'd hold a bowling ball. We shriek at this exaggeration, which makes it so much funnier. Another vignette is how this pal had come up to "me" in Longs Drug Store one day to goose me, the woman wheels around, annoyed, and, so sorry, it's not me.

We are addicted to laughing, Kathy and I, often sharing a dirty joke we exaggerate with each telling. Scatalogical humor seldom fails to amuse me and I love our friends and kids when they are naughty. I always have to take things too far, and Robert has to admonish me when I go to the extreme. Not very dignified or ladylike now, even at forty.

For me, the coup de grâce of the party is my brother (who's antisocial and doesn't usually attend parties) presenting me with a blownup color poster of me on his Jet Ski at the exact moment I hit a big wave going out and fly straight into the air. I feel like a showoff and try not to gush, but I am thrilled with that scene as well as the fact Jimmy captured it.

News comes that Michael Hernstadt was murdered in Aspen, with confusing details about a fellow coming to his house, someone with whom he'd been doing drugs, and shooting him forty-eight times with his AK-15. We receive horrific newspaper photos and articles from the Aspen newspaper, which only then makes it all believable. I hadn't really known many friends who had died except for Billie Weaver, a classmate at Punahou when we were about twelve years old, who had been surfing off Lanikai Beach and was attacked by a shark. It is sobering to lose Michael in this macabre way.

Even more sobering is what happens soon afterward. Todd is accepted at Santa Barbara City College, and we've been planning to take another leave of absence to Santa Barbara for a year, so I ask the Steeles to look for a house for us to rent in Montecito. "Oh, no," Robert says, "that's expensive real estate; we need to live in Goleta." Well, that is the dumbest idea, as Goleta is forty-five minutes away from everything, not beautiful and, when I called to tell Laurie Steele, she agrees heartily. So clandestinely she calls to say she found the perfect house in Montecito for us, and I know this is the one, since she's been looking and there are few homes available. I've already found a tenant for our Kāhala home and know we'll be out of pocket a bit each month, but it is well worth it to live in gorgeous Montecito, at the end of a cul-de-sac, with three bedrooms, a rose garden and lots of land.

So back and forth Robert and I go as he gets more stubborn, and I am more determined to persuade him of the merits of this over Goleta, how can he be so tight and not see we can afford it!? Finally, the week before we are leaving and still haven't decided yet, the afternoon of our going-away party, as well, we are shouting at each other. I scream, "Five of us packing up to go, and no home to move into!" Spittle flies from my lips as I flail at him, a banshee, and, as he puts an arm up to block my fists, I hit it, and hear the crack, and know I've broken my arm. My rage is such I can barely stop even then, me at five foot, six inches, and he at six foot, five inches, and he holds me firmly, his voice dropping to a whisper. "I'm sorry, Chula, I'm so sorry," as I sob.

Horrified at what I've done, I talk about my temper tantrum on the way to the hospital in a daze. Then shame, as reality sets in, the going-away party that night, the week in Idaho where we are all going to kayak down the Salmon River rapids, a special treat. Then Santa Barbara. I think I make something up at first and thereafter I admit how I broke my arm, but I can't remember. Robert and I talk it out for hours, and he comes to realize we can afford it. "Yes, call and book the house, I'm sorry I'm such an asshole, can't believe I put you through this, I'm a stubborn prick, you're right, sorry, sorry." I, too, apologize again and again.

It is a bummer to go on such a fabulous adventure in the wilderness with our four vibrant, fun-loving children with my arm in a cast, but I make up my mind to get over it immediately. Kilia and I ride in the raft with our guides while Robert and the boys paddle their own kayaks through the raging rapids. It is a rush, beautiful, to watch each of them conquering and occasionally flipping and righting their kayaks, narrowly missing the boulders. The azure sky and bright sun are a perfect contrast to the frigid river.

We bought a used car in Oregon on the phone, which we pick up en route to stay with Sis in her cabin on the hill in Neskowin. We were there last when Granddaddy was alive, and it was a lovely reunion with this precious, wise woman who had built her cabin five years prior to be near two of her grown children. They'd gone westward from New England and started a new life with each of their families, and we adore all of them, having camped and fished and hiked together several times.

Our tiny new home in Montecito is everything I'd hoped it would be, and charming as well. Robin and Kilia share a small bedroom, Todd has his own and Rob has gone on to chiropractic college in Oregon, with good grades. The small house is unfurnished, so we buy beds and dressers from Goodwill and use chopped tree trunks from our huge yard for end tables and stools. I've never had a fireplace and was tickled to light a fire on the first cold day. Robert admits we are in the perfect place. Robin loves Santa Barbara High School, which is public, as is Kilia's pretty Montecito School. Robert volunteers to substitute teach at Juvy Hall (a jail for juveniles), at a halfway house and at a school for parolees, which all challenge and expand him.

I join a writing group. (Though I later have no memory of what I was working on those many months, I enjoyed getting feedback on my manuscript from the Edgar Allan Poe Award-winning teacher, as well as the other writers in the class.) I write almost daily, except when we're foraying off to ski for four days with the kids in Yosemite in early 1985, to the Bel Air Hotel to treat ourselves to a weekend in Los Angeles to attend the premiere of Kelly's second movie, *Mischief,* with Jimmy, Steph and Linda; and to Big Bear to ski again for a few days and spring skiing in Tahoe with the whole family.

Todd hangs out with a pretty volleyball-playing girlfriend in his league, plays tennis occasionally with us, until his indoor volleyball season starts, in which he thrives, being six foot five as well as ambidextrous. Robin and Kilia are also keen on their significant others, and all of us are having fun. Having Kelly in her glam world so nearby is a kick; between Charlie Sheen, her recent premiere in Hollywood and bumping into Tom Selleck at the Outrigger Canoe Club when he played volleyball, I think our sons are as good-looking, certainly fitter, more well-rounded and more fun than most movie stars. In fact, many of Hawai'i's youths look like the real deal, with their tanned, sculpted bodies from surfing, hiking, volleyball, tennis, etc., year round.

Todd's wholesome young girlfriend surprises him with news she is hāpai and, because she is a Mormon, this sweet, six-foot-tall woman decides to give the baby up for adoption within her community. There is some discussion over this in our family, we support their decisions, and since she and Todd's relationship is on the wane, he does not see much of her after this, as summer comes on. It is a loss for Robert and me, because we love her, but we wish her well and are glad it is amicable.

It is bliss living in Montecito with the hiking in the cool woodsy mountains, tennis on the rural tennis courts, or just walking for miles up and down lanes of beautiful, spacious lawns, gardens, trees and homes. I foolishly paid a high price for it, breaking my arm, but it was worth it, and we continue renting homes there for the next thirty years. We play guitar and sing songs the whole year with all our friends, have them for dinner and are invited to their homes often. We are temporarily sated with the brisk cool Santa Barbara air when we return to Hawaii's punishing midsummer heat.

My mother is glad to have us home, as are Jimmy and Stephanie, even Dad and Estelle. Robert resumes teaching at 'Iolani, but Robin doesn't want to return there. He asked Robert in Santa Barbara if he could go to a public school when he got back to Hawai'i, and was immediately told no. Robert said he had a free education at 'Iolani, it was a fine school and superior to the public schools around. I pointed out that Robin was well balanced, bright and perhaps didn't need the strict regimen of 'Iolani to thrive, and why not let him? So Robert gives in, allows him to go to Kalani High School nearby. Madcap Robin has his own jargon and antics that amuse us all. When his teacher calls to say, in pidgin, the local dialect, that he isn't sure what to do about Robin when he jumps up on his desk calling out "douche bag," I try not to laugh, apologize if he disrupted the class and say I will have a serious talk with him about it. Robin has begun competing in surf contests regularly as well as dating sweet local girls with long, dark hair and almond eyes, and I never feel the need to scold our fifteen-year-old contented, mediocre student.

CHAPTER ELEVEN

MORE FRIENDS FROM OZ VISITED, and these were our most pupule pals. I'd first met Moni one drunken night in Adelaide when she told me she'd wrapped her Jag around a tree months before and had no idea how she'd gotten there. She no longer drank, just smoked weed. A successful realtor, she was married to Graeme, who owned a pharmacy, and between them, Robert and I shrieked with laughter. We decided at a party we should all go to New Zealand in a week or so, when Robert had time off from Pultney.

Having only just met, it was unusual for us to impulsively go with them to Newzy for three days, but we arranged for Kilia and Robin to stay with my sister, and Rob to be in charge of Todd at home, and off we flew. Driving from the airport to the ski resort on South Island took hours, so we fortified ourselves with beer, wine and guitar, while Moni patiently talked about the weed she would buy upon arrival. It'd been too risky bringing a stash with her on the plane, because they had dogs sniffing all the luggage. As we neared the resort, we saw a roadside food stand with a sign saying, "We can serve you anything!" Pulling up, I hopped out and asked, could he really serve us anything? When he nodded, I asked about some pot. Yes, easy, he replied, come back in a half hour, which we did, right after checking into our hotel. Moni was over the moon and plopped down to roll several joints, calling Robert and me to their room, as we really should have a hit.

"Robert's only smoked dope once, Moni, he's afraid he'll get addicted," I said when we joined her. "Where's Gra?" "Gone down to the pub to have a whiskey," she replied, taking a deep drag. "Oh," she coughed, "good stuff, here Chula." I hadn't smoked pot regularly, but if it were around I'd happily partake. I still smoked cigarettes, so I inhaled deeply and gestured to Robert to take the dubie. To my surprise, he did. "Okay," I drawled through the smoke, "Robert's smoking. After one puff years ago, this oughta be good, Moni." She had several more hits. So did Robert and I.

Moni and I started laughing, about nothing, just high and remembering how much I loved pakalolo. Robert went into their bathroom to pee, finally came out wearing Moni's white silk kimono, most of his tanned barrel chest bursting forth, a sash tied at the waist of the kimono, his underpants, and a white ski cap, nothing else. Moni and I screamed hysterically at the sight and, as Robert sat to take another hit without cracking a smile, Moni and I made a bet he'd never go down to the pub like that. Moni was a gambler and she insisted she'd give him $100 if he would, and, of course, I chimed in, doubling it.

With that, Robert strode out the door and we stumbled after him, cackling till we were choking as we got into the elevator. After only a few floors we stopped, the doors opened and there was Graeme, who took one look at us, stepped in, turned his back to us without a word, his whole body heaving with laughter. Moni and I actually peed a bit as we hung onto the elevator railing, convulsed. The doors opened again, the roar of the pub hitting us, and we followed Robert in, trying not to laugh. All heads swiveled, gaping at this six-foot, five-inch, tanned behemoth in a skimpy white kimono, and I heard the bartender tell his assistant, "Look out for that big bloke in the kimono, could be trouble."

We all bellied up to the bar and ordered drinks, as people stepped aside, staring. Moni and Gra and I were all the same height, and we hovered together in fits, and by now Robert was laughing as well. One by one guys approached us, trying to get a read on the big dude, and Robert chatted them all up as if he were normally dressed. The fun kept spinning late into the night, until we staggered back to our rooms to sleep it off, too exhausted to ski. (Robert wouldn't have skied anyway, and the Halls were very disinterested in sports; their only exercise was smoking and drinking.)

Now, a few years later, we were going to meet them on Maui for the weekend. Robert and I stood outside the Kahului Airport looking for them to pull up in a little rental car. Up swept a white limo, which

I scarcely glanced at, until I saw the profile of a woman wearing a cap at the wheel with head thrown back, mouth wide open. A second look, it's Moni and there in the back sat a sheikh with a white burka on his black, kinky hair, tied with a fuchsia band, Graeme's enfolded in a white caftan. I cackled, pointing, and Robert howled as well. We climbed into this ridiculously expensive rental, giggling all the way to the resort, where we carried on as if there was a drought on, "dry as a dead dingo's donger."

Not only did we no longer have a country home, but '86 brought a change in our lives, Robert giving up rugby. It was not easy, as he loved tackling, charging through the guys with the ball, taking them down, but he still had tennis and jogging. We sometimes even competed together in doubles socially as well as in tournaments, as I was playing several times a week. I hadn't modeled for years, but Kathy occasionally called about doing extra work for movies being filmed in Hawai'i. I did "stunt work" with Kilia in a small raft at a tiny cove called Eternity Beach, from the film *From Here to Eternity*, a stunning rock cliff edging the pounding surf. Another time, when Robert's good friend, Jane Alexander, a stage actress from New York, starred in *Blood and Orchids*, I was an extra with her for four days.

Todd finished his two years at Santa Barbara City College, returned to play volleyball for University of Hawai'i and we were all glad to have him home. His one-liners never ceased to make me laugh.

The first of all the kids to marry was Kelly, to another actor, Kevin Gage, and they resided in Hollywood. Estelle had left Daddy, which was no surprise, since he still chased *pāreu*, old perv that he was. I continued writing intermittently, attending writers conferences a few times. Summer came along, with a family trip to Moloka'i, kayaking for four days along the pristine, remote northern coast, even visiting one night with an almost pure Hawaiian family on the cliff, inaccessible except by ocean or air, who had their seafood diet supplemented by provisions helicoptered in. A new outfit guided us along the deep blue with all the meals and work done by them, and we were immersed in nature, camping with our four fabulously fun kids, the last time we were alone together on a family trip.

In September I took off for a week to hike with the Sierra Club. I'd trained for a few weeks before, carrying fifty pounds of books on my back down Kāhala Beach, the weight our backpacks would be on the hike. Challenged by the steep Sierra trail, I was glad to be in condition and relished the adventure, the camaraderie, the beauty of the mountains and lakes and the fishing for trout. Robert held down the home front with Robin and Kilia and was open to my plan upon returning to put a volleyball court in our backyard. Replacing the grass with sand and sticking two metal poles in cement for the net, we had ourselves a small court. But it was a good place to learn. I had played beach volleyball a few times since Todd had been playing indoor league and wanted to get better. We'd have our pals (Patsy, the Mullers, etc.) and our kids play with us on our backyard volleyball court while having beers before dinner, but Jet Skiing with Jimmy was definitely more of a thrill at this point, whether he invited me for a run at dawn or at sunset.

CHAPTER TWELVE

MY BRAIN HAD HIBERNATED long enough that 1987 brought significant changes for me. Having studied the spiritual and metaphysical realm through books, I'd learned the most valuable concept of my life: All feelings come from either love or fear; every negative thought or feeling came from being afraid of not having something we want. It was so significant, it took months of reading and talking about it with Robert, who was, thank God, open to listening. Robert was my rock, actually my boulder, and we talked about everything. I decided I would teach a class in Oʻahu's men's prison that they called Anger Management. Anger is certainly the most dominant feeling in prison, and most definitely comes from fear.

I began teaching at the Oʻahu Community Correctional Center twice a week. Robert was a bit apprehensive, wondering about me being among crims and murderers, but I assured him there'd be guards nearby and off I went. I had to buy a bra, since it was required I wear one, which amused friends and family that this is what it took to get me to wear one. I'd be buzzed in after being frisked, then taken through steel doors to Module 4, to delve into the feelings of some of the most violent inmates at OCCC. It bothered me not at all to sit in a circle with thirty men whose biceps were like tree trunks, for wasn't Robert as muscled? Or to be among these tattooed, local toughs, for didn't I see similar types out in the surf, on the beach?

I began by asking them what other feelings might be the source of the anger they felt. One answered, "I get all piss off 'cause my fada, he no like my frens, so we yell each otha, and then I bus' his face, break his nose." "Yes," I said, "so you were angry. What else? Can someone tell me another feeling besides anger, like maybe frustration, you feel?" A long pause. "I get so frustrated I like kick my brada's ass when he mouths off to me over and over an' he no listen." I say, "I hear you, so you guys feel angry and frustrated, and maybe vengeful, want revenge?" "Dash right, I want to fucking kill the bastard that tole the cops I broke into that store. I get outta here I goin' find that prick and beat the shit outta him!"

"Yes, that's a strong feeling, wanting revenge, and what about worry, anyone here ever worry?" I ask, looking at these child-men. "Damn rights I worry, what's my ole lady doin while I stay inside hea, you know what I mean?" Several others nod their heads. "Whoa," I say. "Yeah, I get it. What's another feeling you might have about your wife while you're here, you're worried, sure, and what else might you feel, like maybe if she's not faithful, like jealous?" One short guy the color of coffee, with a neck as big as my waist, jumps up and shouts, "That fucker! I goin' break his neck, no, maybe I break her neck!" I pause for a few moments. "Yeah, jealousy is a powerful feeling. Anyone else want to remember what that feels like?" I scan their faces as a few mumble to each other, the short guy still ranting about killing his wife. "And maybe one of you guys has felt shame?" They glance at each other, then the floor. "Like maybe you did something embarrassing or someone else made you shame?" The smallest inmate says, "I tink so Kekoa's shame he not win the arm wrestling insi' here!" "Not!" Kekoa fires back. "That bastad's one cheata!" I nod and say, "So maybe he's shame he has to cheat, huh, he's afraid he would lose." "Yeah!" they exclaim. "Dash right, Milton's shame!" I can see fear isn't a feeling they'll likely admit to.

"You guys seem to know a lot about these scary feelings, anger, revenge, worry, jealousy, shame. Any of you ever feel guilty, maybe something you did, you probably kept it secret 'cause you feel so guilty about it? A hulking, tattooed dude says, "Litta bit. I took some money from my mada, she wen hide 'em in a safe place after work." "Not such a safe place, then, huh?" I said and they laughed. "You such a ratfucker, Kahele, stealing from yo' mada!" "Not stealing, I goin' give it back!"

I was still for a minute. "Now do you mind being quiet for a moment and think what feeling is under all these feelings, a feeling you haven't mentioned yet, but it's the source of all these feelings we've talked about?" "Piss off!" one yelled, and I nodded. "Crazy," said another, and more responses saying the same thing, yet not the one, unsurprisingly, that I was after. "Okay, I'm going to tell you the one feeling going on underneath all those other feelings." "Watchu mean underneath?" I was asked. "Well, sometimes we feel a few different feelings at the same time, but I haven't heard the one feeling that is there every single time we are angry, or jealous, or shame." I got very calm and made eye connection with every inmate I could. "The one feeling is fear. Being afraid of not having something you want."

The class erupted. "Hell, no, I not afraid!" "Lady, you call me scared like I'm one chicken?" "Dwayne's the onliest dude here afraid." Dwayne jumped up with fist cocked. "Bullshit! I'll show you afraid." A guard stepped in toward the group, waiting. I smiled at the men. "I can see why this is spooky for you. Men really aren't allowed to be afraid in our society. Only women, not sure why. Don't take my word for it, but we are all afraid, often, of not having or getting what we want. Yet some anger is good for you, it's appropriate and can help you change." I let myself go still as a pond.

"What do you think the fellow was afraid of when he got so angry at his dad that he didn't like his friends?" I looked at each, trying to remember who'd said this. "Maybe that his father has control of him, that he can't choose his own friends? That his father is the boss, and not a nice boss. He's mean?" My gaze settled on the guy and he looked down. "Our fathers and mothers can seem mean and scary when we're smaller than they are, and this is frightening for a kid." I got no eye contact. "Anyway, I'm suggesting that all the negative feelings we all have come from fear." "I no scared 'em!" one ebony-skinned fellow said, and they all concurred, nodding, talking among themselves. "And if you don't think fear is powerful, just look at the animals, at plants. If you're pissed off or afraid and you go up to a random dog, he growls at you, maybe bites you. Or say a horse, and if you get on the horse afraid of it, he will buck you off. Same with plants. If they're around hostility a lot they wilt, but if they sense singing and laughter, they thrive."

I had my work cut out for me. "So, let's end the class today talking about love. About loving yourself." A big macho guy asks, "Whachu mean, conceited kine?" "No, I mean learning to think loving thoughts about yourself, quietly, not telling others them. Let's try it now, 'cause if you can't love yourself, how can you love anyone else? You always have a choice, each moment, every day, to choose to feel love in any situation. Or fear. Shut your eyes now and imagine yourself at the beach." I cracked my eyes open a slit, saw only a few with closed eyes. "So close your eyes, you're feeling good about yourself. You can have this feeling again later when you start to get pissed off, and . . . " My eyes flew open at the scuffling sounds and I see the guy's back turned to us, his arms crossed at his chest and wrapped around his back, his hands caressing like a lover would. The boy-men roared with laughter.

I reported to Robert how long the road was, though I continued going to the prison a few days a week for months. They could scarcely get past these first steps, which were the foundation of the class as I've outlined it, and eventually I realized another hurdle. The guards working there needed to take the class; they were hugely afraid as well, references to them came up in the class often: "Why you not teach this to the *mākaʻi* (guards)?" Of course, they were drawn to this job because of their fears and their need to dominate and control. Like attracts like. Robert came to one of the classes after a month or so and was impressed with the interaction, and also agreed the guards needed the class. I realized I had to work with the whole, not just the inmates, but prison officials said they could not afford the time slot for the guards.

I considered approaching Aunty Barbie for funding for this, wrote up the request, and was disappointed and hurt to be rejected. Not sure why I was turned down, as she was magnanimously philanthropic. We never spoke about it, but I had to assume it didn't make sense to her, that she didn't see the value. So I took the class out of the prison and into my home.

The first class was for Kilia's age, kids ten and eleven, and they got involved right away, writing up their own lists after I read off mine, of times I'd been angry, making it age-appropriate, like "I was angry when my best friend told other girls stuff I'd confided in her, what was I afraid of?" They chimed in, "That she really wasn't your friend!" "That you can't trust her!" "That now everyone knows your secrets and might not like you." "They might talk behind your back." "When I got angry at my husband 'cause he kept doing our son's chores for him, what was I afraid of?" "That he wouldn't learn to be responsible!" "That he wasn't helping him, he was making it too easy," Kilia piped up, giggling about her dad and brother, "and he won't learn to do stuff himself."

"And when my husband didn't come home from a rugby game till late at night, what was I afraid of when he walked in and I screamed at him?" "That he didn't care about you." "That he didn't call you cuz maybe he was hurt?" I nodded, smiling. How astute these little girls were.

"Let me remind you that some anger is good, it's appropriate. You can use it for change, like when your best friend told your other pals your secret, if you can wait till you've calmed down, you will see how others come from fear, too, and then go to your friend and have a talk, tell her how you feel." "You mean forgive her?" one cherubic girl asked. "Yes. To forgive means to let go of the hurt, to let go of fear. Now think of someone you want to forgive, need to forgive, someone who hurt you." I looked around the circle at their precious, beatific faces. "Let's do an exercise now. I'm asking you to close your eyes, all of you. Okay, breathe slowly, and imagine you are exhaling and inhaling lavender love, or blue or white, whatever color you choose, and it's swirling around you. Keep your eyes closed and imagine a bubble around you, you are inside it with all that gentle lavender love. It's caressing your face, your hair and you can now bring in the person you need to forgive."

I paused a long moment, quiet. "And put the person on your lap." Again a long pause. "Okay, open your eyes. What happened, Sky, when you did that?" "I felt pretty soft and gentle about the person," my niece answered. "Not me, I stood up when I brought her onto my lap," Aubrey said. I chuckled. "So you're not ready to forgive her yet, fine.

But when we hold onto hurt for long periods of time, it only hurt us. It's like tasting tiny sips of toxins, and if there's deep hurt, it will make us sick."

"Anyone else want to share their reaction to the forgiveness bubble?" Nica nodded, lips pursed. "I am so mad at my dad 'cause he left mom." "That's understandable," I replied gently, remaining still. After a time she continued, "And he has a girlfriend already. And I don't want to forgive him. I hate him!" I held my gaze on her. "Yes, I hear you. Lots of fear when we feel hateful. Can you tell us what they might be, or would you rather the others suggest what your fears are?" Her eyes filled with tears, so I asked the group, "Can you help Nica with this?" Kilia said, "Are you maybe afraid your dad won't have time for you, or enough love for you?" Nica nodded, looking at the floor. Another spoke up, "And you might be frightened your mom will be alone?" I said quietly, "And you feel way down deep that if your dad stopped loving your mom, maybe he could even stop loving you." Kilia and Jessica leaned over and hugged Nica.

"Nica, you have been so brave today, thank you. But if you can begin to exhale the hate and hurt in your forgiveness bubble, it will help all of you, your mom, your dad and you. Because you'll learn that your dad won't stop loving you, you're lovable. And do you all remember about change, where it begins?" They all caroled, "With yourself." I waited, then said, "Can you ever change others?" "No," they all chorused. I said, "No, you can't, you can only change yourself. So this leads you to the three Cs." Kilia chanted, "Communication, confrontation and change." "Thank you, Kiwi. And if anyone has questions about the energy of your feelings—do you know the word, what kind of energy it is?" "Magnetic," they all chorused. "Yes, electromagnetic, your feelings work like a magnet, drawing love or fear to you. So your homework is to do your love exercise daily, when you wake up or go to bed or whenever. Let's do one now."

"Okay, close your eyes. And breathe in that lavender love, inhale, exhale. Go to a happy place, the beach, in the mountains, wherever you imagine yourself to be safe, and start by telling yourself all the good things you are. I'm smart, I'm kind, I'm funny, I love to swim, or hike, play tennis, whatever, I'm good in math, in writing, reading. I've got a healthy body, I'm pretty, I have a sweet smile." Long pause. "Open your eyes. Now, remember, this isn't bragging when you tell yourself these wonderful things, is it? It's you creating your most important masterpiece, yourself! Believing all these good things makes it happen for you. And, also, never just take my word for anything here, be open to thinking for yourself."

We knew another family in Kāhala whose son Cooper was troubled, and somehow it was decided he would come to live with us. Before taking in our third foster son, I asked the kids if it was okay, telling them if they ever felt I hadn't given them enough love, they only needed to ask for it. Robin actually did say he needed more attention, which was easy to remedy. Ma had given me milk and honey my whole life, and I was demonstrative as well. So Cooper, an appealing, elfin boy who was easy to connect with and love, came to live with us for several months, and we were actually reimbursed for his food. Thus, we began to take in foster children through Hale Kipa, the shelter for abused children, and we had nine or so girls from then on.

Mary, our first, was from Kūhiō Park Terrace, one of the projects for the disadvantaged, and her mother had beaten her often with a bat. She was tall, willowy and lovely, and my heart ached when she shyly described life at home. She was easy to love and lived with us about six to eight months, and we actually talked about taking steps to adopt her. But, being Samoan, we were told it's de rigueur that mothers hit their children as punishment, and it began to get way too complicated. Eventually Hale Kipa sent her back home. We truly missed Mary and tried to contact her a year or more later, to no avail.

Our second foster daughter arrived while I mowed our lawn in a bikini bottom. It was hideously hot, our yard was enclosed and I'd lost track of the time. When the Hale Kipa woman walked in with Lila, I burst out laughing, apologized, grabbed a towel to cover myself and greeted them. Lila was a tita, a tough, outspoken local girl and, with her kinky hair, big smile and forthrightness, she fit right into our family. She and Kilia hit it off instantly. Foster children stayed for different lengths of time, whether it was a needed break of two weeks, or up to a year, if conditions at home weren't resolved. Lila had been abused badly, but had seen worse abuse by her father to her mother. She was a kick, though, with her deadpan expression, and we all laughed a lot. She told me later, "Ho, I neva believe my eye wen I seen you mowing wit' no clothes on! Wats dis chick doin', I stay shame, but you not shame."

Lila went home almost a year later. I was against it, but Child and Family Services always tries to reunite families. In fact, she called several months later to come live with us again, because she'd tried to kill herself, and she returned in late '91 for a few months. The more kids I fostered, the more against reuniting I became, especially if they'd been sexually abused. I realized that most of these young social workers had not had children of their own, and I knew more about parenting than they did. It annoyed the hell out of me when they'd tell me what wasn't allowed. Since Lila, we'd had six or seven more years of fostering. Why should parents who've abused their children be allowed to have them back, especially a father who'd abused his own daughters? Like the twins that we fostered years later.

We'd had Nangoula from Africa living with us; someone had heard we took in children, and she was at a private school, sent here from Namibia. She wasn't abused, just living in difficult conditions. She was easy, smart and sophisticated, and we were reimbursed by her family financially. After a few months, Nangoula told me that her friends at school, Sophie and Molly who were twins, had confided in her they were being sexually abused by their father. I told her to tell them immediately to run away to Hale Kipa, I'd contact Hale Kipa that minute and tell them to expect them, which is what happened. I picked up the twins that day. They were darling, gentle girls, and the only problem was they were identical, so I could not tell them apart. I didn't know if I'd just hugged Sophie or Molly, if I'd just asked one or the other to do a chore, if this one or that one had just described how she was on the track team at school. Finally, after about seven or eight months, I suddenly saw they were different, I could tell them apart.

Anyway, I confronted the Hale Kipa people often, like being told the girls couldn't spend the night out, or if they couldn't do this or that, and ultimately, when they began talking about the twins going home. I got furious. Why? Hadn't he lost his rights as a parent? And now the twins had already confided they thought their dad, who had remarried and had another daughter, might be having sex with their younger sister. I talked in depth to the girls about their boundaries, how it was wrong what their father did, even had them in one of our classes at home, another thing I wasn't supposed to do, talk about their issues at home. But we talked about everything in our family, how could I treat them differently? I was told their father was going to take some sort of class, but I knew no class would change him as a pedophile. Ultimately, they did return home, and we talked occasionally on the phone, and they (don't know about their sister) seemed to be unharmed. They kept in touch with us over the next few years, with calls as well as cards at Christmas.

I took my class on feelings to Santa Barbara intermittently as well as teaching it at home three times a week for the next few years. I taught it in different formats, one through the Welfare Department and one for paroled girls in a downtown office for six weeks or so. Another time out of the large studio I rented for six weeks by myself in Montecito; then from a gorgeous home Robert and I rented in Montecito for a few months (at a discount, because the owner's wife was in my class). It didn't occur to me that I wasn't qualified to teach this class. I felt knowledgeable from studying (lately Jampolsky, Patent, etc.) and learning so much myself while teaching it. I'd been raised with huge anger from Dad, the feisty bantam rooster, as well as how to challenge authority, which taught me I could choose not to be as angry as I'd been all these years as a mother. Ma had been occasionally angry as a mother, so it came naturally to me, and I'd yelled often at the kids. Not hideous shouting, but an angry, raised voice, which I realized was controlling. And, of course, Kilia mirrored my fear eventually, when we would clash periodically over the years, challenging me and my authority.

"So do you ever have the past?" I asked the ladies of Montecito in our second class. They shook their heads. "Or the future?" No, they murmured. "And yet how often are we really in the present, in the moment?" I gazed into these intelligent eyes and attractive faces. "Never," Teresa interjected, then laughed. "I'm constantly in the past or in the future. How can I stop that?" I smile. "The telltale feelings of the past are guilt, shame, regret, helplessness, anger. And the future? When we worry." Ahhh, they all nodded and chuckled. "You look at a baby, that innocence, do they worry, feel guilt or shame? No. They're pure love. Always in the moment. There isn't anything but NOW for them, which is actually all we ever have."

"But if I'm planning something, you know, for work or a trip or something," Victoria asked. "That's positive, like when you reflect on how fun the trip was afterward," I replied. "It's a creative feeling, not coming from fear." An older woman asked, "But how does one stop worrying? It doesn't feel good, it can't be good for me, and so how do I stop?" "Remember how we learned that all our feelings have energy, everything is energy?" I asked, tapping the chair I'm sitting in, "and energy is always moving, that's its nature, to move. So if you can notice and catch yourself worrying, you can visualize taking out a big pair of orange scissors and cutting the tape you're running. And bring yourself back to the present. It takes practice, like anything. First comes awareness. Because, actually, if you keep worrying you could actually draw the very thing to you you're worrying about."

"Whoa," said Carolee, "that gives it a different perspective." "Uh huh, doesn't it? We talked last week about how the energy of our feelings is electromagnetic. Which is what is implied when you hear: like attracts like, water seeks its own level. What you sow you reap. It's a heady thought, when you begin to see that all our thoughts matter, they add up to loving people and events being drawn to us, or not."

"You mentioned control earlier, Chula," Teresa said, "and I know

I've tried controlling my eldest son for years, which hasn't done me any good, I s'pose." I answered, "To control someone is to come from a fearful place, to be afraid he won't become who you want him to be. But can we change others? No, only ourselves." "But you always hear about kids being out of control," Victoria said. "How does that change?" I replied, "By you talking to them. Communication, confrontation and change, the three C's. Telling them you love them no matter what, which is the only love there is, unconditional. That you're afraid if they keep going the way they're going, they could be in trouble. And by being a role model." I paused.

"We talked about how it begins with a thought, and the thought becomes a feeling, so keep noticing your thoughts as well as how you feel. Notice if you are in denial about your feelings. You need to accept them, which is how you release your fears." I was quiet before asking for questions. Then, "Your homework is your love exercises morning or night. If you cannot love yourselves, how can you love others? And next class we'll discuss how we all create our own reality with our thoughts and feelings."

CHAPTER THIRTEEN

ROB GRADUATED FROM chiropractic college, returned home to practice and fell in love. He met Judi at a Christmas party. I had known her years before, she was the niece of my boyfriend from Punahou. While we lived in Adelaide as a family, I vaguely remembered Judi was crowned Miss Hawai'i, then went on to win Miss America and Miss USA. Blonde hair, blue eyes, tall and slender, she was the epitome of an American beauty queen. She had been living in New York modeling when Robby proposed to her, and they married not long after.

Todd inspired us by playing volleyball for UH, so, after playing for a few months on our backyard court, Robert and I now played on the regulation-size sand court at the Outrigger Canoe Club. It was fast and athletic, quick starts, jumping and diving for balls. You had to be very fit. Todd was a powerful player, quick, strong, tall and he was ambidextrous as well; his opponent never knew which arm he'd hit with. We played as a family often and, of course, Todd dominated the game, but he was good enough to make it fun for us all, and we laughed a lot.

Jimmy had become hugely successful as a commercial real estate investor; he and his partner were the largest owners of office space on the island as well as landholders in the western United States. He and Stephanie had a lovely old home on the ocean at the end of Kāhala Beach. He had all the toys, including a custom-made Ferrari, two new Harleys (which felt like a drug, it was such a high riding with him), even a sleek little speedboat. We had fun in Waikīkī, being pulled on a big "hot dog" toy, several of us astride the rubber "dog" screaming with laughter. Often we saw porpoises diving past us, which thrilled us all.

Sadly, theirs was not a happy marriage. Stephanie confided in me that Jimmy was controlling and probably disloyal. Jimmy had a quick wit (which always made me laugh), but he could also be sarcastic, sometimes cuttingly so. I felt conflicted, because he seldom exhibited this dark side with me, and I had compassion for Steph and could only listen. Outwardly they seemed fine, though, so I'd simply forget about it for long periods of time.

Jimmy and Steph and their four kids had begun taking our whole family—Ma (not Melissa, she still lived in Alaska) but Linda, Lee and Christopher, and occasionally Kelly, and Robert and me and our four kids when they were here—to resorts on Maui and the Big Island of Hawai‘i. The Hāna Maui Hotel and Resort, with its gourmet dining, access to horses and beautiful trail riding for all of us, the beach nearby and tennis courts, offered a playground for the wealthy. Though our family (and Linda's) certainly wasn't wealthy, it only made it that much more exciting. We felt pampered, indulged and extremely grateful to Jimmy and, of course, Stephanie, who planned competitions, events, even prizes.

When they then invited us to the Kona Village Resort, with its more casual but still very fine dining, thatched-roof huts as our elegant rooms right on the clear, shallow ocean teeming with fish, we were thrilled. Adding to our fun was Kelly bringing George Clooney. Kelly had been divorced after her brief marriage and still lived and acted in Hollywood, so it wasn't a surprise for her to show up with the cute, almost awkward actor. He fit right in with our sons and nephews and everyone was merry, especially Ma, who thrived, rejoiced on these family sojourns. Rob and Judi were with us; Rob the robust raconteur, and Judi was hāpai, a big deal, because it would be our family's first grandchild. My cup runneth over. Ma's favorite saying.

I'd been close to Ma all these years, having her for dinner weekly, calling her daily, dropping by her house. Ma's morning job with old kāma‘āina friends as a secretary the past few years was a happy arrangement, so it scared me when, soon after Kona Village, she was diagnosed with cancer of the throat. I thought about the class I'd taught recently in Santa Barbara, and then the most recent one from our home in Hawai‘i. The dialogue with the wāhine.

We'd been discussing beliefs. "So thoughts have energy, '*mana*', and when you think a thought enough times, it becomes a belief for you," I said, "and it's important to examine what our belief systems are. If you believe you are unlovable, perhaps a parent was not emotionally available or even abusive, you would come to believe that, and you keep attracting unloving people and situations that are not loving to you. It is not chance that an abused child will marry an abusive mate, or be raped, say, or . . ." "You're saying there's no such thing as chance?" Kathy interjected.

"No, I don't believe there is. Or coincidence. Or luck. We create everything that 'happens' to us, we draw it to us with the energy of our beliefs." "Whoa," Candy said, "not sure I can buy that." "Well, it is a lot to absorb," I replied. "And we're not eager to look at what we're creating if it's not positive, are we?"

"So what about illness?" Terry asked. "You can't mean we create cancer?" "Actually, I do mean that. If you have deep subconscious feelings, which only means you are not conscious or aware of them, that you hate what your mother, father, whomever, did to you, and you don't acknowledge this and work on forgiving them, it eats at you, like a cancer." I can see these attractive, healthy women are thinking about this. I go on, "You know the whole placebo effect, how that works." Sharon said, "If you know the doctor is giving you drugs to cure you, you believe they will." I smiled. "Even if they're sugar pills. The mind is that powerful. So your thoughts become your feelings, which become your beliefs. If you think you are fat, that fat is ugly, then no amount of exercise will change you from the fat, ugly girl you may think you are. But don't take my word for it, make up your own mind in this class."

"Yeah, makes sense," Kathy said. "Look at all the diet books, always on the best-seller lists. But they don't ever say at the start to check out your thoughts, not just your diet." "No wonder you're so damned skinny, Chula!" Candy interjected. "You've thought all along you're a skinny little bitch!" We all cracked up. I loved this class with so many of my old friends in it. Wāhine are more open to new thoughts, like these are, as the class I'd had for couples proved. Several of the men flat out balked, it could not be this easy, the choice between love and fear. Though I reiterated it was not simple. "It takes practice to be aware. To examine your thoughts and feelings and to change. But, wait, it's only as hard as you believe it will be."

So when Ma got sick, I was surprised she didn't go along the path of natural healing with a shaman, a naturopath, an acupuncturist. It was her belief system to be with nature. She went to doctors here in Hawai'i and started drugs, which she'd never done in her life. Jimmy got very involved in her illness; he actually seemed closer to her, then, and frightened for her. Linda, who hadn't been close to Ma for years, somehow found some type of healer in Tokyo she'd read about. Our mother would go to Japan to this healer, and, of course, Jimmy would pay for all of it. But she needed to be accompanied, and it was deemed Steph would take her, and why not me as well?

I cherished my mom, adored Steph, but the healer information was too vague for me, and I didn't want to go to Japan. I hadn't been drawn to the Asian countries. And yet, of course I went, and Ma was fine with the trip idea. She seemed to feel "taken care of by Jimmy," loved, closer to him. And she didn't feel terribly sick, so it was a bit of a lark for her. Especially since it was all first class. I scarcely remember any of the week, but perhaps it helped, even if it was just a placebo. That week in Japan I wondered why she had created cancer; was it the stifling of her rage at Clark, when she finally divorced him and found he'd borrowed on her small trust fund for business and never paid it back, so she'd had to depend on Aunty Barbie, who bought her the little house in Niu Valley?

I returned to teaching three of my classes at home. The class for couples was interesting, because I realized how similar the men's resistance was to the men I'd witnessed in the prison. Oh, sure, these guys were educated, intelligent, privileged, and yet men in general were not as open as women and children. It was a bit challenging having my brother there as well. Stephanie had urged him to come and he was interested from an academic perspective, not really there to open up with mind, heart and body.

I continued Jet Skiing with Jimmy on the weekends, exciting adventures usually at dawn from his home, continued yoga lessons, tennis three times a week, family volleyball, teaching, writing. And we continued having foster children, before Nangoula, and the twins came into our lives later. (We had four foster sons initially, and seven or eight foster daughters in between.)

Todd starred at University of Hawai'i playing volleyball, and was dating the Italian stallion, Alexandra. She came to UH from Italy, and her English got better and better as she fell in love with Todd. She made the move on him, a familiar concept, as Todd was like Robert, kicked back, not approaching the babes, letting them come to him, which they did because he was so good-looking. A striking six-foot woman, Alex was brilliant, charming, funny, as well as stubborn.

Robin had been competing in surf contests at Sunset Beach, Waimea Bay, Pipeline, Mākaha for the past few years and I'd often pace the beaches, cheering him on. Surfing is a dicey sport to compete in, because it's hit or miss getting "the" wave of the set and carving and shredding it in the allotted time. I'd pace the beach, anxious if he hadn't caught the best wave, or if the surf was huge (twenty-foot faces, triple overhead and bigger), or too gnarly. I'd be stoked for him when he excelled and inspired to surf more myself, which I did on the south shore, where the waves are less powerful than on the North Shore.

In 1988, Robin graduated from Kalani with no plan for college; he lived in Santa Barbara for more than a year, working and competing in surfing in Southern California. He was now a pro surfer, living his passion. Kilia was May Day Queen at her tiny 'Āina Haina School, did a beautiful hula, flashing her radiant smile, so graceful at twelve years old. She had boyfriends, a lovely singing voice, was on the honor roll and would attend 'Iolani, where her dad taught (now the only one of his four kids there), and play on the tennis and volleyball teams as well. She missed Mary and Lila, had gained immeasurably from the experience, as we all had, and they kept coming, though for briefer periods of a month or less. Rob and Judi had a baby boy, Ryan, which thrilled me no end, as I craved cuddling and nibbling him and began to babysit after a few months. Kelly filmed *Twins* and I started the Feelings Foundation. For the classes at home I charged a fee, but all of the State Department of Education (DOE) classes were still voluntary. I approached several generous friends, who contributed for a few years. I had always offered one-on-one counseling after a class, before or whenever, and it was intense, so I was happy to offer teaching and counseling individually now that I was compensated a bit.

Whether in Santa Barbara or home in Hawai'i, our best friends for the past several years had been the Steeles. Storm was fairly short and compact, muscular, with a hilarious, naughty, irreverent wit; Laurie was taller, blonde, with a prominent nose, and though more proper, laughed as readily and raucously as I did. Laurie and Robert were the even keel, and Storm, aptly named, said anything to anyone, and was even more provocative than I. Having loved them in Hawai'i (I'd met Laurie on Kāhala Beach, first with her two-year-old, Jessica, when I was with Kilia, and, when I recognized her from an earlier meeting, said, "I'd know that nose anywhere," and she laughed (I felt I could acknowledge her nose, which was as sculpted as mine). We continued loving them, their *élan*, in Santa Barbara through the years after they moved.

We saw them constantly, always laughing together. They were more elegant than Robert and I, made more money and had beautiful taste that we coveted. Great athletes, Patrick (Storm's first name) and Laurie were tennis players; Robert and Pat played A-league men's doubles, Laurie and I, B-league women's doubles. They had two more darling daughters after Jessica, and we adored them all, as they did our kids. They joined us back at the Cape to stay with Sis for a week, or we drove to San Francisco for weekends, or to Catalina, back to Hawai'i, but usually it was Santa Barbara, where we rented a different home in Montecito annually.

Though Laurie was more ladylike, I amused her, and we told each other everything. In fact, the four of us together told each other everything. One boisterous night early in our friendship, we drove to downtown Santa Barbara to have a drink at Joe's, a bar known for its strong drinks. We tippled and cackled over everything, as usual, and, finally, in the car going to a restaurant, we were on the subject of sex. Our own personal lovemaking was the subject, and somehow Storm egged me on to divulge how Robert had missed the proper opening the last time we got this drunk, how that wasn't fun, and Robert interrupted, denying this. I babbled more intimate details, which Robert called "bullshit," we three were roaring, until suddenly Robert climbed out of the car and left. We looked for him for ten minutes on State Street, still giggling, and finally found him, though Storm couldn't resist pimping him again and again, this irreverent anecdote of ours getting a rise each time until Robert could laugh again.

We felt blessed to be friends with a couple we both loved, knew it was rare. The few differences over the years were that I began beach-combing for volleyball games along the twenty-four courts on East Beach, and Robert turning fifty made him more than a decade older than the Steeles and a little closer to a hip replacement.

Our huge common interests were food and family. Laurie was a superb cook and they graciously had us to dine often in any one of the five beautiful homes they lived in over the years. I adored eat-ing, would salivate all day knowing her menu, and it felt like a warm hearth out of *House & Garden* each time we went. I ate as much as Robert most of the time, and was so appreciative, as was Robert, though he's a low-maintenance guy and could eat a hamburger every other night.

Laurie was from a big family, as Robert and I were, and they were close, so though Pat had nothing like that, he was devoted to his daughters and wife; they were his life and breath. And they admired Robert tremendously as a teacher, coach and counselor, as well as the two of us as parents. Our kids were a big part of our friendship, and the Steeles also were friends with Jimmy and Stephanie. They were a better fit in some ways, the four of them, because they were more fashionable in their tastes for clothes, cars, homes, trips, etc.

The Steeles were aghast when they came just the one time to our country house. Though forewarned, it was not their style; even going camping in Santa Barbara was taken to another level with Storm. We joined him and a daughter with a few of her friends in the mountains. (Laurie wasn't into camping.) Just the amount of his equipment, coolers, food and amenities cracked us up as we piled out of the car. Then, hiking, Storm staggering under his burden, and all of us hot and ready to kick back (except for Robert), had Robert and me laughing harder. Pat shot provocative jokes at Robert's sweating, his strength, his size, as usual, till Robert finally tried to silence him with a rejoinder of "Okay, Little Man," which Pat kept repeating. By the time we pitched camp, it was "Little Man" this, and "Big Man" that. I cackled endlessly, as Storm's humor was always to repeat things to milk it, in variations, and we continued that way through the evening.

As we climbed into our sleeping bags, Storm said, "If I'd known this bag was made for a fucking Lilliputian, I would have gone shopping." We cackled as we watched him trying to burrow into a bag that reached his chest, and I didn't refrain from saying, "You mean it was made for a 'Little Man?'" "Seriously, anyone have an extra blanket?" Patrick implored. Robert said, "You brought all that crap and no blanket? Sorry, Pat, we don't have one either." Robert grinned at me as he snuggled down into his bag and rolled over, content. As we were drifting off to sleep, we heard Pat's plaintive voice, "I'll give you a $100 bucks for a blanket, I'm fucking freezing." "Storm, we don't have a blanket, but, here, you can take my sleeping bag," Robert said, and my eyes flew open. He started peeling it off, but Pat demurred, "No, I'm not taking your sleeping bag, Big Man, thanks anyway," and we drifted off again, trying not to giggle, ignoring his whimpering.

Once when we were both celebrating our anniversaries together, we drove up to an expensive but rustic inn by Big Sur called Post Ranch. Laurie had gone shopping for a sexy little thing to thrill Pat when they got romantic. I giggled when I saw the black lace number that would subtly allow a peek through when clinging to her torso, arms and legs. But most important was the open triangle right where her little tushie would be, and I cackled, because this was so out of character for Laurie. She wasn't as eager as he always was, so we giggled at how much he'd love it that night.

After our hilarious drive, drinks and dinner, we parted for our elegant treehouse cabins, ours right under theirs. I described to Robert what she would be surprising Storm with right about then, which amused him as well. We were going to make love ourselves soon, without any sassy accoutrement to enhance me, and I giggled to Robert that maybe we'd even overhear a real head-banging session upstairs, when there came knocking on our door instead.

Who else? It could only be the Steeles, but why now? I murmured as I strode to open it. Robert had just gone into the bathroom, but turned on a dime when he heard my hysterics. I'd flung open the door to the scantily clad Storm, his muscular body bursting through the black lace, especially through the integral spot, and we only had a glimpse when he turned to sashay up the stairs. Robert howled while I grabbed the camera, capturing a smashing photo of our pal (which I had enlarged the next day and put on a magazine cover like *GQ* at a photo place in Carmel, explaining hurriedly that it wasn't what it seemed, that we'd both celebrated our twentieth anniversaries together, and I needed this to surprise him).

I exulted in our friendship with the Steeles; they defined me. They loved beauty as I did, and though we drove old cars and lived in old houses and wore old clothes, I admired beauty nevertheless. Laurie was a shopper (one of her jobs had been as a buyer for an upscale store) and I wasn't, but I let her urge me into buying occasionally, when it felt like a treat with her beautiful taste. And Storm was always elegantly turned out, which phased Robert not at all. Though Storm and I were inclined to lower ourselves to a puerile level, just to laugh, he also had a true spiritual depth.

When I returned from another Sierra Club hike, the Steeles snorted at my description of sublime: the celestial mountains and lakes, the unexpected snowstorm in early September that locked us in our tents for the morning, and the fifty-pound packs that lightened each day out of ten. They welcomed my brief visit en route home, which was made briefer with Jimmy's phone call.

"Chula, Dad's drinking heavily and I don't have time to deal with it. When will you be home?" Jimmy called from Hawai'i. "What do you mean, drinking? He's not a heavy drinker," I replied. "He is now. Can you help?" Jimmy never asked for help, though Dad had had his eightieth birthday recently and lived alone in that shack, so I didn't ask more questions, said I'd leave right away.

I came home, drove out to Malaekahana and sure enough, there sat Dad with a huge bottle of vodka. I talked to him awhile, though he wasn't making much sense, and told him he'd have to go to Castle Hospital's rehab if he didn't stop. Back and forth we went, I went home, booked him in and took him there, though he resisted. Not a week later he called, said he was ready to go home, he hated it there and somehow convinced me he had quit drinking. He had. He was just lonely, I knew, but he was glad to be back out in the country with a few of his horses around him, dependent on him.

I lined up a series of caregivers to move in and look after him and took over his bills, which Jimmy paid. Jimmy wanted not to be too involved with him, nor was I crazy about it. When I'd call and ask how he was feeling occasionally, he'd say, "With both hands," which was such a turnoff, as the implication was clear, and, finally, after a few more of those, I said I never wanted to hear that response again. I'd tell the prospective caregiver she'd have to have a sense of humor to work with Dad, as he'd come on to her or make rude comments. So I lost a few over the next years, but eventually a picture emerged that was much deeper and uglier regarding Clark, several years later. At least for now he was a task I felt I could withdraw from.

Mummy was also aging, of course, though still independent and healthy, and Melissa had returned a while back to live with her. Melissa was still a single lesbian who seemed a bit unstable. Long ago she had worked for a pool construction company with all men, eventually actually built herself a tiny house, doing all the electrical, plumbing, etc., when she used to live here. She was a comely woman who'd ridden horses in the past, with her hair floating behind her. But then

Melissa moved back to the Mainland, so the timing was right when Robin came home and moved in with Ma. He was fine with the idea and Ma was delighted to have him there, it served them both well, and she actually thought he preferred living with her rather than home with us, though he was paid a small stipend by Jimmy.

It was curious that Robin became ill with mononucleosis over that whole year, he had no energy, was depressed not to be surfing, not to be doing much of anything. Ultimately he healed, and it was as if he'd been at the best college in the world for that year, as he'd been still, thought about his smoking too much pakalolo in the past, wondered what he would do with himself and decided he'd go to acupuncture school. Robin had always been zany, mercurial, with a charming, silly sense of humor, and he regained this finally, went to the local acupuncture school and graduated in three years. I was elated he'd found his path through this illness, and in an alternative healing arena that was finding credibility in the early '90s. The concept made perfect sense: Needles at certain energy points, or chakras, in the body to channel and move blocked energy for healing.

Jimmy and Stephanie divorced after his liaisons became known. On a tip, Steph had gone to the Red Vest one night, the "in" restaurant on a side street in Waikīkī, and found Jimmy with a model friend of hers. She threw a glass of wine on him, walked out and beelined to our house to weep in the middle of the night. It was sad but way overdue, and finally it was over. She and Sky were well-compensated (though it was hard on Sky) and Jimmy's three sons had alternated living between Steph and their mother anyway. It was difficult for me not to side with Steph, as it exasperated me, but I'd been so close to Jimmy and had had such fabulous adventures with him, I stayed as neutral as I could while commiserating with Steph as she kissed her wounds.

Jimmy began dating the daughter of a friend of ours, which wasn't surprising, though it was strange initially for us. Jimmy invited Robert and me to Hanalei, renting a house on the beach, and we had such fun in his speedboat with the dolphin in the bay that he then booked the Big House several months later for our whole family. The

Chula and Jimmy, 1987

*Todd's UH volleyball
game, 1987*

At the Kona Village Resort: (back row) George Clooney, Kelly, Mark, Robin, Jimmy, Todd, Linda, Lee, Robert and Rob; (front row) Michael, Chris, Sky, Matt, Steph, Kilia, Ma, Chula and Judi (hapai with Ryan), 1989

Ma and Chula, 1991

Chula and Ryan, 1992

Kilia as May Day princess at Punahou, 1992

Melissa, Linda, Jimmy, Ma and Chula, 1992

Matthew, Michael, Jimmy and Mark Reynolds, 1992

Book publishing party, 1992

Kelly, Jett and Linda, 1993

Chula with Ryan, 1993

Patsy and Chula, 1993

Hana and Ryan in the backyard, 1993

Big House that Patsy had inherited years before was a lovely, seven-bedroom home with a veranda surrounding it, as well as five acres of manicured lawns. Gracious and gorgeous, it was where we'd go when Patsy's grandparents were alive, and I remembered them with their cocktails playing golf on the lawn, with its enormous pine trees, coconut trees, a huge fish pond and a stunning view of Hanalei Bay. Jimmy had a chef and his jet boat to take us waterskiing on the Hanalei River which hadn't been done before. The next time he rented the house he invited the Steeles to come from Santa Barbara as well for a week of laughter and escapades.

The most vivid adventure was to the Nāpali coast, which Jimmy raced along in his speedboat. Flying parallel to the steep, emerald and purple mountains soaring straight out of the ocean, we smacked against waves that rattled our bones, spray dousing us as we clung on tight. Coming upon caves in the cliffs, we buzzed into darkness, exploring quietly and ducking our heads at the low ceilings, before zipping back out into sunshine and waves again. Finally we reached the end at Kalalau, to the last drop-off possible, with a beach picnic and waterfall drenching to entice us. We anchored and swam twenty-five yards in to play at this remote haven. It was only just becoming known and gradually intrepid hikers backpacked in the twelve miles, some never leaving.

CHAPTER FOURTEEN

I TAUGHT MY CLASS IN about fourteen of Oʻahu's public schools through the DOE, persistent, doggedly persuading them of the value of the class for years. Hawaiʻi's DOE was predominantly Asian, and though I had no prejudice in my life, having grown up with every race, including Asians, I realized that many of the older generation were more close-minded. In the Ala Wai School's fifth-grade class, (under a broad-minded principal), we talked about judgmental thoughts.

"Even if we don't say them out loud, when you are putting someone down, you need to ask why you want to feel superior by judging others. So of all the mean thoughts you have about people, why don't you go up and write one on the board now?" I saw the smiles, unsure, looking around at the other precious little faces. "Okay, you go first, Darryl," I said, which began almost an hour of their naughty words written in chalk: asshole, ugly, fat, stupid, loser, bitch, bastard, shithead (lots of giggling between words, like they're getting away with something), skinny, bad, wrong, lazy, phony, idiot, slut, fag, fuckin'. Then I asked about racist words they used to put down kids of different nationalities, with which this school was rife. "Like when you don't like a white kid, you might think the word haole is a putdown, though that word by itself isn't, it only means a white person, right? So what other words?" They write: haole, nigger, Jap, Chink and a few I hadn't heard of or remembered.

"So let's talk about a few of these, like slut. What makes you say that about another girl?" A tough, chunky girl said, "Cuz she act slutty. She wear da kine blouse, you can see trew it." Another hand shot up. "An' ders one girl lets boys kiss her an she puts little bit lipstick." I replied, "Okay. What if she doesn't have a mother, maybe her mother died, she wants attention, wouldn't know the right things to wear. Or maybe they're poor and can't afford a nice blouse, is it loving of you to put her down?" They looked at each other, getting it, staring at the floor. "Remember, every negative thought comes from being afraid. What might you be afraid of when you're not feeling loving?" "That if you stay 'round that girl you might be slutty, too," one offered. "Maybe you feel you aren't good enough, so you like talk about her," a chocolate-skinned girl confessed. Another said, "It's mo easy talk about her den look yo'self." I smiled. "Wow, I'm impressed with you guys. For being able to look at these fears, to admit them. So wouldn't you think this girl needs loving thoughts and loving people, that you'd want that if it was you?"

I could see much of this had hit its mark. I asked them to erase the board. "And one more thing, why is it okay to dis a girl for being a slut, and not a guy? What word do we use when a guy needs to act cool, or tough, because he doesn't really feel confident?" They murmured among themselves. "It's accepted in society that guys can't be afraid and, of course, they are, right? So there's pressure on guys, makes it harder for them to admit they're afraid." I gazed into the boys' eyes, and most looked away, though a kinky head actually nodded. "So we use 'macho' to describe a man for being manly. But there isn't really a word we use to put a guy down?" One wholesome local boy said, "Moke?" "Ah, moke, haven't heard that word in a long time. Acting tough, aggressive, huh?" There were giggles. "And what about bullies? A bully is afraid. So your homework is to notice when you have judgmental thoughts, when you dis others. And decide you can choose to feel loving instead. Write down when you remember to choose."

Leaving, I think of my own judgmental thoughts, cutting the tapes and noticing how easy it is to judge others instead of being willing to marvel at another unique expression of the universe.

Meanwhile, in 1990, I am writing what I think will be published in two separate, slim books. There is a simple passage on every page, taken from these classes, describing how to choose love over fear, and I find a lady in Santa Barbara to do the illustrations. Though I've been taking life drawing classes at the Art Academy the past year, and am pretty good at drawing people when I have a model sit for a group of ladies at my home, I am not capable of drawing the cherubs she draws to convey the ideas I've written on each page. I decide to co-publish, since I've been rejected so many times by publishers in the past, and find a publisher in Santa Barbara who will take it on. It involves less time but a lot of steps, and I am glad to put it in their hands as I continue editing my work.

It is soon after this that Lila returns to live with us, and we are grateful to be here to love her, as we can see her thriving. I am playing only volleyball now, because tennis no longer excites me, and I even get Lila who is a jock out on the sand with Kilia and me to play. Alex, Todd's girlfriend, is also playing regularly with me, and we all improve by playing several times a week. I'm also happy to have Ryan, an adorable two-year-old I call BabySweet, three times a week or so. Judi and Rob are hāpai again, and I have conflicted feelings about that, because she seems to whine a lot about the demands of motherhood. Though he likes to party, Rob is a nurturing, hands-on dad, like his father, even cooks often, but, as kind as Judi is, that isn't enough for her. Rob has begun to paddle canoe, which makes life dicier in their household.

Paddling in Hawai'i is an age-old tradition. It's usually in a six-man canoe, teams practice a few times a week, and all the different clubs compete. It's a lovely, graceful sport, and takes more than brutal strength, with timing an important factor. All paddles must slice through the water together, in sync, to be a fast crew. At the end of every season, teams practice distance paddling for the big race between Moloka'i and O'ahu, thirty-two miles. Rob is not just powerful, having a barrel chest like his dad and muscled arms, but he has good timing. And the camaraderie is a big draw for paddlers. Rob seems to balance his chiropractic work (now he has his own clinic) with his family, as well as his paddling and surfing. It is impressive to Robert and me, but not to Judi. (Whew, cut the tape, Chu.)

I am a few weeks into a class for adults at nights at Kaimukī Community Center, and am getting paid which is gratifying. I've got all ages for an hour and a half for six weeks, which seems to be as long as

I've ever been able to book a class, though three months, or a semester, is optimum. It's a process that requires looking within, and is not easily navigated by most people. Especially since it includes provocative new ideas that rock their world, with all different beliefs from different cultures. As Asians dominate in Hawai'i, and as I said, are traditionally more conservative, old school, I'm curious to see how this class goes, as more than half the students are Asian. They have been fairly responsive as a blend, and seem to have begun to trust me.

"Does anyone want to say what intuition means to you?" I ask in the third week. "Instinct?" A haole woman answers. "Yes, that's certainly part of it," I reply. "Intuition and instincts are inner influences, right, gut feelings guiding us from within. So it's always there if we listen to it, and it's powerful, can save our lives, actually. For example, I was riding a motorcycle, a dirt bike, in Hanalei a few months ago, racing across this meadow, enjoying the beauty around me, and suddenly something told me to brake, and there in front of me was a metal wire which was impossible to see until I was close up, and would perhaps have decapitated me. I freaked a little that I'd had this close call. What and where did this feeling, this instinct or intuition come from?" They are quiet.

"Yeah, I had intuition help me before," one young lady offers, "when I didn't admit to my friend how angry I was at her, and found out she'd had a good excuse." I nod, waiting, then go on, "And the more we listen, the more we hear it, but where would you say it comes from? I know it's not popular to use the word 'God' in school, but I'm going to say it here. I think it is God, or a higher power. Remember last week we talked about energy, mana, as we call it in Hawai'i? And that everything is energy?" I tap the chair I'm sitting on. "This chair, me, my thoughts and feelings, the trees, the ocean, all are energy. Some of it is visible, some not. Like the wind, it's not visible, but you feel it, you see it moving branches and the ocean, you know it's there, and it can be powerful. So is God. And God is everywhere. I think the more we love ourselves the louder our intuition is, and the more we hear it." I pause a long moment, look at the inscrutable faces of the Japanese and Chinese here and smile. "Which is why I think so many children who have been in unloving or abusive homes stop listening to their intuition. Why would they trust it when their own father has sexually abused them? They can't even trust love, or their own fathers, can they?"

I mention how we have taken in many foster children, some who've been sexually abused, and how damaged they are. How it takes time for them to trust again, and I can see the compassion in their faces, the sensitivity, and I'm heartened I seem to be reaching them though they are not so forthcoming. We do our love exercise and then our forgiveness bubble, and I ask them to notice their intuiton as their homework, to become aware of the quiet guidance, or maybe urgent guidance from within.

Jimmy invites Robert and me to join him and Olivia, his luscious young girlfriend, to go motorcycling on the Big Island. Robert has always ridden a road bike, a motorcycle, and now he has bought me one. I have been riding around Kāhala first, to get used to being on roads with rules, and I've gotten a motorcycle license recently. Hawai'i doesn't have a helmet law, and the feeling of the wind through my hair is akin to flying. It's my new passion, and I'm excited to go to Hawai'i, with its varied topography and climates.

Landing in Kona, we pick up the motorcycles we shipped, Jimmy with his Harley for him and Olivia, and Robert and me with our old Hondas. For miles we drive through the black lava rock, a stark sort of beauty, though its relentless blackness is finally relieved by color as we drive higher. We are going up to Mauna Kea, the dormant volcano, and there will be snow, a startling contrast to the heat we ride through. We stop at a tiny store, I didn't know to bring gloves, which Jimmy and Olivia have, and, as no gloves are sold up here, he buys me some oven mitts, which cracks us all up. Robert buys gardening gloves and I pull on my new oven mitts and away we go. I'm bundled up, we all are, and am amazed to reach piles of white snow piled high over black lava. We've gone from bleak black to the green of plants and now to snow and lava at 10,000 feet. It's exhilarating, and we play here for a bit until descending an hour later to the ocean, where we strip down on the coral and dive into the deep, indigo blue. What a contrast, what happiness.

The next day we head to Waipi'o Valley, and the road slants radically straight down to get there. I'm stunned, and a bit anxious, because it's so steep, like nothing I've ever driven on before, and certainly not on a motorcycle. I follow Jimmy who packs Olivia, and Robert. We all slow down, and I go even slower, feeling it out as to which gear to use, how much to brake. I'm holding my breath, but after a few minutes I realize I can do this, I can drive a heavy motorcycle straight down, like I used to drive my dirt bike down dirt roads, though that wouldn't have hurt if I'd gone down, not as much as this tarmac. I scarcely enjoy the view of this gorgeous valley until we reach the bottom, and now we are going to cross a stream, not a trickle but an actual stream, which would also be different on a dirt bike. If they can do it, so can I, and I zip through the stream after them. I am exhilarated and Robert's proud of me. We all laugh together.

CHAPTER FIFTEEN

MY SISTER LINDA DOES NOT WISH me well, isn't interested in my last adventure whenever we have occasion to talk, which is less and less over the years. Yet I am glad when she calls to tell me her news. "Guess what!" she begins, "Kelly's dating John Travolta!" "Really! How cool is that!" I respond. "I remember she was in that movie with him, whatever." *"The Experts,"* she interjects, "a junk movie." "So they must've gotten tight then, huh?" She responds, "Yup, hot and heavy, I think, and bringing him home for a visit, so I'm having the family for dinner."

Kelly and John take rooms at the Kāhala Hilton and Linda and Lee have us all over. It's a kick to meet the famous face and he seems to be genuinely sweet and gracious. Kelly looks lovely with her cascade of blonde curls and seems enamored though as natural as always. Our family chats him up and gives him space, and toward the end of the evening Robert says to him, "Johnny, just so you know, when you're with our family, you do the dancing and I'll do the singing." Robert chuckles as he tells me this later, but Johnny apparently doesn't. Robert had expected a laugh, and we wondered if maybe he was a bit daunted (he's not very fit) with our chiseled men. Not only is Robert six foot four, so are Rob and Todd by then. Robin, about five feet, ten inches, and Kelly's brother Chris are, too. And though Jimmy, Robin and Chris are slightly built and of normal height, Jimmy is obviously extremely successful, too, which Johnny may care about, who knows? But Travolta didn't laugh at Robert's hilarious comment like I did. (Or maybe he just didn't hear it.)

Anyway, I am glad to have a baby in the family again. Robert and I even take BabySweet, at barely two, camping, just the three of us. It is bliss showing him his first fire, which we always make at twilight to cook hot dogs, while we have beers and Robert plays his guitar, both of us singing. The roar of the ocean lulls us to sleep, and stars blanket us instead of a tent. The sunrise is my private joy to share with him (I'm always the first one up every morning), a bright gold spark blooming into a brilliant ball on the horizon, his tiny finger pointing as we laugh. Making the fire again for coffee, Madam Pele goes through matches before finally coaxing a tiny flame, and I toss on dry ironwood needles from the overhanging trees that catch fire, and BabySweet squeals with delight. A small, blackened saucepan of water begins to boil for my coffee, and Robert rises. I bust out our old pan and fry up Spam, our camping treat, which Kilia calls the salt lick, scramble eggs, fry toast and I'm pau cooking. We saunter down to the other end of the beach from Malaekahana, parallel to Kahuku Golf Course, to the tidepools, to show him the tiny fish and crabs. I hold him close, kissing his neck and biting his plump, satiny arms. "No, Chu Chu," he says, and I laugh, nibbling softer.

In the adult class at Kaimukī, I begin, "So wisdom is an accumulation of feelings. We are here on Earth to learn from our feelings, to learn to choose love through fear. Our lives are learning experiences we create for ourselves. Anyone do their homework, catching yourself judging another?" "I realized I was judging myself, calling myself an idiot," a Chinese woman says, and we all chuckle. "Terrific! Shows you're already becoming aware of those inner tapes we run. Did you pull out orange scissors and cut the tape?" She smiles, says, "No, not yet, I guess I needed to keep scolding myself." The class giggles, nods.

"I believe that loving feelings create ease in your body, would you agree?" I glance around the circle. Most are nodding. "So what about the idea that negative feelings, coming from fear, create dis-ease?" I pick up chalk and write in big letters on the board: love = ease and fear = dis-ease. "Can you open your mind to realizing that all these thoughts and feelings, conscious and unconscious, have energy, mana, and, if unchecked, fearful feelings get stuck in your body. Like if you cannot forgive, that energy can create cancer. It's not for the other person you forgive, it's for yourself, as we discussed last class."

"So even though it's his fault," an erudite Japanese woman says, "and he's done terrible things, I have to forgive and love him?" "Only when you're ready can you forgive," I smile at her, "but you can choose to practice forgiving right away, to let go of the hurt and fear with the bubble. And loving, you can love from a distance once you accept it. You don't have to see that person again, just know he's coming from fear.

"And, remember, energy is electromagnetic, so if you don't forgive, you may attract another person into your life to learn from. To hurt you again. Do you really want that lesson again?"

"You really think getting sick is simply from being afraid? I've been thinking and it just doesn't seem that simple," a shy young man says. I look at him a long moment. "I do think it's that simple. I have been taking treats to a classmate of mine from Punahou who is dying of AIDs, and I've thought how sad and difficult it's been in our society to be gay, like he is, to not be accepted even by your parents, much less loved." I sigh and look at them all. "To feel there is something wrong with you just because of your choice of gender for a mate? I can understand my friend not being able to love himself, can't you? What a lesson we can all learn from them!"

"Do you believe in doctors?" a *hapa* fellow asks. I chuckle. "Yes, for serious accidents, strokes or heart attacks, and infections other times. But I don't have a doctor. My husband's father was on a team of three men who performed the first kidney transplant. If I need a kidney, something like that, I'll find a doctor." The class laughs. "And other than antibiotics for a dangerous infection, I don't believe in drugs, because they all have side effects. I just had another argument with my husband about this, same one we've had many times. The biggest one was when I insisted no vaccinations before going to 'Iolani School. And our daughter has had earaches several times as a child, and the minute she does, he trots her off to the doctor for antibiotics. I think there are natural cures to heal us in the plant kingdom, don't you?"

"Definitely," Nohea, the hapa lady, says. "The Chinese have all sorts of herbs for everything." I smile at her. "Yup, that's what I told my husband again when we argued. Poor kid, we each had one of her hands, and I was pulling one way and he the other!" They smile. "He was rushing her off for drugs, and I was tugging her other hand to get her to bed to rest while I bought some naturopathic stuff." "Who won?" the young guy asks, and everyone bursts out laughing. "He's six foot, four inches, and believes in the Western medical world only, from his upbringing, so you guess," I say.

I have learned so much from this class; I realize you teach what you need to learn, and these concepts I reiterate in every class have really helped me to "get it." I look at my own efforts with forgiveness. Linda has seemed threatened by me and my life for years, has put me down to others, which has come back to me through friends and Clark's caregiver. It hurts, I accept that she's fearful and I move into compassion. I need to be vigilant about practicing forgiveness. It feels more familiar since it happens again and again. I remind myself that Linda has been diagnosed as manic-depressive and is taking lithium or something. Maybe now that Kelly is in love with a sweet guy, a movie star, she'll have more love and fun in her life and be less resentful.

Todd has plans to leave soon to play professional volleyball in Europe. We are proud and excited for him. He's getting paid to play on a team in Switzerland for a year, though Alexandra won't be thrilled he's leaving. Robert and I will have to eventually go to watch him play, which I'm stoked about. And Robert's never been to Europe, so he is, too.

Kilia's going to Punahou now that Jimmy has paid her tuition; we wouldn't have been able to afford it ('Iolani was free) and we're grateful Jimmy arranged it. She is delighted, as Sky and all her pals are at Punahou (as am I, since I loved it there), though she thrived at 'Iolani. She has fun with boys, is a natural flirt, has had a couple boyfriends, as I did, at twelve and thirteen, and her first true love is at fourteen. I'm glad we're close; she seems to share everything, but maybe not. Lila has left, and now I don't really remember where she went after her second round with us, but it feels good to have just Kilia home, who seems to be as active as her dad, running, biking, volleyball, certainly more active than I've ever been. We have more foster daughters from Hale Kipa in the ensuing months, before Nangoula and the twins are on the horizon.

CHAPTER SIXTEEN

KELLY AND JOHN HAVE ELOPED TO PARIS. But the really
big news is they're having a baby. Linda is over the moon and I'm happy for her to be having a grandchild to love. Being Scientologists has
brought, after their marriage, a peculiar dimension into the family,
because Linda has had a long report from Chris, Kelly's brother, who
researched it, and saw it was rumored to be a cult with strange rules
to live by, that L. Ron Hubbard was into sci-fi and other weird gossip.
Linda, like all of us, freaked, we all discussed it, and she got into it
with Kelly, with unpleasant results. So when Jett was born, everyone
was happy, for a time.

Hana Harrison is born to Rob and Judi, a tiny wisp of a blonde
baby, and Judi's overwhelmed, but I help with both Ryan and Hana a
few times a week. Jimmy invites us to Lāna'i, an island as remote to
most of us as Moloka'i, with our motorcycles. Though Jimmy has such
great ideas and is extremely generous, Robert gets a kick out of his
dry, caustic wit, and they get on well. It even seems Robert's learning to be less conservative with money, though Jimmy seldom allows
us to carry our load. We are surprised how dry Lana'i is, with mostly
pineapple fields as far as one can see, but the Lodge at Kō'ele in the
hills is exquisite, and we take off from there exploring on our motorcycles. The gourmet food and quiet elegance is so appealing that
Jimmy books the entire family to stay a long weekend several months
hence.

I've been teaching the class in Ka'ahamanu, Wai'anae, 'Āina Haina,
Hawai'i Kai and other schools, most for a few months, some for a
one-time presentation. I realize how important it is, how it exposes
abuse, bullying, etc., and I'm glad when Robert mentions that 'Iolani's
religion teacher is going home sick and maybe I can step into her
class. Robert has insisted often that I need a degree to do what I'm doing, and that schools would all hire me if I had one. I deny this, as none

have ever asked if I have a degree. The reverend at 'Iolani doesn't ask, either, and I've been teaching here for six weeks already.

"So we all have a universal law of cause and effect. Do you know what this means?" I ask the seventh graders. "If you do something, it makes something happen?" a sweet-faced Japanese girl asks. "Well, whatever we do, everything we do, causes something to happen, which is the effect. And we've been talking here the past month that we create everything that happens to us with the energy of our thoughts and feelings, right?" I study their faces. Some of them nod, brows furrowed. "Question authority, and you can decide for yourself if you believe that, if I'm creating what happens to me, how can I accuse anyone of doing something to me?"

"In other words, are we victims? Should we blame others for something we attract?" A hand goes up. "But you mean if someone kills you or rapes you, then you wanted that to happen?" After a long pause, I say, "Wanting might not be the word to use here, but attracting it, for some reason, subconsciously. For everything is a lesson, which can take a long time to learn. Or not." I wonder if this hapa-haole boy can digest this, if the others can. "I see how this sounds to you, like chaos, bedlam, right? Anything can happen to us at any moment. And yet is it chaotic if we are all taking full responsibility for ourselves?" "But," Keola asks, "what about accidents?" I gaze at Keola's clear green eyes and dark, smooth face. "And what if I said there really is no such thing as accidents? Or luck. So it isn't someone's fault. We can't really blame someone." I write on the board: luck, accident, fault, blame, right, wrong, good, bad. "We can look at these words, see the power they have. See the judgment. If we accept what happens without judging, which isn't easy, we can know there's always something to learn from it. By bringing yourself back to the moment."

I sit quietly. "I'm throwing out a huge new concept today. If you can just be open like you have been, and think about all this." A solemn girl with almond eyes says, "But what about dying?" I nod and gaze at this bright class. "I wondered when that would come up. Isn't that our biggest fear, death?" They look at each other uncertainly, nodding.

"Remember how we learned about God or a higher power being everywhere, and within us, helping us whenever we listen? We create with God's help. So isn't it possible we come to Earth and even leave it with God helping us? To choose who we're born to, if we're rich or poor, if we're loved or abused."

"But why would we choose sad stuff if we have a choice?" the almond-eyed one asks. The doubt, fear, is palpable in the class. "We have free will, remember? And usually we don't learn much about love if we don't have the darkness, the fearful, sad stuff. So as babies we come with love." I pause and glance around the class. "But often lack, being in poverty, being abused, teaches us more about compassion and forgiveness. Gives us a choice to not become abusive ourselves. To help others. If we grow up poor maybe we can learn to work hard, learn not to be jealous, maybe become rich ourselves." I debate going to the next step now, wonder if they're ready. I leap.

"What if you knew death was not final or frightening? That you even choose, subconsciously, how and when you die? Since we are all energy, energy never dies, it cannot die." Mahi says, "My aunty says the soul doesn't die." "Smart aunty you have, Mahi. It's only our bodies that die; our spirits, like our thoughts and feelings, go on. To be with God. He gives us free will."

A serious girl, Kea says, "But what about religion, and what it teaches us? We have different religions, and, I don't know ... " I smile at her. "I think if religion is loving and helpful for you, fine, it's important you go to church. But I think religions are divisive. They usually separate us. Some even say they need to put the fear of God in you! That shocks me. God is only love. But we can continue this conversation next week, it's important and we're out of time."

I love this class, I think as I leave. It's the optimum age to learn this, and in a privileged environment. I smile inwardly about the dialogue we've just had, in the 'Iolani chapel, and will share it with Robert. He's changed, as I have, and I'm grateful we can share these important values and beliefs. I remember how adamant Robert was years ago about capital punishment. Somehow, his belief has changed, and he no longer thinks we must take a life, ever, has even become less of a hawk, believing war isn't the answer. His kind blue eyes are intent as I describe the 'Iolani classes.

CHAPTER SEVENTEEN

THE TRAVOLTAS RETURN (though Kelly has kept her movie-star name, Kelly Preston, which she gave herself years back). It isn't a happy scene when Linda and Lee greet them at the airport after some drinks. Kelly is angry, maybe embarrassed, which seems to begin a shift in Linda's relationship with her. Kelly pulls away, lets it be known she disapproves of their lifestyle, perhaps the Scientology scene influencing her. (I'd had a similar scene with both Robin and later Kilia without the influence of Scientology.)

But troubling as that is, I feel a distinct unease stirring regarding their little Jett. As he gets to be about a year old, I wonder if the fact he won't give us eye contact, that he flaps his tiny hands, means he could possibly be autistic. Robert agrees. My heart is heavy, and somehow it comes up with Linda. Kelly and John have bought a house in Hawaiʻi on the beach near Niu on Kalanianaʻole Highway, where we were raised. Celebrating Easter with them (which is when I think it was), Linda gets angry when I wonder aloud why they haven't come out publicly about the autism, to help others with autistic children.

"Don't you dare mention it!" she snaps at me. "You don't know for sure he's autistic anyway, Chula!" I reply, "I've seen the same symptoms with kids I've worked with at some schools, Linda, and . . . " "It won't do any good you saying something. Don't forget they're Scientologists, they don't believe in terms like that." This is true. They don't believe in psychiatrists, either, as Linda divulged after she'd gotten into a fight with Kelly when she confronted her about their Scientology, why they had to spend thousands of dollars every year to be "audited," and Cakes (which I nicknamed her) had snapped back, "How is that any different from you going to a psychiatrist and spending money on that as well as on drugs?" I saw both points of view.

It is curious that I actually agree with this tenet of Scientology: no drugs. Certainly therapy is hugely important with a psychologist or counselor, but psychiatrists prescribe drugs. Robert often has confrontations at 'Iolani with parents of children with ADD and other conditions. Many of the students are drugged, which troubles him enough to ask that they back off, maybe use other tactics such as less pressure, go to a naturopath, spend more quality time with their child, which he helps with as well. The kids adore him; he is real, down to earth, funny. He tells them how he fucked up as a kid.

Anyway, the Scientology thing is baffling, other than that one belief I know about. Kelly has given us pamphlets written by L. Ron Hubbard. Robert snorts as he reads them, because it is as if a first grader has written them. We are bewildered at how sci-fi it is, how it doesn't seem to be a religion, at the nonsensical wording.

At the last 'Iolani class, we reiterate our talk on bullying in schools. "So you agree the bully that was so aggressive the other day wasn't a happy camper?" I smile at freckled, thin Winston. He nods. "He was mean." "Do you think mean people are feeling loving?" "No!" the class choruses. "They're scared," Winston says. I nod. "So what if you could approach him alone someday, maybe ask him if you can talk. Imagine asking him if he's okay. Maybe you guys could become friends." A girl exclaims, "No way!" And the class laughs. I persist, "Well, if everyone here at 'Iolani spoke the same language, all of them taking a class like this and learning about their fears, if they were not so threatened by it, what do you think?" "I can't imagine me talking to him like that," Winston says. Malia adds, "But it would be amazing. I think it would be easier for a girl to talk to a bully like that, though." Heads nod. "And if they'd taken your class, and if they knew they were acting scared instead of cool, it'd be amazing," Malia says. "Yeah! Like a fantasy school!" Kai responds, and the class chuckles.

"And let's sum this class up with the biggest fears we all share: the fear of failing, the fear we are not good enough." They are nodding. "And the fear of pain, emotional pain. Remember everything is energy, including pain. So we usually try to avoid it, but if you're doing something to avoid pain, then pain is running your life." "Yeah," says

Whitney, "but why wouldn't I avoid pain?" "It's natural, sure," I say, "but if you can just see it as energy, an object, let it pass through you, it'll hurt briefly but then you can move on from it. That particular pain won't rule you. You can relax and release it." They look off in the distance, pondering.

"Well, anyway, can we use the last minutes to write how you feel about this class? Grab a pencil and paper, and just sum up in a few sentences what you learned. The important bits. I'd appreciate it."

And they do. The response is amazing, and I am touched. Insights, observations, lessons learned, how some saw God differently, more loving, and felt they knew Him better. I hand the packet over to Rev. Yoshida soon after this two-month session, hoping, as I ask that he'd want to pass it on to the headmaster, Dave Coon, who I could then approach to legitimately teach it here, maybe even get paid. But Rev. Yoshida "loses" the stack of notes, my feedback. I am furious, feel he is threatened by my class, and I allow myself to be crushed.

We celebrate out twentieth anniversary, me with fragrant pikake lei around my neck and gardenias in my hair, with our kids, our best friends, with champagne and dinner. Blessed.

I am electric. We are going to the San Juan Islands with Jimmy and Olivia, shipping our bikes to Seattle and cruising from island to island on the ferry. It's beautiful when we finally get out of Seattle. But before that I have a scare when my motorcycle stops running for no apparent reason, and they are ahead of me, so I sit and wait. And wait. After twenty minutes or so, I am unnerved I am lost in a city and they have no clue where to find me. Then they appear. When they realized I wasn't behind them, they circled back in heavy traffic. A decision is made to keep each other in sight in our rearview mirrors.

We pull onto the ferries first, talk story (a Hawaiian expression) with the other bikers, and get to disembark first. It is such a different experience, hanging with other bikers, all different ages and from different walks of life. The first island we came to, Bainbridge, we are having dinner at the house of old friends who lived in Hawai'i also.

It'll be fun seeing them in their new habitat. We sweep down their steep driveway for the evening, which reminds me to sip just one glass of wine when driving a motorcycle. Yet I have two glasses of wine, knowing our rooms at the inn are only a mile away, and later I get on my bike after Jimmy and Olivia (who always rides on his bike with him) ride up the hill to leave. I follow, accelerating exactly the speed I need (I wouldn't be able to stop midway or go back) and swoop up the hill. Robert is last, and I gape when he goes down, as he's never fallen on his motorcycle before, a fact he mentioned recently, and now he has, but when I see he was nimble enough not to have been pinned, burned or hurt, then I can laugh. Many times the next day, too.

We bike through lush green fields, forests, along streams, past cows and sheep the next morning. See a sign in a pasture saying, "Don't even think about trespassing, the bull runs faster than you do!" We get caught in a rainstorm, each drop stinging my face like freezing needles, not like our warm Hawaiian rain, but we laugh like children as we pull into our inn for the night. A special trip for a week, going where our bikes take us. Carefree.

Robert's hip continues to hurt and he finally has it replaced during the summer. I knew he should not have played rugby as long as he did, it was predictable, but I've seen how stoic he's been the past year or more, and I am at his side through the next weeks of surgery for titanium hip surgery and recovery. He is the sort of man who downplays any physical difficulty, is self-effacing and uncomplaining. He's never had a sick day off. He continues coaching two sports as well as teaching English lit and history; he eventually takes on the counseling job for a year, as he connects with the kids brilliantly, but he misses the classroom, to which he returns eventually. He also plays guitar (with his colleague Frank) biannually in chapel, and sings songs they wrote as well as old favorites.

CHAPTER EIGHTEEN

JIMMY HAS OFFERED to have a book party for *Cucumber Seeds Don't Sprout Radishes*, which has finally arrived in March '92. (My second book, *Joy Can Be Your Favorite Song*, will be delivered the next month.) His lovely old oceanfront home has been renovated and, at first glance, it appears to be a resort. We walk through the naupaka and hau tree-fringed garden, which slopes gently to the infinity pool, a new concept thus far, admiring how it spills over the edge to the lava rocks and waves below. The stunning vista of the ocean (with a good surf spot in front) sweeps down Kāhala Beach past homes obscured by coconut trees, with Koko Head mountain in the distance. It's the most beautiful home I've ever been in, and I'm tingling, touched that Jimmy will graciously share his home with eighty friends, though I realize his drama is more exciting than my book for the guests. I wear a new, white tailored skirt and jacket with gold accessories, gardenias in my hair (I have taken pains to control the curls) as Robert and I climb the stairs into the high-ceilinged, open entryway, accompanied by the splash of a waterfall tumbling down lava rock in the spacious, open living room. The tiled floors complement the white stucco walls and enormous windows.

My whole family comes, except for Todd, not yet returned from Europe, and Robin is escorting Mummy. Champagne and delicious *pūpū* are served, I feel honored, loved by family and friends as I greet the Mullers, Scotts, Wellses, Mattices, McCormacks, Gileses, Taylors, etc. My books are artfully arranged on a table, signed prior to the party in hopes they'll be sold. (I don't remember how many were.) I hope the upcoming book signing at the Kāhala Barnes & Noble will help it to be read. I have a newspaper article, a radio interview, etc., but not much feedback. In its simplicity and childlike approach, which I felt the best style for the metaphysical subject, I don't know that it works, as I get few compliments.

Eventually I have another book signing in Santa Barbara's Waldenbooks, and, ultimately, a year or so later, I get the most fulfilling review. A German fellow calls to say it's the best book in metaphysics he's ever read, it's succinct and simple, he'd like to translate it into German when he returns home. I tell him to go for it. Wonder if there's a German version of it floating around out there, by Kurt Von Dutz, or whatever.

A week after the book party, we go to Switzerland, where Todd lives. He's had an extraordinary year playing beach volleyball around Europe, but his schedule does not mesh with ours, we won't see him compete there and we're disappointed, as he is. But it's intoxicating for Robert to be in Europe, and we're ecstatic to travel around with handsome Todd, meeting striking Alexandra in Venice. This brilliant, charming woman is our leader, rattling off Italian, gesturing, gesticulating, effusive. We laugh often and marvel at Italy's beauty, the warmth of these pretty people, including Alex's widowed dad at Lake Como. Two hilarious weeks fly by and we come home to Hawai'i, glad Todd will return soon as well.

May Day is Lei Day in Hawai'i, a gay, colorful show as schools on all the Islands perform and sing, adorned with lei, mu'umu'u, aloha shirts and flowers everywhere. It's heartwarming to watch children of all ages and races dance, the boys and girls dancing sweet, endearing hula, each class presenting its own routines. The boys usually have a more masculine version, more athletic. Punahou School knocks itself out on May Day, with authentic *kumu hula* (hula teachers), to instruct for months ahead. I'd danced at Punahou in my clumsy fashion, representing one of the islands, which is a tradition, and now Kilia is dancing, only her moves are so naturally graceful, so intuitively Hawaiian in gesture, Robert and I weep. Her smile is radiant against her mocha skin, her long dark waves of hair sporting a yellow plumeria *haku* lei to match her form-fitting *holoku*. We are grateful Jimmy gave us this gift, as Punahou is truly the most amazing school in many

ways, the arts, sports, academics and campus that make it the largest
private school in the world.

I muse that when I'm in my late eighties or older, maybe lonely or a
bit down, I'll make a point of going to all the schools' May Day events,
as they don't always have them May 1st. It's such a happy, uplifting,
loving and fragrant occasion to see the precious little *menehune* and
the sensuality and talent of the older students dancing and singing.
Another day I shall go to the surf spots, the beaches, to get a whiff of
the joy and energy of Hawai'i's youths pulling in to surf, biking up
with their boards attached, piled on top of their cars or inside, love
and beauty everywhere as they paddle out to carve the waves.

I help with BabySweet and Hana, and plunge back into volleyball
five times a week. I am addicted to this sport: the bump, set and hit,
the diving for a ball, the laughs when we miss. I teach a weekly class
at the Family Peace Center, and a one-time-only at the Boys and Girls
Club, as well as at a home for battered women. The first class has a
powerful message of the choice between love and fear, but it needs
to be reiterated, to go deeper, and both of the latter places have oft-
changing "students," which isn't conducive to my six- or eight-week
class. I even do a class at Calvary and Unity Church, both of which
Robert had attended in the past, for several weeks. (And Unity carried
my books.)

Robin has moved home, now that Ma has a regular caregiver with
the onset of her dementia. Robin was a loving, attentive caregiver, but
Ma needs more now and he will utilize his three years of acupuncture
training. He is as tender and devoted in his practice as he was with
Mummy, and we are impressed. Surfing is only rivaled by his work,
though we haven't needed his needles yet, and we are amazed we have
a second healer in the family, as Rob's chiropractic practice thrives.
We can attest to the fact Rob's a natural healer when we've gone to
him for adjustments, seeing that strapping, gorgeous man stride up to
hug us with a warm smile, though I am seldom in need of his services,
because I keep up with my yoga. Robby jokes that Dad needs to come
in more often, though, since he's a testament to his son's skills, which

isn't looking brilliant, since he still walks with a "carrot-up-his-okole" tilt most of the time.

It's extraordinary that Ma has created dementia, though it seems more like the start of Alzheimer's. She has been saying for the past few years she wants to die when she is eighty. "But Ma, people are living way older than that nowadays, why limit yourself? You can be healthy and happy for years!" But she persists in this, so it doesn't surprise me she is checking out now that she is eighty, heartbreaking as it is. I am already missing who she was. Packing her on the back of my motorcycle to run a chore, her clinging to me happily as we whizzed along. Dropping by to find her swimming laps naked in her pool. On the phone with Aunty Barbie. Coming over for dinner with us once a week.

It is scary for Aunty Barbie as well, as Mummy has been working mornings for her the past few years in her home. In a jesting tone Aunty Barbie would tell me how Ma would forget stuff, make silly comments and errors, that she was going nitty notty. Her tone seemed peculiar to me at the time. Of course, she was devastated when Ma had to quit work, and even then Aunty Barbie was convinced it was only dementia, too scared to use the awful A-word. Not until years later do I realize why her fears seemed to grip this powerful, bright, athletic woman.

Meanwhile, I have been feeding the homeless every few weeks in Aʻala Park on the fringe of Honolulu, bringing chicken soup I've made in a huge pot, along with rolls. It's an experience hanging with these destitute locals, some of whom actually go to work, and we talk story. Eventually that park is closed to them and I follow them to Ala Moana Park, adjacent to the ocean. Quite a beautiful setting in which to be homeless, and I think how much better off they are than in any Mainland scene. It's warm and they can swim whenever, which, oddly they seldom seem to do. If it weren't for the drug use and their health problems, it wouldn't be a bad life camping indefinitely, compared to struggling with a huge mortgage and utility bills.

Months later I take my soup to a homeless shelter downtown, in a building where they come only to eat. "Bill? Is that you?" I ask. The blue eyes are rheumy now, the hair matted and the skin weathered, but I'm certain this is Bill, a handsome lawyer Linda dated twenty years before. "Bill, it's Chula, remember me?" He smiles tentatively, and I'm unsure if he does. I talk story a few more minutes before moving on to the next fellow, stunned that Bill has come to this. Later I discover he had gotten heavily into cocaine, which destroyed his practice and now him.

I have gotten my class into Punahou in a sort of peer group program they have going in the academy, and I feel effervescent to be on this campus for the third week. "So do we ever have the past, or the future? Isn't the past always over, the future not yet here?" The class locks eyes with me and nods. "All we ever really have is now, right? In fact, that's all there is. Now. You have no power in the past or future, only in the present. And yet how often are we truly in the moment? If you only learn one thing this year, learning to stay in the now would be the most powerful thing you can do."

"Anyway, that's your homework for the rest of your life. So this week, let's discuss belief systems. I'm going to throw out a huge belief for you. 'If you don't believe you can have it all, you get to choose how much less than all you will have.'" I am still as they absorb this quote from Arnold Patent. "What do you believe 'having it all' means?"

"Money?" a tall lad says. "Can you write it on the board?" I ask, and he does. "Friends?" Ilima asks, rising to write it. Simon stands as he says, "Health?" and wrestles with Ilima for the chalk as they all chuckle. "Like, a new skateboard and surfboard?" another says, chalk on board. "Yeah!" exclaims Mahi, "Toys! And what about a car?" Quiet little Meiko says, "Fun?"

"Wow, great list, you guys. So, we often hear that you can't have it all. But why not? You don't have to believe that." I point to the board. "Why can't you have money, friends, health, toys, fun? A sense of humor is essential to have. Laughter. I remember at just about your age making a conscious decision to laugh more. Especially at myself.

How's about honesty? With yourself and others." Meiko is still at the board, scribbling away.

"Modesty?" Billy says. I smile. "Humility!" Mahi exclaims, and the class laughs. "You better ask for that, Mahi," Keahi adds, "you need it!" The class roars. Mahi shoots back, "Whoa, dude, how's about silence, knowing when to shut up?" Even Meiko laughs at this.

"Okay, you're a great bunch. Now let's think of other limiting beliefs. If you are overweight, is it that you eat too much, or instead, you eat too much because you believe you are overweight? And if you feel unloved do you fill that *puka* (hole) with food? What about the racist beliefs that hold us back, like if you believe black people are not cool, or, say, Filipino, Japanese, German, whatever. And if you have negative beliefs about a whole race, won't you see what you expect to see in them? Won't you limit yourself from knowing them, maybe becoming friends?" They laugh when Alika lisps, "I'm so glad I realized someone as black as Kanu could be my pal."

"Think of how beliefs in religions limit us." I say after a moment. "If you are not a Christian, you are not worthy. If you are not Catholic, that's cause for war. Do you believe war is the answer? If you aren't athletic, you are not accepted. Do you believe in lack or abundance? If getting old means illness or disease? What do you believe old is, anyway? Sixty? Seventy? Eighty? Ninety?"

"Make a list of limiting beliefs you might have, for your homework. Your truth is created from what you believe. And your beliefs run every moment of your life. They actually create your reality."

As I leave the class I think I'll bring my little stereo to the next class to play one of my favorite songs, "No Matter What," by Boyzo. Great voices and the words are pithy. I had taken it to play in another class at Kalani High School, but the kids weren't responsive in the first place, and the song didn't seem to help: "No matter what they tell us, no matter what they do, no matter what they teach us, what we believe is true. No matter what they call us, however they attack, no matter where they take us, we'll find our own way back. I can't deny what I believe, I can't be what I'm not, I know our love's forever, I know, no matter what. [Second verse:] If only tears were laughter, if only night was day, if only prayers were answered, then we would hear God say: No matter what they tell you, no matter what they do, no matter what they teach you, what you believe is true." And so on. I'm sure this Punahou class will be more receptive to it, as private schools seem more so than the public schools.

Kilia graduates from Punahou, though soon after she too leaves to work for a semester in Santa Barbara before college. Todd is living with Alex in a Waikīkī condo, and Robin with his new girlfriend, so we briefly have an empty nest, other than our Labrador, Kui, who has replaced Mau Mau, and another, a poi dog, mixed-breed, since him. We rent our house and take off for Santa Barbara for July and August, where I beachcomb East Beach for volleyball, and Robert's new hip allows him A tennis again, and we see Kilia, the Steeles, etc. Returning home, I happily play volleyball all week, riding my motorcycle to the Outrigger Canoe Club in my bikini, which feels so free and natural. And I surf. It is at this point Nangoula comes to live with us and, after a month, the twins. Life becomes hectic again, but I feel needed, more so than I really want to be, but I decide they are a gift.

After five or six months working in a café, Kilia returns. She has been struggling the past few years with an eating disorder. With all that exercise, the biking to school four miles though she had volleyball practice in the afternoon (which I had often verbalized seemed excessive), she had been manifesting this condition. Nobody had heard of anorexia, all of her pals at school as well as her cousin Sky, Stephanie, Kelly and me, were thin, and there was always talk at school, at home, everywhere about being thin. Between Steph's modeling world and Kelly's acting world of Hollywood, it was what Kilia often heard, and, though she had a luscious, curvy body wanting to come out, she stifled her hunger to stay thin and kept extremely active. No matter that her father was six foot four and she had his bone structure. So she played sports for hours daily, like her dad. Because she seemed to be replicating what she'd seen Robert do her whole life, I came to accept it. And perhaps Robert's veiled implication of guilt if one wasn't active was an influence. And probably I had implied slender was better, something to strive for.

Ironically I came by my weight naturally, hadn't thought much about it except for a few years starting in college and afterward. Robert roared with laughter when he saw an old video that friends had taken in Australia of me—silly, a vamp, moving my plump body like a siren, even knowing I was "chunky tuna" at the time. It wasn't hard to lose the weight, though I loved to eat, ate whatever I wanted, had hot fudge sundaes most afternoons. And friends often observed this, moaning that they hated me. I had small bones, my whole family was slight, and I had become more active, which increased my metabolism accordingly.

Anyway, it wasn't apparent anything was wrong. Though she would binge and purge with sports, it was subtle and she never made herself sick. When she began calling me, anxious, crying, I would talk her through it, my heart heavy, aching. For half an hour, an hour, we'd talk. Often. In between these crises she seemed fine, productive. So having her return at the end of '93 was good for us all, as she was to begin college the January semester at Boulder, Colorado, where her father went. It is a respite having her play volleyball and surfing, often with me.

I even go with her to college (while Robert holds down the fort with Sophie, Molly and Nangoula), helping her choose her classes, sleeping in her dorm. I feel so close, giggling together, praying this crushingly sad time of her life was past. Though upon my return the calls continue, not often, but the anguish is palpable.

All is calm when I return until Sophie vanishs for a few days. Turned out she was with her boyfriend, but the police and Juvenile Runaway Program had intervened by then, though I don't remember the details. Two close friends of ours suffer excruciating tragedy; one losing a baby to drowning, the other an adult son in a car accident. Heartbreaking. We are always reminded to count our blessings. I continue babysitting Ryan and Hana weekly, our "angels" at four and two.

My fiftieth birthday comes soon after our last three foster daughters leave. I am adamant the twins shouldn't return home (to the father who abused them), but Child and Family Services decrees it. (I'd researched finding land on which to build a boys and girls home, like the old days, big, safe, with teachers, caregivers for these abused teens, but to no avail.) So Robert takes me to Adelaide for his spring break, and after his week is pau, I visit Jane and Ian in Tasmania again, feeling young and carefree. No children, no classes, no homemaking duties.

CHAPTER NINETEEN

ROBERT AND I PADDLE THE USED KAYAKS we recently bought through the channel, past the reef and waves of Kāhala, around Diamond Head to wait for the canoe in which Rob is racing for the Outrigger Canoe Club. From Moloka'i for thirty-two miles, each paddler finishes twenty-minute stints before tumbling out, clutching his paddle, to await the escort boat. It is an art to see the switch, with the fresh teammate ready (having hopped off the escort boat just prior) to pull himself up and into the canoe without slowing its pace. (When the ocean is choppy with waves and wind, it's a challenge to reach up and haul yourself in. It's easy to hurt yourself, which is how Rob breaks a rib in a later race.) It's exciting when we see the red and white canoe approaching and we start shouting, "Go Rob! Go Outrigger!" as they streak through the chop toward us. We are at a distance so as not to hinder the race, for each canoe has an escort boat, and I scream as loud as I can, "You're kicking 'okole! Yeah, go for it Rob! Go team!" Robert and I laugh as the white water splashes off their paddles, all six men in perfect sync, leaning, digging deep, muscles bulging then sinewy, bulging, sinewy, focused. We paddle our clunky kayaks hard and are instantly left in their wake.

Rob and Todd have paddled this spectacular race a few times, and they always do well against the competition, Hui Nalu, Lanikai, Kailua, Hanalei and many others. The teams from Tahiti usually win, because they paddle for a living, full time, but it's a happy rivalry and hugely bonding. I am so proud of our sons, but Stephanie is the most amazing, as she's actually afraid of deep water, yet she trains for the event, in the women's race, and finishes the thirty-two miles.

Robert and I go to Ma's, play guitar and sing to her, which she loves. I go weekly and read to her as well as take her to her doctor. She still knows us, and I am grateful she has such wonderfully patient caregivers alternating around the clock, paid for by Jimmy. Daddy has the same, since he's been physically weak and it's expensive, so I crack up when Jimmy mentions we ought to call in Dr. Kervorkian and have him do a two-for-one deal, or, if Dad starts losing his mind as well, we can move them in together, they won't remember they're divorced.

"Chula," Dad's caregiver calls, "Clark is something else. You know I love him, but he's gone too far." I say, "Oh God, what now?" "Well, he asked me the other day if I'd stand on my hands with no panties on, and I . . . " "Oh shit," I interrupt, "I'm so sorry. What a perv! He's disgusting!" "No, it's okay, I just don't know how long I can last." "I sure as hell don't blame you, he's gross." I've had variations on this call from other caregivers, the last two who were gay, and he asked them if they'd have sex in front of him, you know, like a private showing. His sex addiction has gotten worse as he ages.

Now Dad is in Kahuku Hospital out there on the North Shore, where he lives, for pneumonia or something, I don't remember. He calls me and begs me to come pick him up and take him home, and, finally, I do. I realize he needs that, craves his shack in the country with his horses. All that pasture around him. So what if he's sick, if he's going to die at eighty-five, let him do so at home.

I decide to hold a wake for him before he dies, something to lift his spirits. I call a few friends, which is all he has, and some of our friends, and Robert wheels him across the pasture near our campsite on the ocean. He's cheerful with his upside-down smile trying to actually move into a real smile, a blanket on his shoulders, and we all laugh on this lovely, sunny day under the ironweed trees, then sing a song or two. It goes well, we think, as we camp that night, but Jimmy isn't pleased. He is pissed I took him out of the hospital, says he needs medical care and I am reckless. I let him scold me, knowing he places stock in doctors and drugs, but I ignore it, as Dad gets better because he's much happier.

Todd graduates from UH with a degree in education. We're delighted he wants to teach (though he plans to move to Kaua'i, which I guess we can live with). Two healers and a teacher. Kilia is home for summer, happy and healthy. Robert and I buy crates to pack up our motorcycles, preparing to leave for a motorcycle trip from Seattle (where we pick up the bikes) with my oldest pal Patsy, who will pack behind her husband, Lolo, as well as friends from Sun Valley and a few others. So we ride there to organize ourselves for a day or two, and I am giddy with excitement as we zoom off. I am the only wāhine on a motorcycle, as the others pack behind their men.

We roar along the gorgeous countryside of Idaho through even more stunning Glacier National Park, at speeds sometimes of eighty mph on the straight-a-ways, the testosterone pumping. The vistas are so captivating it's tricky to drive, because I am compelled to absorb the beauty, both around us and below, sometimes way, way below the narrow highway. When we ride open highways I am challenged by the huge trucks thundering toward us, the suction grabbing me as they pass. I feel like an imposter. Until I realize I can do this. Robert is so solicitous, of course, riding behind me, checking on me regularly. We go to Banff and Lake Louise, sometimes staying in little cabins, sometimes camping out with only what we have on the back of our bikes. The brilliant turquoise water of Lake Louise is startling. We hike. Always we laugh. The camaraderie is heavenly during the day, and after riding sometimes 200 miles, I am exhilarated but exhausted at night.

Robert takes charge and changes our course once or twice to accommodate his little Chu Chu. I had begun menopause years before and have been taking Chinese herbs and acupuncture, without huge improvement stemming the flow, which has increased instead of decreased. Finally a gynecologist helped me, since I couldn't have taken this 3,700-mile ride gushing as I'd been, actually in diapers at one point. Now we are stopping by the Gileses, our old pals who'd moved to Montana on Lindbergh Lake some years back. Robert and I had been there a few times with or without kids, and its serene tranquility was as enticing as the Gileses' humor and warm hearth.

We find the turnoff and rumble along the long, shalelike dirt road. The bikers ahead of me kick up clouds of dust, which I eat, and I groan inwardly, remembering how long this driveway is. Robert calls out to

Kathy and Chula, 1994

Rougiers garden, 1995

Rougiers garden, 1995

Chula and Robert in Les Baux,
Provence, 1995

Tyler, Kilia, Kelly and John Travolta, 1996

Anne and Todd, 1998

Ella Bleu, 1998

Family Christmas, 1999

Todd, Anne and Kai, 1999

Chula and Kai at Kalihiwai, Kaua'i, 1999

Rob's family, 2000

Family on Kaua'i with the Travoltas, New Year's 2000

Chula and Aunty Barbie at the Hanalei Big House, 2000

Kai and Chula on her Honda 600, 2001

me and I whine, "How much longer?" He grimaces and replies we're only halfway, do I want to stop and rest? It's easier riding on tarmac, as this rocky, sandy road is gnarly and I have to really focus so as not to fishtail out of control. I am wiped out. And yet I hang on like an 'opihi, grit my teeth and finally up ahead I see their gate, the end of the road and past the other cabins.

Tommy is smiling as he swings his gate open. I cannot endure another second upright, so I slide off my bike and sit on the woodpile Tommy's chopped. He laughs and I actually start crying. Robert tells him we've come more than 150 miles today, after many other long days, and he says, "Whoa, Chu, you should be tired! But if you can ride just ten more yards, Leslie's waiting with a pitcher of margaritas. Which you can drink before or after jumping in the lake."

I always head straight for the lake when we come here, so I mumble that's where I'm going, and dear Leslie, whom I've dubbed Tiger Lily, and she's given me Magnolia Thunderpussy, trots out of the cabin with a big margarita for me as I stumble down the tiny trail, strip off my filthy clothes and dive in. The cold is a shock and I emerge shrieking with laughter. As I haul myself up to the dock to swallow the lovely libation, hugging my dear pal, it actually starts hailing. Tiger Lily and I shout, and I cackle hysterically as we are pelted by grape-size hail, exclaiming how lucky we are it didn't hail sooner.

After a night of tales and tequila, we wake up restored. Our group disperses, and Robert and I head down the coast to Santa Barbara. As we wind past the cliffs of Sausalito, with the ocean to the right and mountains on our left, a fat bug hits my face. Instantly I know it's a bee, because the sting zaps my cheek. I have recently begun to have a slight reaction from bee stings, having been stung all my childhood by Portuguese man-of-war, the last one, as an adult, wrapped around my torso, the bright blue tail leaving welts and stings. I realize I need to pull over, and because Robert's ahead of me, he doesn't know what's going on. I park on the shoulder, and sit until I feel more like lying down. And I wait, wondering when he will notice.

After a few minutes he charges back up to me. "What happened?!

Jesus, Chu, were you hit? What in hell . . . " His face is contorted, so I interrupt, "No, no don't panic. Just got stung by a fucking bee. And I may be having a reaction so I had to stop." He holds me and asks, "Does it hurt like hell, are you okay?"

Then he actually chuckles. "You might want to check out your face." He pulls me up and I look in the rearview mirror of the motorcycle. My face has begun to swell, within the next ten minutes it's a pumpkin, and we both crack up. "Probably not a good idea we camp tonight, huh? I think we should head for a motel, any motel, right away." Which we do.

When we pull into Santa Barbara we head right to the Steeles'. Laurie sees me and snorts, "God, Chu, you look darling. Hair in dreadlocks, face like a moon, sure must've been fun. What a slacker, you only went 4,000 miles." (I don't correct her as we both like to exaggerate.)

Halie Harrison is born to Rob and Judi, another sweet angel and a clone of Rob. We are amazed they had a third baby, because Judi bleated and struggled with two, and we asked Rob when he told us they were hāpai if he knew what was causing this, but we are grateful for Halie. I long to hold her but am bewildered she doesn't come to me or Judi's mother, yet I babysit weekly soon thereafter. Sadly, we don't seem to bond, though I reach for her often.

I have always had family dinners at our house; Christmas, Thanksgiving, birthdays, etc., and it's usually a happy evening, everyone talking at once, drinking, eating, laughing. We sometimes rock out, the whole family, to hip tunes, the little ones bouncing around between us. Kilia is a sensuous dancer with flawless timing, Robin has cool moves and together Judi and Rob sizzle. Todd dances a bit like his beloved dad (who is a lovely ballroom dancer though not much for rocking out) and I am somewhere in between. Though our dinners are usually potluck, Robert and I do the lion's share and Kilia is like having a wife, knowing just where to help without being asked. I love hearing about my kids' lives, though I don't strive to engage Judi, because I'm disinterested in her woes and prattle. It's more fun when we dance.

Todd moves to Kaua'i, to teach English (like his dad) at Kapa'a High School. He rents a studio in Kalihiwai Valley, en route to Hanalei on the North Shore, which could be an ad for Shangri-la. Towering trees a dense canopy overhead, the road swoops over the valley on a suspended bridge, a waterfall crashes into the Kalihiwai Stream below and meanders past a few small houses, one of which is Todd's studio. To surf he need only walk 300 yards to the stream, paddle across it to the beach and walk the crescent of the small bay to the other side. Paddling out past jagged rocks and cliff is the lineup, which only breaks when it gets head high or bigger.

After living a few months with Alex they broke up; an only child, Alexandra was too willful and spoiled for Todd. But I miss her humor, intelligence and charm. He's in heaven at Kalihiwai now. He's also met Anne, a beautiful, blue-eyed brunette who lives on O'ahu, so he comes back weekends to see her whenever possible. She's sweet, demure, a bit passive, but bright and athletic. Robert and I play tennis with them and it's easy, fun; they are a good match.

Kilia still strives to heal her exercise/eating disorder, calls occasionally from Colorado. She isn't into the partying scene there, but she agonizes if she overeats and overexercises, and I feel my heart aching as we talk it through. I have often counseled after my classes, one on one, and I am grateful for those skills now. I begin having massages once a month to counteract the volleyball and surfing and try to be diligent about my yoga.

CHAPTER TWENTY

"ROBERT, I KNOW YOU'RE HIDING my car from me," I say
early one morning as I scurry back into the house, after noticing it's
not in the garage. "What!" he shouts, "What do you mean?!" "Yup, I
can tell you're faking it, trying to scare me." "Chu, are you saying your
car's not there, 'cause I did NOT take it, trust me, and I'm pissed,
Jesus, I've told you over and over to bring your keys inside!" "Yeah,
well, I guess I didn't, 'cause it's gone." "Goddammit! I knew it!" I want
to ask him not use His name in anger, again, but I realize now's not
the time.

He strides out to the garage behind me, furious, yet a bit trium-
phant that he has been proven right, my car was stolen as he'd warned
it would be. "Well," I giggle, "guess it's been stolen. Sorry. So can I
borrow your car?"

Robert laughs. "I know you don't care about cars, Chu, but we can't
collect insurance when the keys are left inside." I run to get his keys,
saying over my shoulder, "We'll get it back, just wait and see."

I don't discern one car from another, nor do I even notice when
Robert washes mine for me. It's years old, don't even know what make
it is, and don't care if it's clean. (My home is immaculate, but my car,
"ai no kea," as the Hawaiian bumper sticker says, written ainokea like
it's an actual Hawaiian word meaning "I don't care.") Another slang I
love in pidgin is, "If can, can, if no can, no can," if you can do it, then do
it, if not, don't.

So I wait for my car to be found, confident it will be. Each day
Robert returns from school, asking, "Well?" And I smile, "Not yet, but
it will." On the third day I begin to wonder. But then, on the fourth,
I get a call from the police. They've found it off Kaheka Street. I ring
up Robert at school after I get a ride to pick it up. "There's good and
bad news." He booms, "They found it!? And I bet it's been stripped."

"Nope. They found it, but it had a dozen roses in it." He laughs. "I'll
be damned. No parts missing . . . what!? You're bullshitting about the
roses." "Yeah, I am, but it had four parking tickets on it, and they said I
don't have to pay for them because it was stolen." We both laugh.

I have begun reading the newspaper to the blind over the radio
weekly, as once again my ADD style of volunteering kicks in. I imagine
all those blind people, rapt, as I modulate my voice. I had interviewed
people on their feelings of high self-esteem a few years before for several weeks on television, people I handpicked for that very reason, so
it's easy now to come into the library studio without lipstick or brush-
ing my hair for an hour and a half the next several months.

I thought we were pau having foster children, but, somehow, we
have sweet Novaa, a mulato teenager who needs nurturing, come live
with us for a month. And another boy after him, a fourteen-year-old
son of a family member who is troubled, a rascal, needs a father figure
for a month or two, and who better than Robert? Who has improved in
the not-enabling department.

I finished a class at Washington Intermediate School, but now I
am ecstatic to be teaching it at Punahou again, in a whole different
capacity. I'd approached Diana, a beautiful, athletic P.E. teacher and
volleyball coach there, with whom I'd played volleyball. She'd played
college volleyball, is smart, easygoing and interested in my class. She
arranges to have six or seven core teachers, who represent all the
classes in the seventh grade, come for six weeks in the afternoon. It
is what I'd prayed for, and I plop down in the circle for our third class
and greet the women.

"I'd like to hand out lists of self-love so you guys can test yourself,
though I'll read some of them now, too. 'Self-love is acknowledging verbally to yourself the good that you do. Self-love is accepting
yourself. It's having confidence in your ability. Loving your body and
admiring your beauty.'" I smile at Diana. "'It's giving yourself what
you want and feeling you deserve it. Letting yourself win. Following
your intuition. Taking credit for what you do. Having authority over
yourself, not giving it away to another. It's creating an abundance of

friends, seeing only those that uplift you. It's doing things for others, serving others. Forgiving yourself of your mistakes. Allowing yourself to have fun, to laugh often.'"

I look at these intelligent teachers a long moment. "Anyone care to comment?" They smile, reflective. A few mention examples of when they weren't loving themselves, then we move on. "Remember, I said that fear is only as strong as our avoidance of it. The more we look at our fears, the easier it is to let them go and choose love.

"And we talked about choosing ease or dis-ease. So disease is a message from our bodies telling us we aren't following our true energy, or supporting our feelings. 'It's the body's way of showing the mind how it needs to change,'" I quote from Emmanuelle and *The Nature of Personal Reality*.

"Chula, what about heredity? Doesn't it matter if someone, your mother, say, has cancer, dies of it, that maybe you will?" asks Grace, a tall, stately Chinese woman.

"If you truly believe that, then it might be so for you. You hear something all your life, from parents, doctors, and you believe it. Why not question authority? Why limit yourself in an unlimited universe? Why not believe there is only now, that's all we ever have. We will go into depth about heredity next week, about changing your DNA. There's documented proof on this, it's been studied for years." They stare at me a long moment. "It's fascinating."

"Wow. It makes sense when you say it like that," Kiana says. She smiles at me, white teeth in a brown face. "Why not change our belief, right?" The class murmurs agreement.

"Imagination and emotions are the most concentrated forms of energy we have," I recite from reviewing it only this morning. "The physically alive body, its activities and condition, are directed through the beliefs of the conscious mind. The body also has 'invisible' counterparts composed of electromagnetic properties and the interior sound and light qualities." I refrain from sharing the last line: "These invisible structures preceded the emergence of the physical body; they also exist after death," which we'll talk about in the last class.

They are still a minute, longer. "What about God?" Simone asks. Her eyes bore into mine. "We don't get to talk about God in school much, but what part does God play?"

"Ah, I love that you brought God up. Your idea of God will determine your whole life. If you believe, truly know, that you create with God. What do you feel is God's part?"

"That if we create everything with our thoughts and feelings, and maybe we create cancer, we can change our mind by asking for God's help. To learn from the cancer, and choose to heal," Simone says slowly, but firmly.

"I could not have said it any better. So dis-ease is not caused by germs, toxins, viruses or any other physical agent. You know never to take my word for anything in here, right?" Diana asks, "Chula, you still smoke, don't you?" I laugh. "Yup, but I never bring that up in class, especially with kids. Too controversial."

"You smoke!?" Kiana is surprised. Diana says, "Yeah, she's a jock, healthy, but she smokes, nobody can believe it. She rides her Harley in a bikini, too." "No!" Kiana says, and the class chuckles.

"It's a Honda, Diana, I always tell people that, but they'd rather think it's a Harley, which has more cachet." Diana adds, "Whatever, but guys are checking you out, you look hot on your motorcycle." I smile, "Good from far, far from good, is what I say. Like when I get closer, they think 'Oh shit, she's an old bag!'" We all laugh.

"But about my smoking. Roll your eyes if you wish, but may I say I only smoke at night, when I have a drink, and I also don't believe it's bad for me. Look at all those people in Kentucky who raise tobacco. So many of them smoke their whole lives and they don't have lung cancer. They die of something else, because they believe smoking won't kill them. I think being fit helps, too, as I think sedentary people can't process stuff in their body as well. I also eat junk food sometimes, love the three staples: fat, salt and sugar, but if I'm surfing and playing volleyball every day, the toxins move through me and out."

We chatter hard and fast about what goes in our bodies, before our time is up in few minutes. I can't wait for the next class with them. I love hanging with wāhine. They're wiser, more open than men, and I feel more connected with my girlfriends, see them for birthdays, lunch occasionally. Of course, Robert is the exception. My girlfriends love him because he loves women, prefers talking story with wāhine at gatherings. Especially strong women. He knows where the fun is.

Fog has shrouded Ma. We have two wonderful caregivers that alternate loving on her. It's unbearable to think about, to see her, but it's perhaps worse for Linda. When she came by a while back after months in absentia, somehow Ma flew at her in a rage. How devastating for Linda. Mummy had made comments over the years, not often, but disparaging comments of Linda not seeing the positive in life, being too competitive. Don't know what they stemmed from and didn't ask. Linda and Lee have divorced; she has not been well, has had to sell their house and has found an apartment that Aunty Barbie helped her pay for.

And Linda hasn't been as close to Kelly, maybe since the incident when she brought Johnny home and Linda and Lee were tipsy. (It was curious that Kelly, who used to party with us all, had cut back. And though she and her mother and I smoked, Kelly had stopped as a result of Scientology, so whenever someone exclaims how bizarre it was, I'd mention the positive effects on Kelly.)

Robert and I babysit regularly and still camp occasionally with our angels, but we are concerned Ryan is so plump. I've seen Judi urge him to have cake, ice cream, even spoonfeeding him. She keeps a huge jar of red whips on the counter for them to have whenever. Robert and I bite our tongues, wonder why Rob doesn't speak up, he's been raised with health in our family. He's a chiropractor, so strong and healthy himself.

Robin is busy with his acupuncture and still surfs regularly. I've felt honored that he's surfed with me, as it takes planning, and Robin's so spontaneous he's like mercury, you can't grab him. He has even come to Diamond Head where I surf predawn patrol (though he chides me, saying, "Ma, that's feeding time!") with a waterproof camera to photograph me, capturing amazing shots on perfect, over-head high, glassy waves. He even comes years henceforth to take a five-minute video of me that he edits, which I get a kick out of, seeing myself surfing, my old-fashioned style.

Kilia returns to Boulder for a month after Christmas before de-ciding to leave the cold. I am glad she's home, and she's ensconced in the apartment we added on to our garage for rentals. She has found a specialist known for helping girls with eating disorders, goes regu-larly and registered at UH for night classes. I hope she will become comfortable, allowing her natural, sensuous curves to emerge. She is gorgeous. We have some amazing surf sessions together, the healing purity of the ocean, the waves, the joy of riding them together. I am able to take the drop on an eight-foot wave, which is a few feet over-head, almost as well as she is. When you are paddling for the wave, looking back at eight feet of moving water, it looks huge. And to paddle hard, stand up and make the drop down the face of the wave all in one motion is a feat for me. It's sublime when the conditions are glassy, malia, no wind. Which is why I surf dawn patrol—less wind, less crowded.

Kilia and I occasionally drop in on each other if the wave's not too big. The surfing protocol, which was hard for me to learn, is that you don't drop in on someone, meaning if the wave is a right, it's your wave over anyone on your right who might go for it as well. But if he's out deeper than you and catches it, it's his wave. If it's a left, the op-posite is true. (I'm goofy-foot, my right foot's forward in my stance on the board, so lefts are more fun, because I'm facing into the wave, not away from it.) If perhaps you don't see the dude and you do drop in on him, and it's a critical drop, it can be gnarly, the board hitting you or, worse, a skeg slicing like a knife, which has happened to me sev-eral times. A few times when this happened it was my fault, but more often I've wiped out and my own board or skeg has slashed me. It can be challenging for me as I age to catch the wave, competing against stronger, younger guys sitting out farther in the lineup, as I have to be aggressive, lining up farther than them to ensure it's my wave. But when the waves are small, surfers are more forgiving, it's not as big a deal dropping in if you're farther away in the lineup; when I'm out with Kilia it can be a fun "party wave."

We play volleyball often together on the mornings she is free. Naturally I get her as my partner, because she's a stronger player; it's such fun to set her well (my forte), and have her jump and hammer the ball. The Jose Cuervo Volleyball Tournament is on. She's got a good partner for the women's division, and I ask a fellow from the club to play with me in the mixed. It's held in front of the Hawaiian Village Hotel on Waikīkī Beach, courts set up just for this. I have fun cheering for Kilia, watching her play, and it's a kick playing with my partners. Mixed volleyball is different, because the net is higher than a women's net, the opponent can drill the ball at each other, and it's usually a harder game. Robert comes, proud to watch "his girls" perform. Don't remember how we did, nor how Kilia did, but there's a big party at the end of the weekend with tequila, of course, and the camaraderie is fun. It'd been scorching playing in the heat of the day, the sand burning hot, sweat sluicing off me, and I'm like a dried-out sand crab.

I am loath to have the Punahou class end with the teachers, as it has been such an honor working with them. "Let me ask you about the concept from the last class, the hundredth monkey phenomenon, do you remember?" Kristin says, "Wasn't that the monkey in Japan, I think the island of Kyushu or something, began washing his sweet potato in the stream before eating it, and other monkeys watched him, then they did the same, until when enough of them did it, that thought or whatever, the energy of the thought was automatically transferred to others."

We are all nodding. "So when enough energy . . . " she pauses, searching for the word, so I interject, "Reaches the critical point." "reaches the critical point like 100 monkeys were that point, thoughts can be transmitted mind to mind." I smile at her and the others. "Fascinating, huh? Imagine if enough of us could believe we had free will, that we could choose love, we all could, how it would affect the world.

And individually how healthy and strong we'd become. No military, but we could help third-world countries with only a Peace Corps." They all look dreamy. "Anyway, moving right along."

"If you want something 100 percent, you get it," I tell them. "That is a law of the universe. And yet, we must remind ourselves to be wholly conscious, to delve into our subconscious. Who knows what belief is lurking there? Perhaps we are afraid we won't have it, or it isn't what society, your mate or your family wants for you. And the concept of prayer comes into play here."

"How do you mean?" Keala asks. "Well," I say, "your thoughts all day long are a form of prayer, and if you have repetitive fearful thoughts, that's what you're praying for."

"Louise Hay's book, *You Can Heal Your Life*—have I mentioned her?—talks about each disease and how or why you create it. She had been raped at five, so it wasn't so shocking she created vaginal cancer as a woman. Sure, she went into total panic initially. But she knew that cancer comes from deep resentment, that she had to reverse her mental patterns. She knew surgery would only cut out that cancer in her vagina, and if she didn't do her mental work, it would appear elsewhere in her body. She realized she'd been blind to her patterns as she began her inner work. As well as forgiveness. And she focused on good nutrition to help detoxify her body."

"And may I reiterate the wonder of water from Dr. Emoto's work, the Japanese guy who used it for healing when he realized the effect of positive or negative thoughts on water. It's just amazing how loving feelings actually change the water, isn't it? You saw the photos. When you think how much water is in the human body, how fear can affect us, other people's fear as well." Simone says, "I know, I bought one of his books and cut out a page that has two pictures, one showing the beautiful shapes in water affected by love, the other the ugly, messy stuff affected by fear." Several talk among themselves and I just listen.

Diana says, "So you mentioned visualization. Isn't that similar to praying?" "Yes. Prayer is more potent when thanking God for what you already have, or what you are in want of. 'Thank you, God, for my health. Thank you for the knowledge that I created it and I can change it. Thank you for helping." I breathe slowly and pause, maintaining eye contact with them all. "And that gratitude fills you while you imagine love pouring through your blood vessels, lavender or white love. Picturing it going where the energy is blocked."

"So the same thing for visualizing other stuff, right? Like a boyfriend?" Keala asks, and we burst into laughter. "Oh, yeah," I reply, "if a babe like you wants a boyfriend, picture him, the babe, with traits that appeal to you, be specific. Be what you want to attract: like maybe fun, healthy, humorous, athletic. Responsible."

"It's interesting," Diana says. "I have a friend who keeps attracting the same kind of guys, and it's not cool. She gets divorced and soon she's dating a guy who looks nothing like her ex, but has all the negative traits. She needs to visualize a different dude."

We all smile and nod. "May I also say again, how the power of our intentional thoughts and feelings influences our bodies, right down to the cellular level. Which means we can believe heredity does not have to influence us, that WE can change our DNA. We have that power, and it's been researched for twenty years! Don't you wonder why it's not in the media more?" They talk among themselves.

I pause a long moment. "Going back to disease, it can be beneficial, a lesson. Real growth sometimes comes from darkness, not light. Louise Hay used it to write a book describing all the mental patterns creating the physical illness. We can all teach others to laugh at themselves, lighten up, cherish each other, each day. We don't have to get sick to die either, we can choose to go when we're ready, a painless, conscious death. Inspiring others to know they needn't create Alzheimer's or whatever. They can believe in miracles that they help create."

All of them have locked into my gaze. "And," I chuckle, "just to throw more food for thought at you, it seems like duality, doesn't it, all this fear and love stuff, lightness and darkness. But really all darkness, or evil, some call it, is the absence of light. All evil is, is the absence of God. All there is is God."

We all hug and say goodbye. I leave thinking of Mummy and her beliefs, my beliefs. The visualization to attract handsome Robert, my knight, on his motorcycle. Visualizing when I was a teenager and drew figurative drawings which ended up looking exactly like Kilia's profile; then pictured her later when I was pregnant: dark, curvy, green eyes, which was exactly her as a cherub, picturing how I'd hold her as we napped. Visualizing health and vitality.

I decide to send off my book to Oprah. I've watched her almost daily, admired her power to help others. I visualize her receiving it, choosing it for her book club, because she's open to everything, especially teachers and, lately, the metaphysical realm.

CHAPTER TWENTY-ONE

"MUMMY, WE'RE GOING AWAY and I'm really going to miss you," I croon in her ear. She smiles vacantly and I hug her tighter, her head propped up on her monogrammed pillows. "We found a minuscule ad in one of those posh magazines, and Robert and I are delirious we're going to Provence for a few months, renting a five-bedroom villa in the tiny village of Rougiers. In fact, Robert's taking a leave of absence and we're renting our house for four or five months, you know how we do, and we're actually making money!" I smooch her soft, wrinkled cheek. "So you know how much I love you, Ma, and I know how much you love me. Goodbye, Ma, I looove you!"

It is July '95 and we start our trip by driving across the country, camping in farmers' fields, until we get to Aspen. We have dinner after arriving late before retiring to a rustic cabin, fall asleep only to be awakened by the manager of the inn pounding on our door. Hearts racing, we go to the phone, and it's Dad's caregiver telling me that Daddy died. Well, I have to admit to some sadness, but I listen as she goes on, and then hear that our Labrador, Kui, was run over, which actually is a bit sadder. This dear caretaker is sobbing, more distraught than I, and I hang up and tell Robert, who is also more dismayed over Kui's demise, and we go back to sleep. We travel on to Boston, stopping wherever we wish, and then, after a visit with family, fly to Paris, ready for romance.

Though I'd rather tarry in Paris, Robert is not keen on big cities (he sweats profusely, which isn't conducive to walking around cities), so we drive right down to Provence to our little village an hour from the sea. I am effervescent. We meet the cultivated French woman who owns this lovely old home in the heart of tiny, medieval Rougiers, with a sprawling garden, grape vines, statuary, pool and barn, all enclosed by a wall. She is charming, doesn't laugh at my fractured French, and even invites us to come down and spend the night with her and her lover in their Cannes apartment.

I have brushed up on my French at an 'Iolani French class to make it negligibly better, and it's wondrous to tuck down to the patisserie each morn for fresh croissants or baguette, or to the cave (pronounced kav) for the local wine, chatting with the locals. There is a tennis court a few blocks away, and we rent bikes for forays out daily. I love hearing the *petite enfants* chattering below our kitchen window each morning en route to school, their little voices sounding like they're underwater. We love everything about this village, even the eight-minute drive to the bigger town of Saint Maximin, with its beautiful cathedral, to do our marketing. We make friends of the owners of that market, who invite us for dinner with their best friends when I see them playing in a boules tournament. They are pleasant, but it's an effort speaking, to be fluent in French (though I speak in the present tense almost always) and, of course, sometimes difficult to understand them. Robert has even less command of the language and usually leaves dialogue to me, while he gestures and speaks as though he's impaired. We have them to our villa a week later, and once again we swill champagne, which helps loosen the tongue, and Robert plays his guitar, singing heartily in English, while they dance along.

Biking to neighboring towns is challenging as most are on top of a hill; thus we drive and then rent bikes in farther-flung villages like Menerbes, Rousillon, Bonnieux, Meustiers, to ride through the gorgeous countryside with vineyards, fields of sunflowers, lavender, meadows dotted with wildflowers. The ancient towns capture ever fiber of my being with their charm, as the French are *très frou frou*, with lace at their windows, profusions of geranium and impatiens on the windowsills, their pastel doors and shutters, their cats napping on doorsteps, windowsills, rooftops. We always pack a picnic and save our big meal for dinner, unlike the French, and we come home for afternoon naps after long hikes and fall into our pool. Occasionally, I talk Robert into making love in our garden. He's modest, the opposite of me, and I had to condition him to this experience when we camped in Hawai'i, as well as when we lived in Montecito that year. He glances nervously over his shoulder at the wall, and I giggle, reassuring him it's taller than any French man is. He gets into *plein-air amour encore* readily.

Robert finds a gym in a nearby town where he goes regularly, as biking ten miles or hiking three hours is never enough. I'm happy to read, stroll around our village and start dinner. He bursts in gabbling away, words he's learned from the gym, which turns out to be his best resource.

After less than two weeks in Provence, I get another phone call. Mummy has died. I weep like the child I am of this wonderful mother and wonder why she departed while I was away. But when we drive down to a glorious restaurant in Antibes on the Mediterranean Sea, singing, "You picked a fine time to leave me, Lucille," for an extravagant lunch in Ma's honor, we laugh and cry, recounting stories of Lucille. I know, certainly, that we are blessed she didn't tarry, that she was so ready to go, and to be reunited with her firstborn, Michael. We return a few more times to Cassis, an exquisite spot on the sea, to hike out over the cliffs and down to the rocks to pique-nique in the sun, read and skinny dip, like the French. Not Robert, *bien sur, mais moi*. I have to say it's arousing to see the lithe bronzed breasts and bodies lolling nearby, and another day at the Cannes beach, I was topless again next to a small, roped-in volleyball court on which I yearned to play. Bare beasts bouncing around playing volleyball, what fun, but nobody was playing.

A week later we are joined by Anne Abel-Smith from Australia, and her dear English, gay friend George. We laugh at myriad events during our week together, as George isn't just erudite, but hilariously witty. It's the tonic I need in the wake of my loss.

After our month and a half *est fini dans* Rougiers, we have another two weeks farther north in Provence, in a cottage next to a fifteenth-century home near Isle sur la Sorgue. Its Sunday flea market is extraordinary, huge, and spread down each side of the banks of the Sorgue River. I am enchanted strolling, looking at their wares, and buy a tiny oval of ancient lace, dallying, eating, tasting, and meet Robert for espresso, as we have been wont to do.

One day we are biking and Robert asks if I'm tiring. I say I'm fine, which I am at that moment, but ten minutes later we pull into a village and I throw my bike down in tears, exhausted, hitting the wall. A little old Frenchman sitting there is staring, but I can't help the tears. Robert patiently hugs me, asks why I was fine ten minutes ago, and looks at his watch, gauging how far we've come. "Okay, Chu, we've biked twelve miles, obviously too far, but from now on I'll just stop sooner. For now though, can you smile, 'cause this poor old man thinks it must be my fault, the big ogre, so let's rest a minute and then find an espresso to perk you up!" I giggle, and we do just that.

We're loath to leave our meandering, mellow days in as-yet-undiscovered Provence, but we are off to London for a week. George is having us stay in his flat with him, and he's brilliant company when we return from touring the city and going to plays. Then we fly back to Boston and drive the more southern route of the United States back to Santa Barbara, then home, filled with gratitude, in early December.

Robert and I are welcomed, as usual, by the fragrant warm air redolent with plumeria. I'm truly glad to be home with the kids, but reality greets me with tasks of packing up Ma's house, which I do, grateful it's been left for me so I can say goodbye (having missed her funeral). I get it ready to sell a few months hence. Robin is busy learning about chakras, energy points for his needles; Kilia is fine and taking classes at UH, dating a cute guy, and we are right back into surfing, volleyball or hiking whenever she's free. But it's the kayaking that gives us the most exhilirating experience.

Kilia, in our garage apartment, eases us into life in our empty nest. I have been doing yoga on the beach lately, at sunrise, when it's quiet and the ocean is still. One morning I rush home to wake up Ki, urging her to kayak with me. "Ma-om, it's too cold and I'm sleeping," she responds. "Yeah, I know, it's about sixty-eight degrees, freezing, right? but Ki, I promise you, you will love it. It's a gorgeous morning!" She pulls herself out of bed and we grab bananas, blueberries and drag the kayaks down the right-of-way to the beach. It's as I told her, glassy ocean, gorgeous, the surface a mirror, and we hop in and paddle out through the reef channel.

I look over to the cliffs of Black Point, near Jimmy's house, and something catches my eye. As I paddle I study the scene. "Oh, my God! Ki! Look! It's a whale, coming our way!" She cranes her neck, squints her eyes. "I see it, I see it! Oh, my God!" she screams. My voice drops, "Whoa, it's a baby whale, Ki, and it looks like it could even get beached on this reef." I am astonished how close it's coming to us. "Maybe we should try to block it, you know how they can beach themselves and maybe it doesn't know about this reef here."

So we part a bit and I line up in front of the reef as she does, and I say, *sotto voce*, "I wonder where the mother is?" "What mother?" she asks. "Anytime you see a baby, the mother's never far behi . . . " I gape, for right then she appears, close, huge, the mother, and the baby just yards from us. I have chicken skin. We are dumbstruck, as both whales dive very near, surface and dive again, exhaling a spout of vapor on each appearance.

For the next hour they enchant us, these two whales, never having seen one remotely this close. We paddle after them, delirious, chirruping. Tears roll down my cheeks as I exclaim, "Kiwi, it's Mummy!" "What do you mean?" She doesn't look at me as we're both absorbed with the spectacle. "Mummy and I used to talk about a sign she would send me, after she died, you know, and I always thought it'd be a bird, she loved birds, but it's these whales! Mother, daughter, as you and I are mother, daughter, as she and I are mother, daughter! Oh, my God, what a fabulous sign!"

"Where'd they go?" Kiwi asks, both of us at a standstill. "I know, I'm wondering that, too," I reply, swiveling my head to look for the wake they'd left. But I don't see a trace. Unless. I look straight down, under me, and *there*, God, is the mother whale, huge, right beneath me, like a submarine. "Ki! Look under us, look, right there!" I shout, as I back-paddle quickly. Whales have been known to surface with a one-man canoe lifted on top of them, so we stab the water with our paddles a few yards backward.

The mother surfaces, exhaling a noisy spout of spray, and we laugh. "God, Mom, this is amazing!" Ki's voice is reverent. I shriek, "Isn't it? Let's swim, I want to get eye contact!" "You go first," Kilia says. I slide gently into the water wishing I had a facemask, eyes wide and staring where I expect the whale to be. Nothing but bubbles and dark shape. I surface. "You go, Ki!" She does the same, but we don't see them. Until, there they are, several yards away, diving, surfacing. "I'm going to eat, Ki; want some blueberries?" I bust out the baggie and start gobbling an apple banana and Ki wolfs down blueberries. "I can hardly believe it, Ma sending this dramatic sign, and you know it was her birthday four days ago!" "Really?! So incredible, Mom, really. You think they might be leaving?" I watch, and indeed it does look like they're heading out back from whence they came.

Suddenly black shapes flash by us, smaller, not whales, but . . . "Oh, God, now we have porpoises! Look, a whole pod of them!" We shriek as twenty or thirty porpoises dive, surface, dive around us. "What next, martians? This is too much, really, how sweet are they?!" "Have you ever even seen porpoises in Kāhala, Mom? Much less whales?" "Never, no. It's astounding." I am weeping again.

After a stretch of exquisite fun we head back, wheeling our kayaks as we hustle home, shouting to Robert. "You won't believe what's just happened! Oh, my God, Robert, listen to this, Mummy sent us whales, a mother and daughter and . . ."

CHAPTER TWENTY-TWO

WE CAMP WITH RYAN AND HANA, watch Ryan's soccer games and I volunteer at the Suicide and Crisis Center. Having asked Todd on Kauai if he'll find us a Labrador as his pals have a new litter, an adorable yellow puppy, our first yellow and first female, arrives. Zelly is more Kilia's dog than ours, but since she is right next to us, we share the duties. Kilia, at twenty-one, says to remind her never to have a baby as puppies are so much work, and I'm amused, am much more into babies than dogs. Though Zelly is so plump and precious even I adore her—it's easy when they're small and not my responsibility.

We see Sophie and Molly for dinner, one of them has a baby; they've stayed in touch as many of our foster kids have. Todd comes from Kauai more often to see his love now he and Anne are engaged, which we are all excited about. Alex has moved away, it was sad to have her go, but Anne is exactly what Todd needs, a quiet, bright beauty, the personification of still water running deep. They marry in June at Hanalei, where we've rented Patsy's Big House, and it's a gorgeous evening, with strands of plumeria wafting from the white canopied tent out on the lawn, a brief rain flurry, wonderful catered dinner and fun dancing. It's a huge treat to be in the Big House four nights, having the rehearsal dinner there as well as surfing, hiking, kayaking, playing in the yard and ponds with the kids.

I am annoyed as hell I let Robert and friends talk me into having a mammogram, as I'd constantly insisted that I would not be creating breast cancer (not having the emotional profile), and don't go to doctors anyway. I go, and it hurt as much as I'd heard they do, but I was furious that they popped one of my breast implants. Why I didn't sue them I don't know, but I stuffed one side of my bra for Todd's wedding, and had new implants a few weeks later. A $10,000 mammogram.

Kilia plays fine volleyball in another Jose Cuervo tournament; Robin is now a professional acupuncturist, competes in surf contests and has sweet, sparky girlfriend Corrina; and the Fourth of July has Todd and Anne joining us in the Waikīkī flotilla. Each year the canoe races are held in front of the elegant Royal Hawaiian Hotel, so we kayak over to watch from the water, among scores of other people on surfboards, kayaks, one-man canoes, speedboats, and really it is a great big party on the ocean. Music blares, kids are dancing, guzzling beers and boat-hopping, and we get a huge kick out of the festivities, as well as the canoe races on a dazzling sunny day.

We are off to Sun Valley for a few weeks of hiking (ten-mile hikes into stunning, majestic mountains), biking and camping before a month in Santa Barbara of volleyball, tennis and fun in the cool, crisp days, typical of that time of year. The Travoltas offer us a ride home on his jet from L.A., which is a thrill as we've never been on anything so luxurious that flies. We have a fun family dinner at Kelly and Johnny's house at Wailupe, except we still feel saddened at dear Jett's obvious plight. They have two nannies to look after Jett, who still won't give you eye contact, still flaps his little arms, still only emits sounds, not words at three years old. Cakes and Johnny are devoted, loving parents, and Jett's every wish is their command. They are so endearing with him, it breaks my heart.

One morning Robert and I walk out to our garage and see the same big, black motorcycle we'd seen before. "Chu! Check this out. Remember it?" "No, should I?" I reply. "Remember when we came out of that Thai restaurant and I told you to sit on it to see how it feels? This is it!" "Really?" I say as I throw my leg over it and perch. "Yup, it's huge and heavy, but I can handle 'cause it's so low, I remember. What the hell's it doing here?"

Just then out strolls a handsome stud, casually leaving Kilia's apartment, and we introduce ourselves to Tyler, who is clearly Kilia's new man. She emerges, smiling sheepishly with a rug rash all over her face, and I burst out laughing. Tyler is from Vermont originally, but is teaching French at the tiny 'Āina Haina school I'd taught my class at a few years back, as well as works nights at the Thai restaurant. He laughs when we tell him how I fit so well on his motorcycle the night we saw it in the parking lot, and I still think it's cool. He says maybe we should do a trade as he's keen on our black Jeep. Which we do a few weeks later, as Robert says it's a good deal and I've needed a bike that fits me better. The current one is a bit too high for me, and I didn't feel all that secure going all those thousands of miles. I am stoked with my new motorcycle, a Honda Shadow, 600 cc (whatever that means), but way more ecstatic about its previous owner.

Tyler is perfect for Ki, I tell Robert. "If I looked the world over, I can't imagine finding anyone so right for her. He's from New England, like you, smart, funny, well-educated with a stint at the Sorbonne learning French, athletic (was a snowboard instructor before he moved to Hawai'i), and so damn handsome." Robert chuckles, nodding, and I say, "But I only wish she'd met him a few years from now. She's only twenty-one, way too young to be seriously in love."

I am so impressed when Diana, the P.E. teacher tells me after taking the Punahou kids to a retreat, that she used the love and fear concept with them. And when asking what they were afraid of, was surprised to hear a neat young girl, popular, smart, tell her afterwards that she was afraid of her father. He was sexually abusing her. She took action, though I don't remember how, and I agreed with her how powerful a tool it is for all schools, that I had children admit abuse to me occasionally during the class though incest wasn't explicitly mentioned.

Meanwhile Rev. Heidl of Punahou wants the class there, is so supportive and asks me to come speak to the chapel service, taking the whole hour. It's exciting, but as I work them through the one-shot presentation that I've done in other schools, I realize it's too big a group. Maybe 100-plus kids, and it's too impersonal, too daunting for anyone to speak up. And yet Rev. Heidl wants to get funding for it as well as a time slot once a week, for the seventh grade, I think, and I wait, expectant, hopeful, praying.

Nothing makes me more ballistic than abuse of children. Especially sexual abuse. So I begin training for the Domestic Violence Clearinghouse, to use my class with women, who often have children. I still help at the Suicide and Crisis Center each week, but realize I prefer physical interaction. I also attend meetings for the Violence Prevention Center at the Women's Coalition office, and hearings at the Capitol in downtown Honolulu for the next few months; to change antiquated laws adverse to helping battered women, regarding consequences for the men who can have the violence expunged from their records. Why? Are we in the Dark Ages that he can have evidence erased? Enraged, I write an editorial for our newspaper.

CHAPTER TWENTY-THREE

WE ARE ALL EXUBERANT we've been invited by the Travoltas to come to Maine for New Year's by private jet. It rivals Jimmy and Stephanie's generosity and we cannot believe Kelly's whole family will be joining Johnny's entire family. If that's not exciting enough, we had already planned to rent the Big House at Hanalei again for a week at Christmas first, as Robert's stepbrother, Sis' son, and his family will be joining us and paying half the rent.

Kilia and Tyler, Robin and Corrina, Todd and Anne, and Rob, Judi, and their three kids, all of us with a mate and Sis' kids and family are thrilled to arrive to see this extraordinary house and acreage, looking out on Hanalei Bay with their two daughters and son in tow. And the surf is up, which it usually is in our winters on the North Shore. We have the most fabulous week, laughing, eating, drinking and surfing, and even set up a volleyball net on the big lawn for rousing family games. We verbalize we'd all have fun together in a shack, but staying here surely enhances it, we feel like nobility, the landed gentry.

It's so over the top to know we are flying directly from Kauai back to O'ahu, and boarding a private jet to fly to Maine. We will fly from the farthest most points of the U.S. as Kauai is the farthest island to the west, and the Travolta's home is on Islesboro, an island off Portland, Maine. We are like children when we board the jet, pointing, giggling, squealing over everything. "My God, how's this bedroom!" I say, looking into the first room off the hall of the jet. We stand and stare, at the perfect queen-sized bed, orchid on the pillows, the décor, its bathroom. "Check out this living room!" Rob says. "Whoa, and the bar!" We all make a beeline for the bar.

A flight attendant grins, asks what we feel like drinking. "Um, champagne?" I beam. "Certainly," she says, pulling out a chilled bottle of Moet et Chandon. "Mom, look at the pūpū platter," Ki exclaims, hustling up to an amazing assortment of shrimp, crab, sushi, etc. We all jump into the treats, until we must sit down on the leather couches for takeoff. John isn't flying us, though he does in the future, but we just feel so pampered, so indulged. Never have I enjoyed flying so much, and I sleep after tippling and devouring the delicious lunch, all the way to Bangor.

There at a private hangar we are taken by ferry to the island to be met by a few chauffeured cars, and within minutes we are gliding down a long driveway flanked by towering pine trees sparkling with white Christmas lights. We are mesmerized looking at the two-story house, for each room, all twenty-two bedrooms, has a candle in the window. We pull up, the chauffeur opens doors, but most of us just leap out into the snow, and the front door is open with that famous face beaming at us. Johnny greets us happily and Kell too, right next to him, hugging, kissing all of us. Someone is taking *our* pictures, as if we are the stars.

Inside the living room with its high ceilings is the hugest Christmas tree, decorated beautifully as the rest of the room is, and up comes someone bearing more champagne. Cakes giggles, "Want some peach champagne, Chu?" knowing champs is my favorite libation. "It has peach liqueur in it, you'll love it." And of course I do. We meet all his wonderful family, his three sisters, two brothers, nephews, their mates, children, grandchildren. It'd dizzying, dazzling.

Escorted to our bedrooms we see each one with its own decorated Christmas tree. We are told to leave any dirty clothes in a laundry bag out front of our room each morning. We are told we will be seated for dinner in a few minutes, no need to change. Robert showers and we rush downstairs and into the dining room, the long table that can seat all of us adults, about thirty of us. Everywhere are gorgeous decorations, and I feel so blessed we get to share in their Christmas holiday though it's three days past. The dinner is lavish, two or three choices, a surfeit of wine, food and lively conversation. I make a point of sitting next to Stephanie, as we're glad she's still included in family celebrations, especially this one. Jimmy is not inclined to show up at most social gatherings, and definitely nothing as big as this one, reclusive as he is.

Part of the days are spent playing in the snow, sledding with the kids, and walking the small island. It is ironic we have been in this neck of the woods before as Robert's dear sister Nina lives in Portland, Maine with her family and their country house is also on a tiny island nearby, which we've been to a few times. It's quite different being back here in the winter, however, and there isn't skiing available so our kids get a bit antsy just eating and partying. And Kell and John sleep 'til almost noon daily, as they are night people, so this is also different though it doesn't affect us. I'm happy, content, thrilled to have all my family in this wonderful, gracious home, and so grateful to the Travoltas.

It is as if every night is New Years Eve as we are served scrumptious pūpū, drink champagne, and sit down to a wonderful dinner party. We feel feted as Kelly changes the dining room tablecloths, the slipcovers, the candelabra, table decorations and adds dangling streamers for New Years, everything sparkling white and silver, so waltzing into this room feels grand and we feel glamorous. The wee ones sit at their own table, are seen and not heard as we dine late each night, and some of us are keeping similar hours to the Travoltas. If so we are hungry again by midnight or later in the morn, and are urged to ask the chef, who is on call day and night, to cook a cheeseburger, etc. as that is Johnny's favorite midnight snack. One night we dance in line next to John to "Chain of Fools" from the movie *Michael*, all of us singing along. That's my favorite movie of his, and I realize Johnny is just as endearing as Michael.

We are one big 'ohana, family, and we get to know his sisters and brothers well; Margaret is my favorite, so easy to talk to, bright, and funny. One of the nephews is kolohe, and Robert and I are drawn to him and his beautiful wife. We quiz him about Scientology, but they are neither in the "church" nor enthusiastic about it. It's not a question we can ask Margaret as she is so dignified, and it seems taboo. It is strange Cakes and Johnny are Scientologists, as Robert and I don't see its appeal, but after this year of '97 I think I remember that Kelly and John stop drinking and Kelly quits smoking. So perhaps they are getting something good out of it.

Don't know the reason it gets away with being called a religion so they are not taxed; L. Ron Hubbard is deviously clever. As are the Catholics, the Mormons, etc. What is wealthier than the Catholic Church, which has spent millions protecting their pedophile priests, shunting them off to different diocese rather than protecting the children they abuse? And the sect of Mormons that invented rules allowing them to sleep with young girls, then marry all of them. I agree with John Adams: "This would be the best of all possible worlds if there were no religion in it."

I no longer am close to Linda, so don't get into it with her, because she had been diagnosed with fibromyalgia about this time. She's been in pain for a few years and is finally relieved to have a name for it, hoping drugs would help her. I had compassion for her; I also believed she created these conditions for a reason, as we all do, to help her cope, and to learn from. Perhaps painful thoughts had manifested this illness, and Kelly sent her off to a Scientologist setting to be "purified" (or whatever the term was), to cleanse her. Sounded reasonable, but I don't remember anything else about that period for Linda; maybe she and her daughter became closer during this time.

Though skeptical of its sci-fi nature, I try to remain open to Kelly's discourse on her "religion," and one day was actually amused at a turn it took. Cakes, Steph and I were walking along the beach past Niu by Maunalua Bay (near where I'd grown up), when I got stung by a bee. I yelped, said I was allergic to bees, would need to pee on it (it was supposed to help, the the pain of Portuguese man-of-war stings were lessened by urine) and instantly began to whip off my bikini bottoms, but Kell said she'd pee on it for me. I giggled, as she did, and she insisted she would do an "assist" when she was pau, which she proceeded to do after she peed on my foot. The Scientologist term meant retracing our steps before the sting, and then something else, I don't remember, but the moment before it we heard laughter from the kiawe trees several yards away. Looking up, I saw these local firemen leaning on their fire truck, taking a break, having a ciggie. I don't know why they were in this rather removed area, but, of course, they got a huge kick out of the babe peeing on her aunty, and now we were convulsed over it ourselves. It occurred to me later they'd have been even more delighted to know the babe was the movie star Kelly Preston.

CHAPTER TWENTY-FOUR

THE YEAR 1997 STARTS OUT MELLOW, with occasional camping with Rob and two of his sweet blondies, Ryan and Hana. Judi isn't interested in camping and is staying home with Halie, which makes it easier. We go to Hana's soccer games now, as well as Ryan's, watch Rob's canoe races and Robin's surf contests (he's thinking he may phase out his acupuncture practice and just shape surfboards to compete full time), are thrilled Todd and Anne are pregnant and due in October on Kaua'i and see Kilia and Tyler often even though she moved out last September. She's happy and in her own place, but it isn't long before she and Tyler move in together, which is so gratifying, because they are a wonderful couple, plus he always has me laughing.

Having sold Ma's house, we have each inherited a fourth of the price and Robert and I feel extravagant, are euphoric to be going back to the romantic villa in Provence, with Ki and Ty joining us for a week. He speaks French fluently, so I'm motivated to listen to French tapes for our early June trip. In late August, we are going to Ketchum to teach in an alternative school, started by an old classmate of Robert's from New England, for three months. Meanwhile, I continue surfing, kayaking and playing volleyball (with Kilia occasionally), and am stoked when Tyler surfs with us; he's so athletic, he is a quick study.

Tyler's parents divorced after twenty-five years on their 100-acre farm in Vermont, because his dad, fell in love with his mom's best friend. Painful for her, but fortunate for Ki and all of us, because his wonderful mother moved to the Big Island, which is why Tyler came to Hawai'i. Furthermore, not only did she learn hula and swim with the dolphins in front of her cottage on Kealakekua Bay, she eventually fell in love with a young Ozzie screenwriter seventeen years her junior. Go, Mom! Ty describes (in his deep, rich voice) his meeting

with his future father-in-law, who's a few years his senior, having us
in tears at the vision of the pink Mohawk, tats, pierced ear, etc. Now
Ty's father and stepmother have come to Hawai'i, and we adore them,
see how well suited they are.

We are granted a sabbatical for six months, as 'Iolani teachers are
supposed to have one every ten years or so, but there have been none
available thus far, so we've only taken leaves of absence (no salary).
We are enchanted to be back in the antiquity of Provence in early
June, in "our" villa in Rougiers, where we hike and bike until Kilia and
Tyler arrive a week later. We show off our favorites, biking to Bras, Val
and pique-nique one day, and hike to Mount Pilon and Saint Baume
the next, sitting under a tree wolfing Brie, salami, baguettes and fruit.
Tyler insists we only speak French that night as we prepare dinner at
home, and we laugh nonstop at how pathetic we are, how superb Ty's
accent and command of the language. Sipping champagne, once again,
lubricates the tongue and brain, and I feel quite clever blathering on
to Tyler, though I don't understand him anymore than he does me, for
different reasons.

We spend another gorgeous day at Cassis, with its sheer cliffs and
seaside boulders, the clarity of the Mediterranean's rich blues and
greens inviting us. Of course, I am not nude this time, but Ki and Ty
slip away to be on their own after lunch. I cry a week later that my
best friends have left, (though we know we are not their best friends),
feel blessed they shared a week of their holidays with us. Sitting on
our tiny terrace overlooking the garden and pool with Robert, I am
reminded of the fight Robert and I had a year and a half ago, in this
same spot.

After a few glasses of wine, we talk about how much fun it'd be for
our whole family to come here, and somehow we segue into talk of fi-
nances. Robert and I decided years back to buy each of our four kids a
house, it was the only way they could afford nice homes in Hawai'i and
we had Robert's trust fund, though mine was pau. So we bought Rob
his (he knew he had to pay the mortgage) and had just bought Todd
his home in Kīlauea on Kaua'i. Of course, they were all so grateful, but

already it seemed Rob and Judi were living beyond their means. His chiropractic practice was thriving, but insurance was not easy to get for his services, which was beginning to affect business, and many chiropractors had moved away from Hawai'i.

"Well, you know how much he appreciated that $12,000, it was a lifesaver," Robert says. "What $12,000?" I ask, startled, dragging on my cigarette. "Remember last year, he didn't know how he'd keep his practice going with his debts, so we helped them out? I told you about it." My eyes are slits. "You certainly did not tell me about it, and ..." "Yes, I did, Chu, I know I did." "Robert, do you really think I'd forget something like that, and what happened to us discussing everything, including money matters!?" I bark. "Yes, I did tell you, and anyway, you would have been glad to help him through lean times, and ..." "No, I'm sorry, Robert, I'm so pissed at you, you are still enabling! We've already bought them a house, let them figure out how to make ends meet. Let Judi go to work or something! Let her family help them out! It's not a loan, and you know it! Like they are ever going to pay us back?" My jaw clenches. "Okay, so it's from their future inheritance, when we die ... " "So do you think we can keep forking out that kind of money to Todd if he needs it—Todd, who makes way less than Rob as a teacher, or Robin or Ki? I'm so angry you didn't discuss this with me, as we've always done. Is it because your trust fund was bigger than mine? You know I almost used mine up on trips we took with the kids, right, skiing at Tahoe, that Moloka'i kayak trip and the river trip in Idaho with the kids?" "Calm down, Chu; no, I don't think it's 'cause I had a bigger trust fund." Around and round it goes. Finally, he agrees, again, we'd always make big decisions together. He promises. And I say I'd tell the others to remember Rob's legacy is going to be that much less than theirs. It is one of our worst fights, I think (after the *big* one), and in this pretty, romantic place, too. Well, that's history and we learned from it, I hope as I wince.

Now that the kids are gone we rally to walk around Saint Maximin, the nearest village, with its gorgeous cathedral, noticing there is a concert here the next night, which we attend, though oddly their lovely voices soar to Christmas songs. (Reminded me of the last time Robert played guitar to Mummy, me cuddling her in bed as we sang "Kaimanahila" and she hummed a Christmas carol next, which we had to play for her, so funny, in August.) We sip espresso in the open-air market piazza where we'd met wonderful new friends from Oz and U.K. our last visit, such fun eavesdropping, hearing the accents then chatting up these cosmopolitan people and having them to lunch later at "our estate."

Now we meet some of them again and make plans to tour more villages together. I had bought a book after our last trip here, *The Most Beautiful Villages of Provence*, and we loiter in many of them, enthralled, until our month in Rougiers is up. Then we go to a tiny, charming wing of an old house in Mirabel, in northern Provence. We see Gordes, Venasque, Crestet, Vaison la Romaine, Rousset, etc., then back to beautiful Lurs, near all the blazing sunflowers. I feel steeped in the beauty of hundreds of years; we make new friends. *Au revoir.*

We celebrate our twenty-fifth anniversary in Santa Barbara afterward for a month before camping in an ancient, huge redwood forest en route to Oregon. We stay with Sis' kids and grandchildren again in Neskowin, on a beautiful cliff overlooking a strikingly different coast of the Pacific Ocean, with enormous boulders and gray, freezing water. After a week we are off to Ketchum, where we've rented a cabin for three months to volunteer-teach at the Silvercreek Alternative School in Hailey.

We live down a long driveway flanked by occasional rustic homes ending in Greenhorn Gulch, which we hike immediately. Wildflowers, streams, birds and a coyote entice us through the quiet hills. We are delighted to watch an authentic Wagon Days Parade, a throwback from the Wild West. It's a very different Ketchum and Sun Valley from our first time here in winter, the white replaced by brown, yet it's still chilly and there's snow on the higher hikes.

We start at the school right away, and I adore Barge, Robert's old pal, whose insight and drive have put together a fabulous school for youths expelled from Hailey High School (which was run by a Mor-

Kai, Wyatt and Noa with Robert on his Honda 1100, 2003

Sky and Kilia, 2003

Olela and Chula, Chula's 60th birthday, 2004

Robin at Pipeline, 2004

ROB HARRISON
WEARS A SHIRT BY
ORIGINAL PENGUIN,
$70; SHORTS BY OP,
$55. RYAN HARRISON
WEARS A T-SHIRT
BY TROVATA, $55;
SHORTS BY THE
NORTH FACE, $80.
SURFBOARD BY
ROBERT AUGUST.
SUNSCREEN:
NEUTROGENA.
PHOTOGRAPHED AT
THE OUTRIGGER
CANOE CLUB,
HONOLULU.

Rob and Ryan, sportswear ad, 2005

Robert, Ty, Rob, Ryan and Todd at Waimānalo Beach, 2006

Bronze surfer girl, 2006

Family canoe race first place, 2007

Robin and Reena, 2007

Todd's family, 2007

Family Christmas, 2007

*Barbie Anthony's
memorial, 2007*

Introducing sensuous scupltures by...

Chula

March 9-April 13

Mu'umu'u Heaven
767 Kailua Road #100
808.263.3366
Opening reception March 9, 2-5pm

www.muumuuheaven.com

*Chula's sculpture
show, 2008*

mon or two).

These fifty or so outspoken, gregarious haole characters are a contrast to the Hawai'i classes. Robert is teaching and tutoring a combination of studies, though mostly English and history, as he does at 'Iolani, and I teach my class on feelings, calling it an E.Q. as opposed to I.Q.

"Last week we talked about change, how we can never change others, so where does it begin?" I glance around the room. "With ourselves!" a smiling boy announces. "And then we can communicate and confront the other assholes." Everyone cracks up. "Yup, the three C's; communication, confrontation and then change. And we don't confront when we're still angry, right, which comes from . . . ?" "Fear!" a couple of girls shout. "Excellent, you guys are sharp. So we do our forgiveness bubble, filling ourselves up with love beforehand."

"Soon as I can forgive the Mormon dick that kicked me out, maybe I'll confront him," a young cowboy says. We all laugh and I say, "Yeah, that's one you for sure want to approach when you're no longer angry." "That'll take years," the cowboy says, "it's weird he's running a school when he doesn't even like kids." I smile. "You do have to wonder. Sometimes people are drawn to positions of authority to feel superior, maybe even to bully those under them. They feel insecure, afraid, from being on the other end of it in childhood. So maybe you can forgive by seeing him as that scared little kid."

"You know," I address the class, "all our relationships are like mirrors for us. Reflecting what and who we are. Start noticing your relationships with your parents, girl or boyfriends, your schoolmates. See what they are reflecting back to you. Like if you keep drawing into your life selfish girls, or guys, why is that? What do you have to learn about this? Or rude, mean, unhappy mates, what is it about them that attracts you? Like attracts like, yet don't we often blame the other person, not looking at ourselves?"

"Yeah, Cliff, listen up," a sexy girl blurts. "All your girlfriends suck." "Bullshit!" Cliff retorts, "and, anyway, what about you?" The class chuckles. "Okay," I interject, "no blaming here. How might you have said that to Cliff in a friendlier tone to help him, if you two were quietly hanging out." I look at the unnamed girl. Cliff says, "Yes, Gina, let's hear a friendly tone, you know, the one you use when you're on the prowl for dudes." More laughter. "Okay, you both made your point, but now can you look at each other and get real gently? And honestly? Which is what love feels like, right? In fact, let's role-play right now, and Gina, you and Cliff talk to each other as if you're talking to the one you're in a relationship with. And then we'll get two more out here," I point to the middle of the circle as I pull a chair into it, and they begin confronting, playing the roles of parents, siblings, teachers, friends and lovers. I conclude with, "Remind yourselves that these people are also choosing to come from fear, it's not personal, you needn't take it personally, though it's easy to do." An energetic, instructive class, and I leave feeling honored to work here.

Robert and I can't wait to camp at Lake Alturas for the night, and it's as we heard, a lovely big lake surrounded by pine trees, but more tantalizing is the sign BEWARE OF BEARS, listing the ways not to attract them. I am hopeful we see one, as I've wished for this excitement when we go to the Gileses' cabin on Lindbergh Lake in Montana, where I chummed for them with hamburger meat on a paper plate, and actually heard one snapping twigs down the hill behind the cabin and I saw it up close and personal through the doorway, huge! But with no cabin to protect us, I'm not foolish enough to chum here, and we have a peaceful, romantic campout.

Back at school twice a week with these bright teenagers, I begin class, "So last class we talked about relationships. Do you think you'll attract the kind of guy or girl you want if you yourself are not happy and healthy? You need to be what you want in the other person, so if you're a skier, hiker, etc., are you going to be attracted to someone doing drugs and drinking too much?" A few of them smirk, look at each other. "No," a husky guy answers, "like attracts like." I reply, "Excellent!" A wholesome girl asks, "But what about 'opposites attract?' I've heard that before a lot." "True, it's a saying, but don't you think there are many ways to be opposite from someone? You might be shy and yet attracted to an outgoing, popular guy, yet underneath he's got similar value systems as you. He is healthy, honest, has a similar sense of humor." They nod, ruminating.

"You know, my man, Robert, is a Taurus. I'm not into astrology, but since I'm an Aries, it's not meant to be a good marriage. We are both fiery and can be intense, so we're actually similar, and yet not supposed to be good mates." I chuckle. "And we have really gnarly fights, but we have so many similar interests and values, it works. I am definitely the feisty one, but I realize the way he sweats, which he's legendary for, is a metaphor for putting out my fire."

"My father," Neil says, "was such a prick to my mother, he totally controlled her and she let him. She was so passive." "Are they still married?" I ask. "Hell, no, after twenty years of him ruling her, and he even pushed her around, hit her toward the end, I told her she had to leave him. Told her to stop being a doormat." "Very good advice. You're a supportive son." "But then she began dating this asshole, a quiet wimp, and he went agro on her, same shit." "Interesting, isn't it, how we keep attracting the same qualities until we are ready to learn the lesson they offer? I hope she left him as well." He nods. "Finally, and she was scared to be alone, but she's managing." "You must be proud of her, as that's her lesson, to learn to be independent and strong by herself."

The students talk among themselves now, sharing stories. "Do you mind if I ask you, Neil, what you think you learned from your parents, their marriage?" He looks off in the distance. "I guess I can say I figured out he was nobody I ever want to be like. Jesus, what a son of a bitch he was. And Mom, I would not be interested in a girl who is a doormat either." He glances at one of the girls, who blushes. "You know you guys are a great class. We have about forty-five minutes to role-play, who wants to go first?"

They get into some deep stuff, different kinds of abuse, and, after half an hour, I decide we should discuss what was revealed, because it was painful. "You know," I say, winding down, "we are all energy, as I've mentioned, and energy cannot be divided, so we are all connect-

ed." "I've heard that expression and don't get it, that we're all connected," a pretty, shy girls says. I smile. "It's curious, isn't it, you don't see
how we can all be connected, what does that mean? But if you erase
the physical body in your mind and just imagine all of us as spiritual
beings, which we are, we are energy, everything is, and can't *not* be
connected. There's that saying by the wise Indian, Chief Seattle, I
think it was, 'Humankind has not woven the web of life. We are but
one thread within it. Whatever we do to the web, we do to ourselves.
All things are bound together. All things connect."

They are quiet, musing, until Randy says, "Yeah, those Indians are
wise fuckers." We erupt with laughter.

I sometimes hike Imperial alone, or Adams Gulch Loop, Fox Creek
Loop with new friends, or with an old friend to Mill Lake, these spec-
tacularly dramatic, gorgeous hikes, ten or twelve miles, with pan-
oramic views. Robert and I have dinner at Grumpy's and hear music
at Bigwood Bread, camp again at Alturas Lake. Through my old friend
I meet Jack, an older cowboy who rides horses in 100-mile races, so
I'm stoked and nervous (don't remember when I last rode a horse,
fifty years?) to ride with him from the neighboring gulch. The scariest
part is when we come to a steep side of the mountain. "Are we riding
down that, Jack?" We stop, staring at the long, straight-down incline,
spotted with trees. A man of few words, Jack finally says, "We can
lead them down." Whoa, why not go a different route, I wonder? But
we dismount and grab the reins and my behemoth starts trundling,
crashing and sliding down, scaring the shit out of me, until I can get
sideways of him. Finally on flat ground, we gallop through crisp air
and beauty. A different rush.

We see other old friends, running into apple-cheeked Mia with her
five dogs on a hike. She is a funny, pretty young woman, with platinum
flaxen hair, has moved here from Hawai'i with her husband, Matt, and
started a pet store where everyone loves her and hangs out with their
dogs. She cracks us up instantly with her pidgin dialect, "Ho, I neva
went know you was hea, whea you stay?" Reacquainted, we are de-

lighted to be invited for dinner, later run into other transplants from Hawai'i over the next few months.

I hike to the top of Baldy for five hours with a random new friend (while Robert plays tennis or goes to the gym), hike Harper's Trail, Pioneer Cabin, on many trails that are patchy with snow. It's exhilaratingly cold, sometimes gnarly when the snow is deep, and fall colors are emerging on the Aspen trees. Again we camp at tranquil Alturas, though I no longer want to jump in the lake, as Robert does.

Mia greets us in a crowd of dogs as we arrive for dinner. "So what, brah, long time no see, but garans we talk story now." Matt hugs us; he is handsome, taller than Robert. We hardly draw a breath laughing, talking, and Mia and Matt describe the bears that have been cruising their house, getting into their garbage cans in the middle of the night. I perch in front of their window, hoping to see one.

Back at class, I say, "So we talked about drugs last time, how they have side effects. Whether they're recreational or prescription. And they interfere with dreaming, which is meant to be beneficial. If someone is sedated by their doctor when they have a trauma, like losing someone close, they have to deal with their grief eventually, they have to move through their pain, and taking drugs only delays it and inhibits dreaming."

"What about depression, though, you don't think a drug can help?" Cliff asks. "Yes, if that's your belief, and you are deeply depressed. But I think drugs for depression can be harmful as well. It's said depression is anger turned inward. So I would go the natural route. A naturopath has a cornucopia of herbs from the plant kingdom, but don't take my word for any of this." They all have eye contact with me. "But I will take words from *The Untethered Soul*, where he describes blocked energy, an impression from the past which is called *samskara*. A Sanskrit word. A samskara is when you resist releasing painful feelings, which build up within you and restrict the energy flow. Which can cause depression, because too little energy is coming into your heart and mind.

"I'd like to ask who would feel ready to talk about any of their fears on their list from our first class. Someone who hasn't contributed yet, maybe?" My eyes rest on each of them and I exhale and wait.

"I know someone," Maggie says, "who has been sexually abused." Her eyes are pools of sadness. I say, "Well, that's one of the most horrible things to happen to anyone, isn't it? Only thing to make it worse is if the abuse is by a family member or a priest." I look at her with my heart full, wondering how close she is to this "someone." The silence rests on us all for a minute and I allow it to stretch out longer. I look again at Maggie, who has ducked her head but looks up now, tears rolling down her plump cheeks, and I guess she is the someone. "You know, Maggie, I offer individual counseling when it's needed, but may I say that this kind of fear can grip like a vise. It's hard not to take it personally. Really hard to trust again. Extremely hard to forgive. It might be easier to release this fear by getting a bat and whacking a big pillow, over and over. Somehow this allows the release. Of the tears, the pain, the sadness. Suppressing painful feelings, as we were just saying, will block your heart, and eventually unfinished mental and emotional patterns that are stored there get reactivated."

The wholesome girl, Sierra, says, "But if you forgive the pedophile, won't that mean he's back in her life?" I shake my head. "Not at all, unless she allows it. When you finally forgive you can begin to accept it happened, from a distance, from far away. Begin to love yourself again, to acknowledge it. I personally feel if someone forces sex on you, they've lost the right to be in your life ever again. And I feel that not forgiving only hurts you. Holding onto that pain will make you sick, because it closes the heart, constricts your energy." Curious how such a rowdy group can be so sensitive, so quiet. I ask if anyone else wants to speak, suggesting that each person here is a teacher as well. A few more speak until the end of the class, at which time Gina goes over to Maggie and embraces her. They hug a long time, unabashedly. I am touched at how powerful this class has been and remind them of their homework, noticing when they're judging and cutting the tapes. I mention I'll bring my book, *Cucumber Seeds*, next class for them. I think Maggie may have gained her weight for protection, like armor, which seems to happen to abused children. Hopefully she'll release the weight when she releases the fear.

More gorgeous, sometimes twelve-mile hikes to Pioneer Cabin, Norton Lakes, Chocolate Gulch, Prairie Creek, Corral Creek, Summit Creek, Hulen Meadows. An elixir, this wild, quiet beauty. Dinners and beer at Ketchum Grill, Sun Valley Brewing Company, Sawtooth Saloon, and I decide I prefer this season here to winter, because it's more outdoorsy, and Robert doesn't ski anyway.

Exciting news from Todd and Anne at the end of October that baby Kai is born. Stephanie calls us to say we have all been invited again to the Travoltas in Maine in a few months. I'm feeling like a spoiled brat, but a lucky one. We leave Ketchum in mid-November for Santa Barbara for two weeks, returning home in time to go to Hanalei to meet adorable Kai, a clone of his pretty mother, with her blue eyes and dark hair. I get to snuggle him, irresistible, like an opiate.

CHAPTER TWENTY-FIVE

"YOU DON'T WANT TO GO TO MAINE, Robin?! How can you miss out on the fun and pampering?" "I'd rather surf, Ma, it's s'posed to be big, and . . ." "But you can surf anytime, this is our whole family together!" "Yeah, no, I don't want to just hang out, there's not even skiing there. And I'm competing again, Ma."

I insist I stay home to help Robert after his second hip surgery, but he argues he'll be fine, since the replacement is a week before our departure for Maine, it'll be easier this time around because the device and procedure are more sophisticated, and Robin will drop in to help when needed. Turns out Robert is in much less pain than last time, doesn't even need crutches. So I leave on the chartered plane with everyone else to the Travoltas for New Year's '97, a festive, fabulous week even without Robert. Extravagance and graciousness are personified in Kelly and John.

I return to a vibrant, happy husband who's almost ready to resume tennis, to grandchildren, feeding the homeless monthly (sometimes with Kilia helping me to make the chicken soup) sports, camping, sometimes even with Todd, Anne and baby (who come to Oʻahu) and our whole family as well. Robert and I still feel anxious that Ryan has gotten obese, and we try to bite our tongues (Rob's been working out with him). Robert begins taking him to hit tennis balls. Kelly comes to town occasionally alone for brief visits, and Steph and I hike Mānoa Falls with her, play Password and have fun together.

My first lover, from Kahuku, is in the hospital and I visit him right before he dies. Strangely, Monte Goldman (who was married to his second wife and has sired two children) also dies in '98, but this feels way sadder and more shocking because it's suicide. I don't ever learn the whole story.

I finish writing another book (perhaps the one about a child who could not speak or hear, therefore saw the world through nonjudgmental, innocent eyes), which sits in my closet. A brief depression descends on me, because I am mystified my prayers have not been answered regarding my class and books getting into schools via Oprah. I begin a new craft (having drawn and painted nudes from live models years before), painting animals and Hawaiian wāhine on ceramic tiles that I give for gifts and hang in my home.

Robert starts a community service class at 'Iolani. He had tried convincing the headmaster and head of the English department how important it was to get students out and helping others (as Punahou had been doing), especially the privileged 'Iolani kids, and they did not support him. He pursued it, did some research on many other schools that had this in their curriculum, until they finally approved it. But when seventy-six seniors signed up for it, they wouldn't allow Robert more than one class per semester, so he had just twenty seniors each class for the next two years (typically myopic and ignorant of 'Iolani's powers that be). The students chose to volunteer at an old folks home, a hospital, a school for severely handicapped children, the deaf, at Juvy Hall, etc. It was a huge hit, both for the kids and the people they served, everyone benefitting.

I have Kilia's twenty-third birthday party with her pals and our family, which is great fun. I hope her struggles with her eating disorder have lessened, realize I am looking into a mirror with Kilia that reflects my errant behavior or attitudes. She and Tyler are crazy about each other, though, such good company, and remind me of Robert and me. They are honest with each other, work, laugh and play often together.

It is June '98, only six months after the week with the Travoltas in Maine, and now our family's invited to the Hyatt on Kaua'i with all of Johnny's family, which is delighted to be coming to Hawai'i. It's almost embarrassing to be treated again so soon. Almost. We rarely stay in hotels not since Jimmy would take us, so we get a big kick out of this resort with its pools, waterfalls, luxurious grounds and rooms right on the ocean. We even set up a volleyball net on the beach and have fun family games. I get to hold adorable baby Kai often, we are feted by a fabulous *lūaʻu*, the wining and dining never seem to stop and massages are available as well.

Robert and I are going back to Ketchum for a few days in July, staying with Matt and Mia before kayaking down the Salmon River again, just the two of us on a guided trip with strangers. We are in a two-man kayak and are excited to paddle the rapids together. It's fun meeting new people and, though most are men, Robert and I are just as skilled in our kayak. I remind Robert to communicate with me, because he's in front, the power of our team, and it's crucial he calls out what he sees, that we're in unison. We never *huli* (flip) on the gnarliest rapids, crashing through the white water unscathed, glancing off boulders, whooping and laughing. The afternoons are mellow in that majesty except for a fun hailstorm once, and we enjoy the camaraderie over drinks and dinner at each campsite.

We return to Ketchum for a week at Mia and Matt's, then drive off to Montana and the Gileses, then to C'oeur d'Alene to stay with old friends, to Neskowin, Oregon, with Sis' kids and camping at Waldo Lake en route to Santa Barbara for a few weeks.

Life is bliss, as usual, returning home in late August, after which I start my class at La Pietra, through Beth, the health teacher at this small, gorgeous private girls' school, an old estate on the slopes of Diamond Head. It is a replica of an Italian villa, well preserved with its courtyards, lawns and statuary, and is financed mostly by my Aunty Barbie. Many of the girls are haole from privileged families (except for a few on scholarship), are all sixteen or seventeen years old.

"So at the end of last class we mentioned how your beliefs can be limiting yourself in an unlimited universe. I brought my book today," I hold it up, "and want to quote from *Joy Can Be Your Favorite Song*: You must dissect facts to see if they're only images that have become your 'truth.' Like asking yourself if you believe love can run out. If you believe being alone is lonely. If you believe losing is not okay. That spankings are ever necessary. That money's hard to make. That life's not fair. If you believe that you are a victim. That you've got to prove yourself to Mom or Dad. That sharing meals is unimportant in a family." They are listening, some smiling.

"Everything's energy, right? 'Visible or invisible, the invisible energy of your thoughts becomes an invisible medley of feelings. Together they compose the chords of your beliefs. As your beliefs become visible in all that surrounds you, see if what you've attracted is what you want. If not, why not believe you can orchestrate more joy? For, in time, a heartfelt new thought becomes a belief.'"

"Would anyone like to read the next page for us?" I ask. A ponytailed Asian thrusts out her arm. "Thank you, Elsa," I say, hoping I've remembered her name, and hand her the book.

"'Challenge if you believe some people are wrong,'" Elsa reads boldly. "'That the world out there is a dangerous place. That dis-ease can happen to anybody, anytime. That all rich people are smart and happy. That it's never okay to be dirty and messy. That you cannot re-invent yourself. That everyone seems to be humming a song you don't know.'"

Dawn waves her hand, "What did you mean 'believing some people are wrong'?" "Okay, if you believe in right or wrong in any way," I begin, "that would make some things wrong, some people wrong. Instead, why not let go of judgment? Instead, why not accept that there is no wrong or right, but thinking makes it so?" I have their full attention. "Whoa," says Dawn, "that's pretty trippy. Tell my mom that!" The class giggles. "Yeah, that's a big one. I mentioned it in an earlier class, but that takes reiterating, again and again. When someone acts 'wrong,'" I make quote marks with my fingers, "aren't they just coming from fear? When someone is hateful, cruel, dishonest to you?"

"But if they rape you or kill you, isn't that wrong?" Mehana asks. I hold her gaze. "That's what society calls it. But what if we all began to see it's fear, that it's almost never personal, and that the fearful person needs to be institutionalized in a school-type prison to learn from his actions, to take responsibility for them. And that person stays however long it takes to learn his or her lesson. To eventually learn from their fear."

"So there is no wrong or right?" Elsa asks. "It sounds, I don't know, too simple. Impossible." I nod, "You might want to be cautious quoting this at home out of context. Pick a mellow moment if you do, both for your parents and yourself. Dawn, Mehana, anyone else want to read the next few pages?" I wave my book, Mehana takes it and reads, "Ask if you believe you need approval. That it's too simple all unloving feelings stem from fear. That guilt is a fact of life. Challenge if you believe it's hard to lose weight. That low grades in school mean you are stupid. That if it's their fault, you don't need to forgive. That wealth makes people superior. That you can ever escape the consequences of your actions. That you cannot have it all."

"Anyway, it's a lot to absorb. Your homework for the rest of your life is to notice your thoughts and what you believe. Just because your parents, your teachers, doctors, religion, the media have stated 'facts,' decide for yourself if they are your truth."

"We're desperate," Beth says, calling from La Pietra to ask if I will coach their junior varsity volleyball team. I laugh, replying that I had never even played indoor volleyball, much less coached it or any sport. "You must be," I chuckle again. "Seriously, Chula, you've got all the skills, the girls will love you and all we've ever won was one game the past few years." "Okay, why not?" I chirp, and immediately call Todd and ask Robert how on earth do I coach these girls, what are the rules? Very different sport with six on a side, rotation, etc., but I take notes and begin coaching.

Don't remember when this was, probably after I taught my class there, but we practiced several afternoons a week, which challenged me, as I never enjoyed even warming up and bumping the ball when I played beach volleyball myself. Actually found five or six minutes enough of a warm up, since I wasn't one to work on any sport if it didn't come easily to me. And now I had to put these girls through the drills I'd found tedious, but they were novices, needed to learn. When we began playing games every weekend it was difficult dealing with the parents, for their daughter may not have come to practice regularly, thus she would not play until the diligent girls were rotated in. And some of these girls were just not athletic, were passive, disinterested, yet I had to play them sometime. Whew, thank God we won one game during the season.

Simultaneously with La Pietra I teach at the Adolescent Treatment Program weekly as well as surf with Ki, sometimes Robby, who also plays volleyball with me, Tyler and Kilia now and then. Robin's surfing in contests in Portugal, later in Japan, South Africa, France, the envy of his pals and brothers. I gasp when we are given a photo of Robin on a forty-foot wave, astounding to see him on this blue mountain. We go to Kaua'i for a weekend with Todd, Anne and Kai, and I get to hold this mellow, delicious, year-old baby. It's easier to leave knowing they'll come to us for Thanksgiving and Christmas, when I'll be able to spirit Kai away to our beach in Kāhala for sunrise each morning. Not since Ryan have I held a baby like I cuddle Kai, as Hana and Halie would not let us. Our family's happy to be home for Christmas, we play volleyball together, Todd at the helm, and tennis, surf, camp. Of course, I realize my life is a wonderful distraction from my big plan with my class, yet I still visualize it getting onto Oprah, going mainstream.

The Adolescent Treatment Program class continues throughout 1999, while I begin one at Holy Nativity School, a one-time class for Child and Family Services, at Hale O Ulu and later at Kaimukī High School, the only school I've ever walked out of. The kids were so inattentive and rude, I said bye-bye and left after the second or third class.

We are thrilled when Anne and Todd have their second son in June. Wyatt is a smiley, outgoing blond baby, and Kai at three years old is as endearing with his baby brother as Todd and Anne are great parents.

I still help occasionally with dear Ryan (who is slimming down), Hana and Halie at our house; Robert has his sixtieth birthday; Rob is venturing into a new chiropractic clinic of his own, only a mile from their home, and gives me treatments occasionally; Todd still competes in volleyball for the Outrigger Canoe Club and plays in the volleyball nationals in California, if he can get away from teaching at Kapaʻa High School; Robin competes in surf contests, is sponsored, a semi-pro; Kilia graduates from UH with a BA in Arts and Science, is sexy and seems to be healing. We are going with them to visit Tyler's parents on their farm in Vermont, and go to Cape Cod to Sis's sprawling old house for July, then she and Tyler will move to Santa Barbara, where Kiwi will get her master's and Ty will get a job. We return after a month in Santa Barbara to Zelly, our granddog (yellow Labrador), who will live with us in their absence.

A clever invitation comes in early September from the Travoltas to have the big 1999/2000 New Year's week on Kauaʻi for the combined families, which fills us with anticipation. The millennium.

CHAPTER TWENTY-SIX

Aunty Barbie and Aunty Ole Lady, now going just by
Olela, who had been Mummy's best friends, became closer to me, a
sweet result of Ma's death, and I feel so blessed. Olela and I stop after
some outing (like a canoe race of Gaylord's) to eat, which I love doing
with her because we are both happy to eat anytime, and she orders
several different dishes to taste each, whether we are at the Outrigger
Canoe Club or a plate-lunch place, commonplace in Hawai'i. She has
Robert and me to dinner at her lovely old house on Noela Drive, so
Olela from Noela has soirées, with delightful Uncle Butter, her brother and his mate, perhaps with Gaylord and Carol, or Patsy, if she happens to be here from Hanalei (where she lives now, having divorced
the philanderer), or close friends, but mostly she likes having youths,
like us. She often gives her guests ginger lei, so gracious, as one is in
the habit of giving the hostess a lei, not the other way around, and I'd
bring her pikake lei or gardenias.

An ingénue, Olela is sweet, almost naïve in some ways, and unin-
tentionally funny, as well as quirky and coy. A coquette until she dies
in her late 80s, she always has a handsome man like Robert at her
table. She has been married since divorcing Patsy and Gayla's dad (Albert Wilcox, who inherited huge land holdings in Hanalei) as a young
woman, and then outlived John, an attractive California gentleman.
Her rude edge has softened with age (I'd feel compelled to apologize
to Kenji, her longtime, doting housekeeper), though she's never been
rude to me, usually just her help, as people of her era seemed to do.
Her home, garden and courtyard are charming, chock-a-bloc with
family photos, paintings of old Hawai'i, driftwood art, colorful knickknacks of a bohemian nature, plants, orchids. And she slides deeper
into eccentricity, still gets away with marvelous fashion combina-
tions, always has fun jewelry on she's just found after many years lost,

and flowers in her hair. I hope to be like her at her age, though she is much more of a lady than I.

Olela was an athlete, playing tennis into her seventies, summoning someone like Robert, strong and steady, to play with her. He'd always come home with a vignette to share, as I did when I was with her. And we laugh, she always makes everyone laugh, whether we are with her or not. Not sure Gayla laughs much, but even sweet Patsy, though annoyed and put out with her vicissitudes, has to laugh. And it isn't just Olela who reeks of charm, but her siblings as well. Three of them, for starters, are gay (and have the best stereotypical attributes of gays), though it is not spoken of, because they've all been married at one point, everyone accepts it, and I'm uncertain they ever acted out gay urges while married. Aunty Red, the oldest, Uncle Butter and Uncle Seymour were all exquisite company, well, not so much Red, a tough cookie, but definitely Seymour and Butter. Being with their family was deliciously entertaining, a feast, especially out at their Punalu'u estate on the North Shore, stamped with their foreign flavor, their unique undiluted elegance. Their panache. I always felt I was breathing rarified air in their presence, especially with the whole family, and Mummy fit right into their lives. Lucky her, lucky, lucky me.

I became extremely conscious of five extraordinary women in my life. Mummy is the first, of course, and she came with Olela and Aunty Barbie, but then my dear Rosie in Kentucky, and lastly Robert's precious stepmother, Sis, all giving me more character, flair, wisdom and love than any one person could possibly wish for. So much love and such role models.

Aunty Barbie eventually leaves us at eighty-four years old, in 2007. She was the wealthiest (along with her sister) woman in America for much of her adult life, and her obituary says she was worth 12.6 billion. A dramatic figure. In the pecking order, Olela saw her at the top, especially since they were neighbors in their last years, living across from each other on Noela Drive on the slopes of Diamond Head. So, though Olela may have been a bit daunted, it changed her not at all, she was so truly who she was. And Aunty Barbie got such a huge kick out of Olela as we all did. But Ma was definitely awed by her younger pal, Barbie Cox Anthony, as Lucille was raised in Kona in the country, in a modest lifestyle. So perhaps Ma was more comfortable with Olela, who was part Hawaiian as well, and whose whole family she'd been around since before she was married to Clark, but she was drawn to Aunty Barbie's keen intelligence and lofty, sophisticated background. And they laughed a lot together. Lucille was undaunted by her imperiousness, also, accepted it as her due.

Aunty Barbie was a good athlete, skiing and playing tough tennis into her early seventies. She had ranches, one in Australia, one on the Big Island and another on the Mainland, was an equestrian and loved horses as she did dogs. One day driving out to Punalu'u she explained to me in detail the whole story (much of which I've forgotten) of her husbands, of which she'd had five, and it may have been the first who had died, the second she was married to when she met Ma, but I'm uncertain. A polo player as well, Kennedy was the father of her son and daughter. Jimmy Kennedy had raced motorcycles professionally in college, came often to windsurf on Maui before marriage, kids, his career in the media, and Barbie's daughter had married and lived in Australia with her family. After divorcing Kennedy, she married once or twice more before Garner, her current husband of twenty-five years or so.

Aunty Barbie got a kick out of my driving a motorcycle, and I would sweep into her driveway to pick her up for lunch at the Outrigger Canoe Club. Garner, a lawyer several years her junior, comes out. I wasn't keen on Garner, a gut feeling, so I just smirk when he says, "Don't like you taking Barbie on your motorcycle, Chula; she's not as young as she was, you know." Out hustles Aunty Barbie. "Pay no attention to him, Chula," she decrees as she swings her leg slowly over the back of my bike to climb on.

"You really are hurting in that knee still, huh?" I ask as we take off. "Damn it, it hurts. I'll have to have it replaced soon. Can't play tennis like this, so might as well." At the club I help her off carefully, blinded by her pear-shaped diamond, the size of a grape, and we chat and giggle through a delightful lunch on the gorgeous ocean, imbued with its spray and tang. Watching surfers paddle out or in from the lineup at "Old Mans," the one-man canoe paddlers, the catamarans and canoes moored on the reef in front of the Hau Terrace.

Mostly, though, we talk on the phone, because Barbie is no longer as social as she is chatty. She still has a huge wardrobe, from which she'd given me several dresses years ago when I needed to dress up in Kentucky's winters. And she still has the jewelry to go with the clothes. In fact, she'd once told me to come into her bedroom when I was there visiting, and she pulled out bags and boxes of treasures, sapphire and diamonds dominating the rings, earrings and necklaces. Eyes out on stalks, I was awed, because she was so casual about hundreds of thousands of dollars' worth of gold and jewels. It may have been another time that she tossed a choker toward me on her bed, asking, "Want this?" I giggled, feeling like a kid playing dress-up, and put on the cabochon jeweled choker in bright heavy gold. "Looks better on you, anyway. You're young and taller than me." I thank her profusely, though I'm unsure it's me.

One of the most memorable dialogues I had with her on the phone was when I called her from Santa Barbara. She always knew when I was leaving for a trip or I knew when she was, so we stayed in touch. It was during the whole political race before Obama got elected, and I've never been politically inclined, but since Obama had attended Punahou, was a Democrat and half Black, I'd been interested. "So I don't even know what you are, but I wanted to ask, no, I probably shouldn't ask, 'cause you're probably a Republican and . . . " "Hell no!" she interrupted, "I've always been a Democrat, don't you know that?" "I might have, but don't remember. It's just not important to me, politics. And I guess I assumed that since you're so wealthy you'd be Republican."

She cackled, then launched into a description of her companies, such as Cox Broadcasting, and how many people are employed there, etc., and how they're all Democrats. Her son Jimmy had taken over her empire years ago, and she talked about their politics, etc. "For some reason, Aunty Barbie, I feel so close to you because of this conversation. I'm so naïve but it seems that most Republicans are wealthy, and here you are, the wealthiest, and you're a Democrat. Most of Robert's and my friends are Republicans, so we just never talk politics."

It's curious how wealthy, famous people can admire other famous, wealthy people. So when Aunty Barbie called to invite me to lunch with her, Kelly and the Travolta's daughter, I was delighted, intrigued. I had described Ella Bleu to Aunty Barbie. She was beautiful even at three. Barbie hadn't been close to Linda for years. I knew Barbie was curious to see Kelly, and now even more so, with Ella Bleu in the picture. Barbie read prodigiously, mostly nonfiction, as well as a few of the tabloids, which cracked me up. I was given her old *HELLO* magazines from London, which were gossipy and fun stargazing, so she'd seen photos of the Travoltas all along, as we all had, and she'd known Kell as a child and young adult. "Come to lunch with Kelly and Ella Bleu next Monday, will you?" she asked.

"So, Chu, Aunty Barbie told me you're coming to lunch," Kelly said later on the phone, "and I just want to ask you not to say anything when I ask her to help Narconon. Don't, you know, react, okay?" I replied, "No, of course not, Cakes. In fact, I'm excited to see Ella Bleu, so I won't hang out with you when you do ask, I'd rather be surfing with her in front. Will she like that?" "If she doesn't get sprayed in her eyes, she will. Go easy, she's not been in the ocean much."

I was still intrigued, though now my big question was answered: why they were having lunch. We all knew about Narconon, of course, as Kell announced at Peter's, her stepfather's recent funeral, that Scientology was opening a chapter here in Hawai'i (with its epidemic of crystal meth) for Narconon, which had helped loads of kids and adults at its other chapters. So after hugging Barbie, Cakes and Ella, I enticed the adorable three-year-old into the ocean on the surfboard. The shore break in front of the club was tiny, so I just pushed her on the wavelets which she enjoyed, while I chatted away, surreptitiously kissing her nectarine-cheeks and plump arms as well as glancing up at Kelly and Aunty Barbie. I wondered how it'd go, Kelly asking for what, maybe $100,000 or $200,000 as a donation? And when they beckoned to us to join them after a half hour, I wolfed down my Cobb salad, taking all the bits Aunty Barbie's gave me from hers and watched her interact with Ella Bleu.

Afterward, when Kelly told me, I was shocked to hear what she'd asked for. And got. One million dollarinis! She just asked and she received. That should help a lot of kids, I thought, but I have to say I felt a prickling pang that I hadn't pushed it with her to help my classes get into more schools, even for the prison guards. Would she have helped? She hadn't even responded years ago when I wrote a letter describing the class.

I had approached Oprah several times, even sending a video, at one point, of my class out at Wai'anae, which is not a fine public school. In fact, it was in disrepair, but a friend who taught there was glad to have me drive the hour to teach the class, which I was happy to do, because I could surf Mākaha afterward when scarcely anyone was out. The girls were all local, underprivileged and most were pregnant or already young mothers. I thought it'd melt Oprah, because she was a champion of teachers and underprivileged kids. And she seemed so into the spiritual, the metaphysical, I was baffled I did not hear from her.

So I kept praying, believing, visualizing my class on her show, with handpicked local kids from Hawai'i, maybe eight or ten of them, and Oprah, realizing its value, how schools across the country needed the simple lessons of identifying fear and knowing one can choose love. I wouldn't have to delve too deep, no life after life stuff, if she didn't think her audience was ready for that. I even thought if she supported it financially in a select number of schools across the country, I might've been able to ask Aunty Barbie to pony up dollar for dollar. Why not?

All to no avail.

So when Kell burbles that Barbie wrote out the check, I chewed on this for days. Until Barbie called. "Chula," she said, "Can you come to lunch today at the club?" Today? My mind raced, as I seldom "do lunch" and I actually had planned to meet friends at the Art Academy, where I'd signed up for sculpting lessons. "What time?" I asked, stalling. "At noon. Sorry I'm calling so late, but Jimmy's here and he thinks I'm going nitty notty, so I need you to come assure him I'm not." I was stunned again. Her son, who was running her empire, was in town and obviously not pleased with his mother's choice of donation. "I can make it," I said. "Oh, good, because you've got to damn well tell him I'm not going nitty notty, okay? He's worried."

Well, actually, so was I. Not that she was losing her mind, but why such an enormous amount of money for Narconon, something she really didn't know that much about? Certainly Kelly would've given her statistics and been persuasive as to the needs of the underprivileged kids, at the huge rise in crystal meth in Hawai'i, but I sensed it was an extension of her love for Ma, and this was her granddaughter.

So I trotted into the club and, as timing would have it, I saw Jimmy alighting from his car. I greeted him. Years younger than I, he was warm, handsome, smiley, so I said, "Jimmy, just so you know, I had nothing to do with that whole lunch. Your mom invited me, I had no idea why, and I was stunned to hear what she gave my niece."

He looked me in the eye. "So was I. And I did think you had something to do with it." Whoa. Lucky my intuition prompted me to mention it, I thought. "No, absolutely nothing, and I can honestly tell you, I was shocked." "Well, we'll see what we can do about it, though I think it's too late. The damage is done." I replied, "And Jimmy, I don't think your mom is losing it, she has seemed strong and clear all along, except for this. Really." He smiled. "Thank you, Chula." And we went to lunch on the *lānai* with no other mention of it except Aunty Barbie's comment half way through, "Tell him, Chula, tell Jimmy I'm not going nitty notty!" Which I reiterated.

But, in the aftermath, I vaguely remember it was a big deal to Jimmy Kennedy that his mother gave a million dollars to Scientology's Narconon.

CHAPTER TWENTY-SEVEN

Hawaii's light, love, fragrance and beauty continually enchant me. Friends have mentioned I'm like a newcomer, not a kāmaʻāina, because I am always so appreciative and observant of Hawaiʻi's natural gifts, the ocean, beaches, mountains, flora and fauna. Because Goat Island is at the tip of Mālaekahana Bay, we have had fun taking grandchildren there, which means walking the bay, then wading the shallows across to the strip of flat island, which has nesting birds but no goats. It's a lovely vantage point from which to view the whole of Mālekahana Bay, a perfect white crescent fringed with ironwood trees, and, on the backside, one gets a glimpse of Lāʻie Bay.

The Mokulua Islands, encircled by surf and capped by pointy, rocky hills are a short canoe or kayak paddle from Lanikai, the tony beach residence on the northeastern shore of Oʻahu. A more dramatic, accessible jaunt, it beckons with adventure for older children. I haven't availed myself or my children of Rabbit Island off of Makapuʻu Beach, but as adults my kids have ventured there by boat and board to surf. There is definitely an allure that draws one to uninhabited islands, even though we live on an island, to which sailors, surfers and the innerchild are drawn.

Hawaiʻi's mountains, mauve or forest green, have a different mystique. The myriad mountains of Oʻahu had not appealed to me before, until the end of the century, in 1999, when I joined a group of ladies who hiked regularly. Chatting, laughing and sweating, we climbed different paths monthly through moist ginger, strawberry guavas, ti leaves, ferns, forests and streams. New friends were made effortlessly, as in Sun Valley (which is what inspired this different pursuit for me), and, though the peaks in Hawaiʻi weren't nearly as high or dramatic, they were happy, fun mornings ending with potluck picnics.

One of the wāhine, a talented watercolor artist, became ill with
ALS, Lou Gerhig's disease. Peggy Chun had a ready laugh and a thirst
for fun, so it was crushing to watch her deteriorate over the next few
years. A year or more after I joined this group, she could no longer
hike. Soon after, she was in a wheelchair. She kept painting, even
taught classes in her tiny, charming home, eventually painting with
the brush clenched in her teeth from her wheelchair. She was such an
inspiration many of her pals helped her, calling themselves Peg's Legs.

While she was still in the wheelchair, I and several others began
helping Peggy, rolling her on special wheels over the sand into the
ocean, floating her out of it and around, like a big, happy baby. When
she became bedridden, I began reading to her. I was only one of many
helping, because, at this point, she was hooked up to machines to help
her breathe, and eventually to help her communicate. I read one of my
favorite books to her first, *Bel Canto*, a poignant story in itself, but,
in that environment, with Peggy prone in bed, with a nurse day and
night, including her lovely son and his angelic wife and baby, I teared
up often.

One night I lay in bed imagining what it would be like to be captive
in your own body. Inevitably, even her eyes, which had enabled her
to communicate through a machine spelling out her answers, could
no longer move. Not even to open or close her eyelids. It would be the
most terrifying, unceasingly traumatic way to die. But Peggy's spirit
remained vibrant even longer than her caregivers' and family's. She
just wasn't ready to go yet, captive or not.

One happy memory of those years is of when Peggy was still able-
bodied enough to attend an ALS charity at a hotel, which I also attended, joining a big table of Peg's Legs. I had a few glasses of wine, as we
all did, and bid on an unusual item at the auction, a sexy white Honda
motorcycle, which, (hiking up my dress) I had mounted earlier to see
how it felt. Robert's old, ugly (maroon) motorcycle had faltered, was
on the brink of expiring. I asked my pals not to let me bid too high, but
I was determined to buy it, a great way to give to ALS as well. It was
thrilling to snap it up for a reasonable price to surprise Robert with

his new ride, and so out of character for me to shop for a vehicle. He was shocked. And pleased.

I am not a big shopper, nor am I not keen on being shopped for. When Robert gave me a pretty little watch for our first Christmas, I smiled and thanked him. The next day, I said, "You know, darling, I'm not a watch person, never have worn one, and I wonder if you'd mind if I exchanged it for something else." A brief hint of hurt crossed his face, and then he smiled. "Of course I don't mind. I should have realized that. Take it right back and get something you want."

So I took it back and, as I walked past the other stores at Kāhala Mall, I glanced over at a black feather boa on a mannequin. We had New Year's event coming up, a big glam party, and that was just what I needed to go with my simple black dress as few wore boas in those days. I bought it, feeling flouncy and festive already, and put it on with the dress to model for Robert. "Oh! Of course!" he exclaimed, "Why didn't I think of that!? Much more you, a boa you'll wear one night instead of a watch you'd wear every day." We both laughed, and I told him I'd saved him money, too. But when I wore it the next night to a pre-New Year's party, getting some mileage out of it, some of the feathers floated off. When I called the swish store to ask if that was to be expected, the clerk said, no, bring it back after I wear it for New Year's Eve.

At 11:45 on New Year's, standing under a huge kiawe tree, we all counted down the minutes as a long string of firecrackers crackled over us. When one splintered off and flew at me, it took a few seconds for Robert and me to see it was sizzling my boa. I yelped and yanked it off, proceeding to stomp out the fire, laughing hysterically. The next day I took it back, though half of it was simply a black cord, explaining to the owner what'd happened, how everyone got a kick out of it, and she said that was worth the free advertising, what did I want to exchange it for? I giggled, picked out a tiny black marabou feather jacket that Robert and I found amusing, as all this began with a watch.

I often gave away gifts I wouldn't use or care for, long before the word re-gifting was used. It just didn't make sense to hold onto something, and, if I didn't like the gift, I simply threw it out. So when my closest friend Laurie gave me a sweet little music box, opening up to a ballerina or something, I thanked her and gave it away. The next time she came to Hawai'i, she was at our house and wondered aloud where I had put it. Oh, oh, I thought, now what? She followed me into my bedroom while I stalled for time. "You gave it away, didn't you!?" she snapped. "It was darling, Laurie, really it was, I just didn't have any place to put it, so I . . . " "No place to put it!?" she shouted. "Well, if you moved this," her arm swiped some framed photos off our dresser, "and this," she swiped off some ceramic critters and trinkets, "you'd have room for it!" My mouth hung open as she laid bare the dresser, until I burst out laughing. My cackling didn't appease her for several minutes, she was so annoyed. It's peculiar that she's never given any gift away.

In fact, the diamond engagement ring Robert gave me had a similar fate. When we were still separated, years back, after three months or so, I was so hurt, felt so unengaged, I had the diamond put on a gold chain around my neck. When we were reunited, he looked at it, laughed and said, "I guess that's better than my balls around your neck!"

About this time Alfred Goldman killed himself. It was shocking in itself as he'd seemed happy (though I hadn't seen him in years), but also because his brother Monte had committed suicide the year before. I didn't learn the reason for his death, but at least he had never had children who'd suffer, as Monte did.

'Iolani School owned a cabin on the top of Pālehua that we had never stayed in, and when I saw it nestled in the eucalyptus trees on one of our hikes with the ladies, I suggested we all stay there for the night. After signing it out, we went up loaded with food and drink and never stopped laughing, eating and imbibing. Of all the cabins on that mountain, it had the most amazing view of both Mākaha, on the distant west coast, the mountains and valleys between, and, way off to the southeast, a view of Waikīkī. A one-bedroom cabin with a *pūne'e* (sofa bed) in the living area near the fireplace, a tiny kitchen and lānai, it was chilly, tranquil and imparted the feeling of being on a remote island, with hikes through the forest in either direction.

Thus began almost a decade of family nights at Palehua, as it was a bit like camping, just not on the ocean, and Robert and I adored going there with the kids and grandchildren. Only an hour drive from home on the best real estate in that neck of the woods. Robert playing his guitar and us singing. And then I also began taking my old pals up to Palehua, five or six of us who'd been hanging out for twenty-five years or so, with gourmet food, doobies and libations. Ready to play Password or Cranium. Giggling for two days.

CHAPTER TWENTY-EIGHT

OUR FAMILY IS EXUBERANT about the end of the century festivities. Not only is it cool to have the Travoltas invitation for a week
at the Kaua'i Hyatt, but prior to this our family will ski ten days in
Tahoe for Christmas. I've rented us a house big enough for Robert and
me, Rob and Judi and their three kids, Todd and Anne with their two
babies, Robin and Corrina, Kilia and Tyler. Ki and Ty drive up from
Santa Barbara, where she's in school, and he's bartending in a hip bar
downtown, having quit his job teaching French in Hawai'i a few years
ago, and had worked at a Thai restaurant for a change. They find a
Christmas tree and set it up for us to decorate.

It's the most expensive holiday for us, because we're paying for the
flights, car, house, food and ski lifts. I feel so blessed to be able to afford this, that we can all ski together. There are a few wrinkles, as big
families are wont to have, but we laugh from the first moment we arrive. Tyler has the exact same humor as his three brothers-in-law, and
each eggs the other on. Just going up the ski lifts is a spectacle, and we
fight over going with Ty, taking turns to laugh.

Tyler has brought a pair of false teeth, clever ones molded to fit
over his own, yet snaggled and stained. We've never seen anything like
these, and the moment he slips them in, we shriek, as he, the linguist,
has every accent down pat, and, with his new look, he becomes a
hillbilly hog farmer. His first ride up on the lift I sat behind in the next
chair, watching him work the guy sitting between him and Rob, who
was unaware that these were brothers. Rob strains to stifle his snorts,
nodding, listening to Ty's repertoire, asking questions. The fellow's
head bobs between them, and finally Rob throws back his head and
howls. I seethe with jealousy, dying to know the patter, which I made
Tyler repeat on the top of the mountain afterward.

Whooping with laughter, we charge down the black runs together, all of them on snowboards except for me. Next one up with him is Kilia, and again I snag the seat behind to giggle vicariously, having no idea of his storyline. My turn is with a bright woman, and it is a bit tricky maneuvering her ahead of us, then between us on the chairlift. Tyler, on the left, smiles at the woman between us. The teeth are classic, almost not believable, but Ty pulls it off, saying, "I bet I'm the only snowboardin' pig farma' on the mountain. From Oklahoma," he adds, nodding with a wink. "Where you from?" he asks. "I'm from NASA," she answers. "Well, that's nothing to be ashamed of." I snort. "Where you from?" He leans toward me and I reply, "I'm from Hawai'i." "Oh, out ther' in the middle of the ocean, huh? When I'm cleanin' the pig pens sometimes I feel like I'm in the middle of oceans of pig shit!" I giggle, he smiles, then addresses her. "Can I ask you a pers'nal question?" She looks at me before nodding. "I'm thinkin' of having a little work done on my teeth. I see people lookin' at my teeth sometimes, you know, and I was wonderin', you all think they need fixin'?" "No!" she answers. I'm poker-faced.

Then Tyler laughs and plucks them out. "Oh, my God," she says. "I wondered if you were putting me on at first, but then . . . " We all crack up.

The snow is excellent and I am over the moon, skiing with grandchildren Ryan and Hana, while Halie and Kai start out in the ski school. Anne and Todd take turns with baby Wyatt, and Robert, not a skier, happily plays with them in the snow after his workout in the gym.

They also amuse themselves snapping photos of each other, one of them positioned below a hillock chosen for jumps. Ty (having been a snowboard instructor in Vermont) was the master, glad to be in his element after years of occasionally surfing in Ki's wake, metaphorically. After gaining speed, the brothers take turns jumping, getting air, swiveling their bods and swooping down while we cheer. I was glad for the break, because it is impossible keeping up with them. We meet for lunch, which we packed ahead of time, and recount stories before returning to the slopes, while I ski down, meeting Robert and the babies before going home for naps. Nights are a bit chaotic, trying to organize dinner for everyone during beers and wine, while hilarity prevails.

A few days after Christmas, we fly to Kaua'i for a week at the Hyatt. Lots of socializing with our huge 'ohana ensues, with the varied personalities and characters, and, of course, playing tennis, volleyball, sliding down pool slides with the kids, relaxing on the beach. Johnny and Kelly have their two nannies for Jett (as he's gained weight) and the muscular fellow is necessary, to help. The big night, the end of the century, with all the hoopla implied, is set. Johnny has rented out the hotel's best restaurant exclusively for us. We are all decked out, buzzing, and meet for champagne and cocktails before a sumptuous dinner party. A raucous night, and Tyler's brief, subtle vignette with a glimpse of teeth cracked up Kelly, John and his family before we rocked out, dancing to fun tunes to bring in 2000.

Alcohol had been an issue in our family all along. Robert brought it up regularly, his three siblings had all stopped drinking through AA and he verbalized caution about his own intake. Hartwell and Robert were about the only ones in the family who weren't alcoholics, so he had discussions with Rob, Todd and Robin often how it ran in families. Robin's father, Stephen, had been a good example of how not to be. Every time Robin returned from visiting my ex-husband, he described his intake of drugs and liquor; it obviously bothered him and he'd confronted Stephen many times to no avail. Stephen had gone on to marry a few more times and had sired other sons and a daughter who were in complete agreement with Robin that their dad was in serious trouble. Robin still smoked weed occasionally, had a few beers, but was fairly grounded, apparently not addicted.

We weren't so sure about Rob and Todd. Our family loved to party, and with Robert and me as their role models, who sometimes would go over the line, we had to be vigilant and aware to handle it. If I had a hangover, as I did many times over the years, I'd vow to cut back, and I still smoked, which didn't help the hangovers. Rob and Todd, strapping young athletes like their dad, would get high, but were usually capable of reining it in. Until it seemed like trouble. Anne quietly talked to Todd about his drinking until he took charge; Judi harped on Rob. Her own dad was an alcoholic so she was understandably anxious, but it was all out in the open. Until later, when it wasn't.

In late February we took a semester's leave of absence. Robert replaced himself at 'Iolani and I rented our house before leaving for another six-month hiatus in Santa Barbara. I took a sculpting class at the Santa Barbara Art Center, and dallied in creating wristbands to remind oneself to stop negative thoughts. A simple rubber band, colorful, thick, with a tiny button stitched on that could be snapped whenever a fearful thought emerged. Not the best invention (though it helped me) and I only sold a few as the ADD kicked in, but I stuck with the sculpting, which I loved.

Todd and Anne had taken a sabbatical to live in Santa Cruz near her family for a semester, so we drove up there as well as them coming down to us, which gave me my fix for adorable three-year-old Kai and precious tiny urchin Wyatt. We are Chu Chu and Umbi to all our grandchildren, as Pat Steele (Storm), dubbed Robert "Umberto" when we went to Italy, shortened to Umbi, an endearing name for an endearing man. Ki and Ty were still in Santa Barbara, but Tyler had decided he wanted to go to Florida for training at a flight school to become a pilot, so Kilia dropped out of her master's program and they drove across the country with Zelly in May. We then drove up to Oregon to Sis and her kids, Montana to the Gileses cabin on the lake and Sun Valley to Mia and Matt's (who had a second home now in Santa Barbara).

Everything was hunky dory upon our return to Santa Barbara until I stopped ignoring a nagging anxiety about our tenant in Hawai'i. I had rented the house to Peter, a German fellow in his forties. He was smart, personable, and into computers and software. The checks were deposited on time each month until perhaps mid-May, after which I called to ask him why they'd stopped. Oh, he said, he was busy negotiating to buy a house in Kāhala, on the beach, and described it to me. Yes, I knew just the one, and was impressed he could afford the three- or four-million-dollar home and told him I hoped it worked out. A few weeks went by, I called again, couldn't get a hold of him for the next week or more. Finally I spoke to him in early June, and, oh, so sorry, he'd been busy with the stray dog he took in, as well as putting up new rain gutters on our house. And he had to replant the ficus tree in the pot by the pool. He'd deposit the check right away. Another week or so went by, it was late June, and we asked our eldest son, Rob, to go to our house and deal with Peter. We said to tell him he had to get the hell out if he didn't pay up.

But Rob reported back that he couldn't talk to him, the gates on our fence were locked. (Locked? Nothing on our house had ever been locked!) And he heard a steady noise coming from behind the pool, maybe a generator. Turned out he'd let our pool guy go, so we had nobody to ask what was going on. We asked friends in Santa Barbara, who were lawyers, what recourse we had. Unbelievably, we were told we could not kick him out, or he could sue us. Sue us? Really?

By now it was the beginning of July and Robert was seething. He called an old friend in Hawai'i who was a private investigator to ask if he could arrest Peter, but he could not make contact either, to serve him. He called us to say maybe he could help by meeting us at the house when we returned. The chords on Robert's neck bulged when he told me this. "I'm going to jump our fence and grab that little fucker and break his neck!" Robert snarled. I burst out laughing. "Oh, yeah, uh huh, I can just see you jumping our fence, when's the last time you jumped anything higher than the curb?"

We imagined different scenarios as we flew home other than breaking his neck, cheering ourselves up. Rob picked us up at the airport, we spent the night at his house, and early the next morning we went to our home, which, sure enough, was locked at the gates. We called out Peter's name several times. Robert's eyes were like flint and he was pouring sweat, and then out came the little wimp, casually smiling and saying hello like nothing was wrong. I asked him what the hell was going on as we followed him into our home, why did he have a generator, why had he let our water service lapse? The pool is disgusting, out trots the dog Peter took in, and then I walked into our living room and stopped in my tracks. The carpet was filthy, the couches looked like the dog's bed and the upper living room was packed with computers of every kind and shape. I don't remember the dialogue, but fury spilled out and I spit venom at Peter, who was still kicked back, until the P.I. arrived and took over.

The upshot was that we would keep his Mercedes and he was told to vacate that day and haul his computers away. He said he had no place to go, and how was he to leave? "Boo hoo," I said, "how dare you ruin my home! Take the bus, whatever it takes!" Unbelievably, Robert had now mellowed out and agreed with the con man that he could drive away in his Mercedes Benz and come back the next day for all the computers. "What!? No, Robert, he cannot leave in that car," I protested, "are you crazy? What happened to breaking his neck? He hasn't paid us for three months of the rent." Robert pulled himself up to his full six feet, five inches (when he stands up straight), and glared down at Peter. "You're meeting us here tomorrow at 7 a.m., right Peter?" He promised he would and hightailed it out of there. I asked the P.I. why in hell they thought we'd ever see him again, and he replied that the computers, etc., were expensive; he'd have to return.

I wasn't sure at all, I knew nothing about computers as I'm the lowest-tech person, and I warn Robert not to let him elude us again. I was relieved to see Peter the next morning. I immediately called the water company to reinstate our service and hired someone to come and clean while he hired someone to remove his equipment, and Robert announced that we would now take possession of his Mercedes, which would almost cover his debt. I relaxed.

Peter moved his equipment to a storage place in Kāhala, and we tell the P.I. that we were going to sell all of it to cover upholstering and cleaning costs so please get the storage receipt. He agreed, saying he'd have someone on it right away, and somehow in the next day or two, Peter snuck back to the storage and removed everything. Don't

Chula and Kilia, Chula's 64th birthday, 2008

Robin and Reena, 2008

Robert and Chula, 2008

Olela and Chula, 2008

Robin at Waimea Bay, 2008

Rob's Molokaʻi canoe race (Rob in second seat), 2008

Punahou classmates at Mālaekahana, 2008

Chula buys Robert a motorcycle at the Peg's Legs ALS charity event for Peggy Chun, 2008

Chula's 64th birthday, 2008

Ki, Tyler and Kawela, 2009

Christmas 2009

Kilia surfing at Diamond Head, 2009

Inside the image (magazine cover), text includes:
YOUR EVERYTHING GUIDE
101
THINGS TO DO
www.101thingstodo.com
Island Maps pgs. 24-36
Lu'au pg. 41, 43, 104
Ocean Excursions pg. 64
Dining Directory pg. 106
Shopping Guide pg. 118
Featuring: Cycling the Coconut Coast Page 14
KAUAI
Kilauea couple Todd and Anne Harrison cycle the path on Coconut Coasters rentals • Photo by Geison Dwight

Anne and Todd, 2011

remember how. But thankfully we had the Mercedes that we sold so we weren't out of pocket too much. (And through all the years we'd rented our home we'd been fortunate.) Detectives and cops kept coming around though, for they had been following Peter for months and he'd eluded them locally as well as on the Mainland. It was sad when different charities would call over the ensuing months, as it turned out he'd ripped them off somehow. Such a cunning, sly dog.

CHAPTER TWENTY-NINE

I RESUME SCULPTING CLASSES at the Honolulu Art Academy, as enthralled with the sensuousness of clay as I was the first time I touched it in Santa Barbara, and begin sculpting nude ladies. But the exciting event of September is Kilia and Tyler's engagement and their plan to marry the following August in 2001. I am no longer teaching classes, which I miss (and have sent my outline, video to Oprah again), but I am weary of feeling like the trout swimming upstream, always initiating it into schools. I am happy to veg surfing, playing volleyball, hiking, babysitting, camping.

Handsome, merecurial Robin is grateful it's his turn to buy a house and it's fun driving around the North Shore looking for one he likes that we can afford. He's stoked to find one a block from the beach at Velzeyland, a good surf spot near Pūpūkea. He will live in the tiny studio, rent out the house and start organizing a room there to shape surfboards. He's been dating a sweet Filipina, Thelma, who is bright and gentle, but we are baffled he seems serious over someone who has nothing in common with him, and cannot even swim.

Jimmy and Steph have been friendly the past year or more, and we sometimes dine with them and Linda. It's lovely to have this again, though gorgeous Steph is dating younger guys, studly, sexy young men. I'm happy for her, wish Linda were dating someone. I am so glad to have Olela in my life, seeing her for meals, and talk to Aunty Barbie on the phone daily. Kelly returns to Hawai'i occasionally, this time with pouty-lipped baby Ella Bleu, whose huge blue eyes peek out through dark, thick bangs. Jett is fine, still severely autistic. He has never spoken. I go to the Palehua cabin monthly, either just with the wāhine or with family. In April, Kilia and Tyler return (hitching a ride on the Travoltas' jet) to live in our rental off the garage now that his flight school is pau. He gets a job with Trans-Air Cargo flying interisland, we address handmade wedding invitations by Ki, a few showers are given for Ki by my pals, culminating in Steph and Sky's lovely May shower at Stephanie's little house on the ocean at Niu.

Happiness reigns regarding the upcoming wedding of my daughter and best friend. Family and friends trickle in in late July and it's festive right up to the second week of August, when we all drive the hour to the west coast, to Lanikuhonua, a gorgeous oceanfront private property owned by the Campbell Estate next to the 'Ihilani Hotel. We had been invited out to Lanikohonua several times for camp outs with Olela's grandchildren (who Kilia and I played volleyball with), which was truly upscale camping, with its manicured lawns, large bathrooms and grill, and electricity. It is Patsy and Olela's gift to us, such a treat.

A small wedding of 140, it is being catered by our pal's (the owner of famed Buzz's Restaurant) son. Guests can choose to stay at the five-star 'Ihilani or camp with us. Of course, our family and the younger locals camp, including Ty's family and friends from Vermont and elsewhere. There's been some anxiety for Ty because his mother (married to the much younger Ozzie) has not seen her old friend since she fell in love with her husband, Ty's dad, and married him fifteen years earlier. Naturally, weddings bring out the love (or not) and, at this one, Ty's mother and stepmother are happily reunited.

The rehearsal dinner is Friday before the Saturday wedding, and I'll not forget the deep joy I felt as I played volleyball on the lawn, looking out at the ocean through the coconut trees, seeing the caterers arrive to set up for a delectable dinner. God, thank you, how blessed am I to have this union of my beautiful, vibrant daughter to this marvelous man after four years of living together, here in the country, and then to know I didn't have to do anything all weekend except cherish each moment and breathe in the tang of the ocean.

Kilia, breathtakingly beautiful in a strapless white fitted gown with a rope pikake lei as a necklace, and Tyler in a white long-sleeve shirt and cream-colored slacks rolled up on his calves are stunning as they are married, the ocean as a backdrop. Intimate and surrounded by beauty. Then we're served scrumptious pūpū while rocking out to hot tunes by the DJ before dinner.

Again we awake the next morn with the sun and begin the day with a swim, volleyball and eventually beers. A few days later the newly-weds hike the Nā Pali coast into Kalalau, the remote, sheer cliffs on the North Shore of Kaua'i to camp for five days for their "moon."

Robert and I go to Todd and Anne's on Kaua'i, as they've just given birth to their third son, delectable Noa, two years after Wyatt. Kai is an extraordinary athlete, able to make baskets on a regulation basketball court at four years old. Crouched and holding the ball near his knees underhand, he'd toss it up and into the net, almost making twelve baskets in a row, missing just a few. Now he's bumping, setting and hitting a volleyball with dexterity at five. Not surprising, and strong, muscular Ryan and Hana have become agile athletes at soccer, surfing and tennis as well.

All of this, our life, children, grandchildren, Hawai'i, is a dream, a *huge* contrast to the horror of a few weeks later, on 9/11. An incomparably different reality. So much hate (fear) causing it and the effect as well. Will we ever learn to choose love? Understand we are all connected? One?

I meet with the Childrens' Advocacy Center to work with them a few times, but have no memory of what I did, still cook huge pots of chicken soup with rice for the homeless every few weeks, help Peggy with ALS and sculpt on my own. I find out about Sunny Buddies, an organization that pairs you up with a Down syndrome buddy. Thus, 2002 begins a ten-year commitment with a young woman, taking her to lunch and a movie weekly. I see Aunty Barbie and Olela for lunches, sometimes dinner, and often Steph joins us, which makes for more laughter. Hiking a different mountain with the ladies' group monthly, I realize I'm aging and can no longer do two sports back to back on the same day, as surfing is strenuous when the waves are up and beach volleyball is exhausting in the heat with Kilia and her contemporaries.

Tyler and Kilia have found a small, old house with a spacious back lawn in Waimānalo, a block from a still undiscovered white sand beach, a stunning view of the soaring, undulating Ko'olau Mountains. They immediately have a third bedroom walled off into a rental, with its own entrance, bathroom and lānai. They are as grateful as their siblings, and we are happy to buy it. Kilia is substitute teaching in different schools, another contented teacher in the family.

Robert has always been a low-maintenance guy. He's happy to eat a pizza or chicken pot pie from Costco if I'm disinterested in cooking (though I'll have a treat for myself), he cares less what he wears (and I am sometimes his valet, laying out nice outfits), never seems grumpy from fatigue yet will nap falling asleep in four minutes as well as at night, is unfazed by heat or cold. I continually marvel he isn't aware when he's tired, hungry, hot or cold, but it has its downside. We are out at Ki and Ty's house helping in their yard. I am clipping dead areca palms and Robert is using an electric saw on an old hedge. I stop work to see him sweating profusely, water sluicing off his head, shoulders, arms and chest onto the saw and begin to yell at him to turn it off, when, oops, too late. He drops the saw, shaking his hand violently back and forth. "Oh, my God, Robert, you were almost electrocuted!" He looks at me. "Yeah, that was quite a shock." "No shit, Sherlock. Seriously, what were you thinking? I've got to tell the kids we have another one on the list."

And a year later our cleaning lady had just sprayed our oven with cleaning foam, when he pops in a croissant to heat up. When I came into the kitchen a bit later she whispered to me what had transpired. "Robert!" I say as he showers, "The oven has chemicals sprayed in it, you can't eat that croissant." "Too late," he replies. "Couldn't you smell that spray? I know you're a deaf mofo, but you can smell!" "Nah, no big deal," he smiles. "Oh Lord, you don't know when you're being electrocuted, don't know when you're being poisoned." The list grows longer.

We summer in Montecito and Montana before returning home to

our thirtieth anniversary party. Australia beckons again at Christmas for a few weeks with old friends, especially Anne Abel-Smith in Adelaide and Jane and Ian in Tasmania. But we are deeply saddened when Kathy Muller's husband Joe dies while we are away; though he's been sick for years, he was one of our best friends and had a delicious, dry sense of humor. My heart aches for Kathy and her daughter Baba. It reminds me how blessed I am to have healthy, robust Robert, how much I cherish him.

CHAPTER THIRTY

LIFE FLOWS ALONG IN '03 and, to our surprise, Robin marries Thelma mid-June at a friend's house on a cliff overlooking the ocean at Lā'ie. We finally meet Thelma's family, who are Filipino, and Robert has had an 'Iolani colleague translate a welcoming speech into Filipino. I weep watching him, Thelma and her family as he reads it.

A few weeks later I, Magnolia Thunderpussy, venture off with five old, dear pals (who have been going up to the Palehua cabin the past few years with me) to Montana to play with Tiger Lily (Leslie) for a week. We are the Frunions, and though Tommy is in residence and told Les he wouldn't hang out with us, he can't resist. Whether canoeing, swimming in the freezing Lindbergh Lake, hiking, eating, drinking or just talking story, we think we're so hilarious he is sucked into the gaiety.

I then join Robert in Santa Barbara through July and most of August, and coming home I am happy to be greeted for lunch by Aunty Barbie and Olela. They are a kick together, as Olela's naïve remarks followed by Aunty Barbie's crisp rejoinders crack us up, though Olela isn't sure what's so funny. Robert and I go, as we're wont to do a few times a month, to see the Kaua'i kids, merrily having our usual bonfire/picnic on Kalihiwai Beach (where Todd used to live). It's our favorite thing to do. Robert plays his guitar, we sing, swill and chat while I cook hot dogs on the fire. Kai and Wyatt surf the shore break or romp on the beach with happy Noa until I call them to eat raw veggies with dip before their hot dogs. It's a night off cooking for Anne, then she and Todd have a date night, which they need because she has no family there to help. Mornings we play volleyball on the most beautiful volleyball court in the world, the mountains a dramatic backdrop to Hanalei Bay. Kai, almost six, has just begun to play with us at this point, with Todd for his partner, and Anne and I take them on. Robert plays a few games, but moving quickly in the sand isn't easy on his hips.

In September, Robert and I are going to Tuscany. The year we took off in Santa Barbara Robert was given only a half-sabbatical (a semester's pay), all 'Iolani could afford back then. So now, after teaching thirty years, he'd asked to have the other half of a year's salary for a semester off, which took negotiating because the senior master in charge of sabbaticals was neither obliging nor respectful of Robert. In fact, I think he was threatened by Robert's adoration from the students, his skills and accomplishments there. And perhaps some of the faculty were envious we'd taken leaves of absence to marvelous places, which required only initiative (and renting our house).

We have a Santa Barbara couple joining us for a few weeks in two different villages, then old Hawai'i friends for a few weeks in the wing of a fourteenth-century home overlooking Firenze (Florence). I am entranced. Each day is spontaneous, fantastic, but the highlight is the Cinque Terra. Not yet discovered (then) as they are inaccessible by car, the five villages on the northwestern edge of Italy perch along the cliffs of the Mediterranean. As we trek the four-hour hike, I gasp and get chicken skin at the first glimpse of each exquisitely charming pastel, storybook village. Tiny vineyards lace the hills between, it is as if time stands still, and we absorb the view of the startling turquoise sea through deep breaths. We stop for an espresso, later lunch in another village, full immersion, then hop a small train back to the first village, where our car is parked.

Loving Italy passionately, we tear ourselves away to come home in time for Thanksgiving at Kilia and Tyler's home in Waimānalo. I'd passed the baton to Rob and Judi for the prior Thanksgiving at their home.

After Noa was born, his brothers asked if they would ever have a sister. No, probably not, they were told, since three kids is quite enough, thank you. Months later they asked again, and dear, patient Anne told Todd perhaps he could locate the daughter that he'd sired while at Santa Barbara City College. Not enough that she had a baby and two other sons, she encouraged Todd to seek her out. It only took a few phone calls to the Mormon community (his college volleyball coach knew everyone around) and, to our astonishment, Todd discovered his twenty-year-old daughter had been adopted by parents who lived in Lāʻie, in the Mormon community there, ten minutes from Mālaekahana (where we still camped and had our country shack years before). She played water polo at Kahuku High School, had even played games at ‘Iolani School. Turns out her parents knew about Todd, had even watched him play volleyball for UH.

So Todd found his daughter, who was thrilled to hear from her birth father, and, after a long phone call, Todd asked if they could meet at Thanksgiving on Oʻahu. It was arranged that her birth mother, Todd's long-ago girlfriend, would join her. Her husband and family would come also, but she alone met with Todd and their daughter quietly a few days before Thanksgiving. Todd described the wonderful meeting and we couldn't wait to meet her at Ki and Ty's.

We come with my standard Caesar salad and pūpū, serve ourselves beer for Robert and wine for me, with, of course, Todd's and Rob's family, and Robin and Thelma, and we all babble and giggle in anticipation of our new, oldest granddaughter until their arrival minutes later. In walks this striking, tall young lady as lovely as her mother, who comes in next, and we fall on them with kisses and hugs, till we break off to meet the sweet, short parents as well as the other daughter they'd adopted. We all cry, then chat out back on Kilia and Tyler's big lawn, the Koʻolau a quiet presence to this newly enhanced ‘ohana for a most loving Thanksgiving.

Turns out our "new" granddaughter works at a clothing shop in Ala Moana, commuting the hour each way to the North Shore, so I suggest she spend the night with us occasionally to save herself the drive. It is an easy, fun way to really get to know her, and she has a glass of wine with us, though she is Mormon. On one occasion, she and her beau spend the night, and Robert and I giggle, wondering if this is allowed in their religion. Typically kolohe we were, supporting such wayward behavior. Robert has a few brief exchanges with her suggesting she

might not need to rush into marriage and children, but, when she
moves to the Mainland not long after, she does just that. So Todd is a
grandfather. We are great-grandparents.

We are thrilled in January '04 that Tyler gets a job flying for Aloha
Airlines. I have launched into sculpting, having made a tiny upstairs
bedroom into my studio. I sculpt in meditative silence and have the
clay pieces fired at 'Iolani's art department. Like her brother, Hana
is an excellent surfer, has been competing in contests under Robin's
tutelage with us in attendance. While on Kaua'i for the weekend we
get to watch Kai in a gremmie surf contest at Hanalei. The three boys
delight us as they never fight, and, in fact, play tirelessly with Noa
bouncing between them. Aunty Barbie's out of town (as is Patsy, who
lives mostly at Hanalei since her divorce), but Patsy comes when
Olela hosts my sixtieth birthday party at her charming home with all
my wāhine pals and a delicious menu that we choose together, catered
to the queen's (Olela's) taste. I tend to milk my birthdays: have
another party for couples, one with the Frunions, and yet another for
my Volley Dollies, a bevy of seventeen or so babes that play volleyball
with me.

Robin and Thelma separate to divorce. She is sad, but I think sees
they are not a good match, and they part amicably and easily. Santa
Barbara beckons for July and August and Kilia gets free travel, now,
so joins us for a week, and Tyler for a few days. I am so addicted to
sculpting and carry on even when I'm away, packing my piece carefully to return.

What the Bleep Do We Know? comes out on the big screen in the
fall, a movie about science, spirituality and quantum physics. I'm
excited because it's been like a secret, something rarely even in the
media, and covers much of my class contents. Robert sees it with me,
though maybe is not as tantalized, and I decide I must take Aunty Barbie to see it. If one hasn't been introduced to this realm, it would be
tricky following it, and I'm not sure how much she has absorbed when
we discuss it afterward. Certainly not the dialogue with the spirit
entity from thousands of years ago (like Ramtha, who I'd listened to

when I began this path), yet I was glad she was open to it, as somehow it validated me. "Don't get stuck on who was pouring out that wisdom, it's just the messenger," I told her.

I wished Stephanie had been in town to join us, a different voice and feedback. She'd bought a darling cottage in Venice, California, having sold her house on the ocean here, as well as a small condo on the ocean near the Outrigger Canoe Club. I have seldom seen Sky in the years since she's moved to Los Angeles and opened a clothing store, but when she returns we are always eager to have her for dinner. She has fallen in love with Brett, a wonderful, bright entrepreneur. I also see Jimmy less, though we are invited to dinner with him and Linda occasionally. When Kelly comes we get together with Steph for dinner as well.

I have the bags under my eyes surgically removed at sixty years old. I think I look younger and know I shall never have a face lift because it's too scary, and probably I won't care by the time I really need it. It is at this point in time that Aunty Barbie calls me for lunch with her, Kelly and Ella Bleu, and *voilà*, the contribution to Narconon. Weeks later, I'm asked to lunch with her and her son Jimmy Kennedy to prove to him she's not going nitty notty. Afterward I am invited to a charity at La Pietra School with Aunty Barbie, their biggest benefactor, and Garner (whose compliment annoys the hell out of me) and I watch them bid on auction items and realize her million-dollar donation was like a hundred dollars to her.

We still camp with Rob and his three dear ones, always a fun getaway with the allure of the ocean, Rob playing his guitar along with Robert singing together in harmony near our campfire. I have begun to teach my Sunny Buddy to have a sense of humor; when we walk into an empty theater after lunch for the movie, I take her arm and exclaim, "Oh, no! Where will we sit?" Her brow furrows as she looks at me, and I laugh, saying, "Seriously, there are not enough seats for us, are there?" Finally, I eke a smile out of her. At this point I've been reading to Peggy weekly, realizing it's my best way of contributing; have begun selling my unglazed ceramic sculpture; join Hana in a surfing television commercial for a surf shop.

I fly back to Santa Barbara for the Steele's daughter's wedding for a week, and feel lucky to stay at Mia and Matt's cottage again. Robert and I have rented it (for a song) the past few years, and we feel like they are our children and love their two children as well. I sculpt one of my best sculptures there, an eight-inch-high girl sitting and playing the 'ukulele, feel creative and eventually have it cast in bronze to sell it many times over.

But I am bereft after that week, as Laurie has announced on the phone we are no longer friends. I am stunned, crushed, mystified. Why? What have I done? I had seen little of her, as she had one daughter's wedding going on and also two other daughters at home. Perhaps I hadn't asked enough about the hoopla, the behind-the-scenes ambiance when we had lunch? I didn't know. It was even more peculiar because she and Pat had been having strife with their eldest daughter, it was a most tormented saga in their family, and when Robert and I were last there, Laurie called to ask a favor of me, to be a sort of intermediary. I was happy to help. But how could her feelings have changed so dramatically for me so soon after that incident? Only a few months ago?

I mull this over for weeks, introspective. It felt like a divorce. And I can only think it was me. Perhaps too forthright, opinionated, too dramatic? I was outrageous, like Storm, and Laurie, aging, was more conservative. I finally accept it, come back to the Now. Yet some years later I hear she dropped other friends, which somehow helped me to understand.

Robert is more comfortable with our grandchildren as they get to be four or five, and in the past has taken Ryan, Hana and Halie at that age on a "boogy," fun ventures, playing age-appropriate sports and stopping for a treat. When Todd and Anne come from Kaua'i, their three boys were swept off on the boogy as well, to swim in 'Iolani's huge pool, play racquetball there, run around the gymnasium, play softball or Frisbee in the park, tennis, volleyball, lunch. Umbi is still the camp counselor/dad/grandfather from heaven and all six grandchildren adore him. They come home sweaty, tired and happy after four hours, and I am in awe of his patience, his stamina.

Robert and I have been at Hailey's soccer games lately (though I was weary of soccer by now) and know we have another athlete in the family. When Todd brings his family again from Kaua'i to us for Thanksgiving, Umbi takes them on boogies, our whole family body-surfs the smaller surf spot called Baby Makapu'u, even teeny Noa goes for it with his floaties on his arms. We all walk Kāhala Beach the next day to the Kāhala Mandarin hotel (used to be Kāhala Hilton), to watch the dolphin show they put on for their guests. It's a marvel, these dolphin diving and leaping in the lagoon, though it bothers me they are captive. Being with our children and their mates, six grandchildren in such glorious beauty, satiates me as we adjust to a quiet Christmas, now that Todd's family needs to stay home on Kaua'i with the huge expense of interisland airfare for five of them.

CHAPTER THIRTY-ONE

MY BROTHER HAS DISTANCED himself from me. He has married a lady younger than two of his sons with whom we have little in common, though I'm not sure that's the reason. Jimmy is at his best when he is helping, rescuing someone, which I don't really need. Perhaps it's partly attributed to his friendship with Linda. I am glad they have become close, it's a relationship she's craved for so long and probably prefers it to be exclusive of me. It would seem she has made comments against me as she had in the past to others, which have often come back to me, this time from Aunty Barbie. But Jimmy is his own person, knows exactly who I am, and chooses to love me from a distance. I miss him, though we hadn't had our adventures in years, I got a kick out of his humor.

Linda is pleased she's had her own home built by two friends whose blueprints and estimated price for a two-bedroom house in Pālolo had seemed impossible. She ignored everyone's input that it wouldn't work out, and she was right, we saw at her housewarming party, it was darling and just what they said it'd cost to build. I described all this to Aunty Barbie, told her she should see it and she thought about it. When she calls me to ask if I'd take her to see it, I am glad. When I call Linda, as Aunty Barbie asked me to do, they haven't talked in years, Linda asks why the hell was I calling, why not Barbie? And declined the offer of the olive branch. How sad to turn this reunion down. Her loss.

I sculpt a naked woman who resembles Christ, called "Christa," have her attached to a wood cross (from a milo tree in our yard) in the same iconic pose seen worldwide, and have her cast in bronze. A few friends make no comment, but, of course, Robert says, "Perfect. Women have died for men's errors for thousands of years." Eventually it is sold, the second one of two cast, for $1,200 at a charity auction.

We still have marvelous nights up at the Palehua cabin overlooking Mākaha to Waikīkī, sometimes just me and the Frunions, have lunches with Aunty Barbie, Olela and Steph, get invited for weekends to gorgeous Lanikuhonua, where Kiwi and Ty married, have massages every few weeks. Ryan is paddling with Rob in two-man canoe races, which are great fun to watch. Ryan, as strong and fit as his father and grandfather, is just as sweet. Hana is sponsored, one of the top surfers in Hawai'i in her age group, and I take her and Hailey to lunch occasionally. Sometimes surf with them.

Romance is in the air in '06. Robert and I are ecstatic Robin is dating Reena, an Indian treasure who graduated from Punahou, whose parents are both physicians and who is studying to be a veterinarian at Colorado. She is a dark-skinned beauty, surfs and has the same lolo, charming humor Robin has. He is already in love, and for good reason, as her quick wit has us laughing often.

Unsurprisingly Robin's dad (my first and second husband) died, drugs being the cause. He is sad but knew it was inevitable. An interesting result down the road is that Robin inherits some of his trust fund which makes life even easier for him. I reflect how fortunate it is he's had Robert for his role model, the antithesis to Stephen.

Dear old pal Kathy has been dating Ben, a sweet, gentle man who is the opposite of Joe (her husband who died a few years ago), who had a quick, dry humor but was not demonstrative.

Kilia has been teaching science at La Pietra School for Girls, happily becoming a respected facet of that charming, beautiful setting. It seems appropriate as Aunty Barbie was their benefactor and I'd taught and coached there myself.

Yet our big news is Robert retiring at the end of May after forty years of teaching, coaching, counseling at 'Iolani High School. Though he'd wearied of the stacks of papers to correct, spending at least two hours or more nightly with his red marker making explicit comments, he kept wondering aloud why friends asked when he'd retire. I replied he was at that age, why the hell not? Not only free days, he'd also have his nights free. What would he do, he mused, and I said he'd be so busy he'd wonder how he'd ever resisted it. Which ultimately is exactly what happens.

Santa Barbara and Sun Valley draw us in the summer. I sculpt in Santa Barbara as well as play volleyball daily. I am pierced with envy in Sun Valley when I read the book *The Secret*, which covers all that I've taught and written about, and Oprah has the book and authors on her show. It's the only thing I've wanted and not gotten in my life, and I'm mystified. A few years later Oprah moves to Montecito, to a property where I used to sit to meditate; it is huge, quiet uninhabited, and I hear how she's been seen when in town to restore the house. One day I ask God to show me a sign if I'd ever reach her, or how to reach her with the class. The next day I go to Pierre La Fond's, a deli I frequent often. As I get in my car to leave, I see Stedman, her mate, looking at the car next to me from the curb. Oh, I think, I can go talk to him! Explain who I am and what I hope for. I am torn. Then I decide it was rude, intrusive, he was here in Montecito with Oprah to get away from it all. I don't approach him but wonder if I should have.

After a month in Idaho we leave for Italy. I had found out about a small town in northeastern Italy that is a mecca for sculptors the world over, near Carrarra, where Michelangelo procured his marble. I questioned if Robert would have enough to do while I sculpted, but he insisted he'd be fine. We drive an hour or so to Pietrasanta from Pisa, arriving Saturday morning, parking near the apartment we have rented for the month. I feel euphoric, with its spacious, high-ceilinged living area, its two bedrooms, views of pretty, antiquated buildings out huge windows, the fact it's on a narrow walk-street to the main piazza two blocks away. I immediately find a ceramic store with a terraced garden where I can sculpt, owned by handsome Franco, with his assistant available should I need help, and, of course, kilns where my clay pieces will be fired. He has no classes going on, which is perfect timing for me, as it's quiet, like it's all waiting just for me. Serendipitous.

We meet an amazing American couple our first morning, she has sculpted marble here for many years, and he's just published his book,

The Reluctant Tuscan. She has some of her marble pieces in the Metropolitan Museum of Art and he's written screenplays in Hollywood for television before, quitting and renovating their house in a town near Pietrasanta. They are bright, funny and a wealth of information. They have us to dinner at their pretty hillside home, we marvel at their innovativeness, all of which is chronicled in his charming book. We join them for prosecco and dinner in the piazza often, meet their friends, some of whom are English, some local. Robert plays tennis with him and his pals. But Robert finds the tennis pro and has far better tennis regularly with him, goes to market, plays his guitar, finds a café from which to send emails.

I walk the few blocks each morning to my garden studio, and with photos in hand of what I will sculpt, enlist Franco to make the armatures for each. Thus far, I have only sculpted reclining or sitting pieces, as the concept of all that heavy wet clay balancing on two tiny ankles is beyond me, and I feel a frisson as I begin to realize my goal of sculpting a surfer girl in the "cowabunga" position on her board. Franco closes his shop daily for the two-hour lunch, so I bring mine, strip down and sit naked in this glorious garden to eat and sculpt into the afternoon. I'm unused to working such long hours, and come home happily tired to my "wife," who's already gone to market; I am free to lie down to read, then ask what time we can go to the piazza tonight.

"Again?" the "wife" asks plaintively. "We've been out the past four nights. And I bought hamburger for our dinner . . . " "Thanks for going to market darling, but why would we stay home alone together when we can be out people-watching every night in that piazza? And, why would I eat a hamburger in Italy, instead of their scrumptious bruschetta and pasta?" He smiles, "Yes, you're right, why would we?"

So he dons his aloha shirt, I attempt a sassy if not arty look, and we restrain ourselves not to leave before 6:30 p.m., which is still early for Europeans. We saunter down our cobblestoned lane bordered by shops and restaurants to the piazza, and perch at Café Michelangelo. A wedding is imminent at the grand cathedral, we watch the precious Italian children on the steps, their lovely coiffed mothers, their handsome daddies milling about smoking, the corseted bride. A gorgeous young lady bikes by, with her four-inch stiletto heels, gracefully alights, and carries off her infant from its baby seat. Most Italians seem to be well dressed, all in precariously high heels, most smoke.

An attractive local smokes next to me; I'd cut down on cigarettes before we came, but this is when I want to smoke, along with my prosecco or red wine. I catch his eye, drooling, and he offers one. I smilingly accept. He whips it out, lights it and Robert quietly admonishes me again, saying, "Why don't you let me buy you a pack, Chu? There's a Tabac shop right over there." "I know, but I'll smoke more if I have them, Mr. Enabler." Which is what happens when I let him buy me a pack. But after this trip I *know* I will never smoke again, so I smoke 'em while I got 'em.

I have finished "Surfer Girl," and am sculpting "Joy," a woman standing with her head thrust back, her arms reaching to the sky. I am in the habit of walking around Pietrasanta in the morning for an hour, early (which means more energy to sculpt than the surf sessions or volleyball allow), and I've checked out the huge open studios of the marble sculptors. They never mind my cruising, and I feel honored to be in the midst of this creativity, this realm of beauty, awed to bear witness to their gifts, their skills. I introduce Robert to a few. One comes into the piazza and we buy him a glass of wine. We hear several different languages in this open, cosmopolitan setting, wish we at least understand and speak some Italian. One night a fun concert is scheduled with a known Italian cowboy, who charms us.

Our first weekend there we drive the mile or two down the hill to the beach. I can see the rows of endless lounge chairs roped off into clubs, the last thing we'd want to do. But wait, what's that sound? I look over and there's a volleyball bumping above the hedge, and I dart over to see what's up. To my delight I see three darling Italian men warming up, and they can play. I watch for several minutes, then venture over to ask if they have a fourth, and no, what a bummer, he didn't show up! I ask if I can play with them, as I play in Hawai'i regularly, and the one who speaks English says they play on a team in Firenze, and are as pleased as I am. They see I can play, too. Robert sits and watches us, smiling. (I momentarily have a pang I am playing, he's not, but remember all the years I watched him play rugby.) I am stoked how I lucked out, though I don't know how to score in Italian and let my partner be in charge of that. It's fast volleyball, we actually win a few games, are even with the opponents, and we laugh a lot.

Another day we're touring past a beach and I spy a large striking sculpture and ask to pull over to photograph and gaze at it. It's beautiful, the verdigris bronze men in athletic poses, and then I notice some waves, and look, there're a few surfers going out. "Oh, God, I've lost her now," Robert exclaims, "she'll want to move here and live in Pietrasanta." I laugh, watching the surfers in below average surf, am not even tempted.

When I finish "Joy," I start on "Dancing Girl," she is on one toe, the armature holding her. Another weekend we are excited to take the train to Cinque Terra, which happens to be only a few hours to the west. Robert and I are beaming as we begin the four-and-a-half-hour hike, notice it's a bit more crowded, but revel in the intoxicating beauty of the pale jade Mediterranean below, each seductively charming village. Sweat splashes off Robert though, and I am nervous, again, he'll plummet off the cliff into the sea in his low-tread tennies.

Anticipating the arrival of Kilia and Tyler, who will join us our last week in Pietrasanta, I push to finish three sculptures in three weeks, and have been working on a fourth at home that Franco will be firing in the raku fashion, not to be cast in bronze. He has taken me to the foundry he uses nearby, a large, noisy place that manifests how labor-intensive bronzing is, why it's expensive, and helps me choose the patina for each of my three pieces, which he'll ship to me later. Foundry workers jabber in Italian, gesturing excitedly, explaining to me the process, and I wish once again I knew the language of these wonderful people.

Each night we giggled, smoke cigarettes, drink wine and beers with friends or alone, and each night we totter home, me clutching Robert to steady me. I'm still giggling when we go up the stairs to our third-floor apartment, wondering if I'll have a hangover, which I never do, perhaps because there're less sulfites in the wine here. Rising early as usual, I cruise the studios of Pietrasanta, grab brie and salami for my lunch, kiss dear Robert and I'm off. I feel at home with these gesticulating, demonstrative Italians.

Finally we get the call from Ki and Ty to meet them the next morning at Vernazza, the prettiest of the villages in the Chink. We drive as far as we can, park in the place above the village, rush down to the piazza and throw our arms around gorgeous, sexy Ki and Ty. Cappucino, cackling, chattering, and then we begin the hike again, happy to show if off to the kids. They marvel at the antiquity and startling beauty, as we did, as we stop for lunch and swim, then follow them to the villa where they are staying. A Punahou pal of Kilia's lives here, has rented the most perfectly situated one overlooking Vernazza with her Italian lover, and we have drinks with them and their friends before dinner, gazing at the spectacular view. Kilia and Tyler had spent the night here and Robert and I are staying as well tonight, so the gaiety continues. Next morning, thank God, Tyler, the pilot, drives us home, as the circuitous, steep, narrow, dangerous road back has us hyperventilating when Italians race toward us.

They are contentedly ensconced in our spacious apartment with its crimson walls and peculiar art, I hike with them above Pietrasanta to Capezzano and Capriglia, they join us for wine in the piazza a couple nights before dinner at the Gato Nero, our favorite restaurant. They meet our pals but have evenings of their own alone, as they certainly did for that special opportunity in the vineyard on one of their hikes.

CHAPTER THIRTY-TWO

It's wrenching to leave Italy this time, like plucking an 'opihi off a rock, yet I know how spoiled I am when we return home to the Pacific Ocean. We go out with old pals, the Scotts, on their boat to speed along next to the canoes in the Moloka'i race, looking for Rob in the Outrigger boat. It's fun charging nearby, and we scream, "Go Rob!" over and over, hoping he hears us, though it's bedlam out there, with escort boats for each canoe and a few helicopters overhead. Robert has taken up paddling canoe himself, and he's as driven as usual to achieve excellence, realizing it takes more than just strength, now he's one of the boys paddling short races at the club. Having paddled at the Outrigger Canoe Club for a season or two, he tired of the "paddletics" and changed to the Hui Nalu Club. He loves the camaraderie, says it's not important to compete as they can take all day, then gets stoked to compete after all. An ex-football player from New England, who would've thought?

Kilia calls to say she's hāpai. I scream into the phone, this is the best news, my only daughter having a baby, at last, due June '07. Conceived in a vineyard above Pietrasanta.

I am wary to receive my bronzes from Italy, as I've been turned off to some of my work after completion, wonder why the gesture or pose doesn't work, why I didn't see it earlier. Trepidation lingers, having spent huge bucks on the bronzing and shipping, and I wonder if I'll wish that I hadn't had at least one of them cast. But I love all three of them, even the raku ceramic, and feel a sense of accomplishment, amazed how productive I was.

I plunge back into volleyball, surf a special morning with Robin, Rob, his son Ryan and daughter Hana, three generations surfing together at Suicides, not the name of a surf spot I'd be drawn to if it wasn't for the kids. It's gnarly but thrilling and we all cheer each other on the waves.

We have dinner at Olela's, she loves hearing about Pietrasanta, and lunch a few days later with her and Aunty Barbie. I always thank God for giving me Mummy and her two pals. But Aunty Barbie has had a knee replacement that isn't healing well, and she's in pain. Strangely, I cannot remember how it was disclosed, but apparently her marriage was over when she realized his infidelities. When invited to lunch the next time, it's just the two of us at her house and I remember telling her how sick and sorry I was, no histrionics, just acknowledging it, as she bravely divulges she'd asked him to leave the day before. I am moved, I love her so much and wish I could spare her this.

Rob separates from Judi, and comes to stay at our house. We think he's making the break, but after ten days he goes home. He's definitely been drinking too much, self-medicating, and Robert and I are concerned again, tell him so, a few times. He denies it.

We all go to Kaua'i to Todd and Anne's extraordinary family for Thanksgiving. Kai, Wyatt and Noa have never once had a fight around us, which is the norm, we come to realize. We rent the small house at Kalihiwai where Todd first lived in the attached studio, which has a big yard where our family plays softball with lots of screaming, laughing and carrying on. It's potluck at our house, we surf Kalihiwai, play volleyball on our mobile volleyball court we put up on the beach. It's bliss being around Robin and Reena, Kilia and Tyler, who are uncomplicated.

I have found a good foundry in L.A. and send "Ukulele Girl" that I'd done a while back, the "Surfer Girl" I'd done in Italy, cast from the mold, the recently finished "Prone Surfer Girl," and ultimately I sell them, the "Surfer Girl" (mounted on lava rock, unlike the block of Plexiglas in Italy) for thousands of dollars (which pays for our airfare to Italy), "'Ukulele Girl" was sold several times, as well as "Prone Surfer Girl." I have a showing at a local restaurant nearby that sells several, as well as one at a darling clothing store in Lanikai that does the same. The last pieces have been cast in bronze/resin, which is less expensive to produce, thus to buy. I have them in several Honolulu stores and marvel how much better my sculpture does compared to my books.

Robert organizes a family boat to compete in a canoe race in Waikīkī, is excited to have Rob, Ryan and Todd as well as two cousins paddling, and they win, which is thrilling to watch from a friend's boat, get great photos enhanced by dolphin diving around them much of the way. (Ryan graduates from high school soon afterward, is smart, handsome and going to college at Cal Maritime near San Francisco.)

I am unnerved after my recent brief visit, which turns out to be my last visit with my godmother, and Aunty Barbie seems fragile and a tiny bit confused. The words "nitty notty" came to mind, and I know now why it terrified her so when Mummy started losing it, thinking it could happen to her. She never really healed from knee surgery, never truly was mobile afterward, and the crushing blow of her marriage ending on an unpleasant note shook her. It is not long after that we are unable to see her, Olela, none of us, apparently she is weak, bedridden. And then she dies. I am consumed with sadness, unsure of the cause of death in medical terms, but I know instinctively she died from heartbreak. Not because she was so deeply in love; no, it was that he betrayed her.

Robert decided to get his license online to marry people when Kathy asked him a year before to officiate at her and Ben's wedding on Hanalei Beach, very private, just family, and Robert was wonderful. I was anxious I'd have to get "the hook" in case he rambled, but he was poignant and tender, Kathy loved it, as did I. Now Sky was marrying Brett in Santa Monica and they'd asked Robert to officiate. Kilia and Tyler were there, Ki very hāpai and happy, helping me give Sky a fun shower two days before, then their lovely garden wedding at Sky and Brett's home (which was sweet, eloquent), before the big reception at the Bel Air Bay Club.

Seeing Jimmy at these warm, family occasions, and later the Steeles at the reception, I was comfortable, giving each a peck on the cheek, "d'ere you go," and rolling smoothly away.

One door closes, another opens. Now I'm tuning into the joy of Kilia's baby with a big shower in her honor by dearest pals Patsy, Kathy, Jackie. Olela comes, is adorable and we fuss over her as much as Kilia. Another shower is given by the Frunions, who elicit shrieks when a huge purple dildo is unwrapped. Stifling giggles, I quickly distract Olela, who wouldn't have had a clue what it was but would have surely asked. I can hear Aunty Barbie cackling at the sight.

It's decided Ki will have a home birth by a dula, midwife, and I'm not thrilled, but it's arranged she will go to nearby Castle Hospital if problems arise. She tells me not to come, the dula and Tyler are enough, which is fine with me. The big event begins with mild labor for the day, escalates the second day to hard labor and we anxiously await a call, which doesn't come. (Since my babies took an hour and a half with Robin and forty-five minutes with Kilia, I'm perplexed and actually worried.) Sitting until early afternoon without news is making me crazy, so I *hele* on out to surf to distract myself, rush home after a few hours to hear from Robert that Robin has been helping her with his acupuncture, thank God, but now she wants me to come, so I hustle out to Waimānalo.

The scene startles me, does nothing to assuage my fears. Ty and Robin are taking turns talking her through labor. She is bent over with pain in the bathtub, panting, exhausted, tearful. Ty strokes her head and back. The dula whispers she has not dilated past seven or whatever. I calmly tell Ki that I'm here, that I hope she is going to deliver soon, tell her how much I love her. An hour later I hiss at the dula that she might decide to take her to the hospital NOW, what is she waiting for? It had been thirty hours of labor. Finally, a few hours later, they go. A sleepless night for us wondering when I'll hear something. Why haven't they given Kilia a caesarean? Again I vent to Robert, as usual.

I am frantic at dawn, cannot endure the waiting so I surf again, big waves, very distracting, and mid-morning I finally get the call she's had a C-section and Kawela is born. Whew. We grab flowers and food and race out to visit my weary, happy daughter and grandson. Tyler is just as exhausted, not a great way to greet their new baby, and part

Kilia and Chula, 2011

Robin and Reena's wedding, 2010

*Robin and Reena jump off the
big rock at Waimea Bay and
wade ashore afterward.*

Chula and Kawela, 2011

Chula, Linda, Annie and Kilia, 2012

Brett, Sky, Mehana and Malia, 2012

Chula surfing, 2012

*Teacher and coach Peter Cole (left) joins Punahou's Class of '62
at its 50th reunion.*

Chula's 69th birthday at home with the Volley Dollies, 2013

of me wonders why she wasn't taken to hospital sooner. When it's divulged that she couldn't dilate past eight, and I realize later that mothers have died in childbirth for this very reason, I am aghast again that she had to endure the grueling pain and exhaustion for no good reason, and in fact both she and her baby's lives were endangered.

I am grateful, ecstatic to have succulent Kawela in my life. It dawns on me how different it is for the simple fact that Ki is a daughter, and I remember Ma telling me she loved all her grandchildren but that it was different when it was her son's children. A bit of a remove compared to her daughters' kids. Also, eventually, I came to realize that it was my first "real" grandchild, though that didn't change anything. Weeks stretch out with me going there to visit precious Kawela, trying to help. Finally, I babysit him weekly at home, have him to myself.

Meanwhile, Patsy invites us to Olela's birthday at Hanalei in the Big House, with family, a few of her pals but more of her kids, Patsy and Gaylord's pals. It's a lovely, four-day celebration, loving on Olela, punctuated by a canoe paddle out in Hanalei Bay surrounded by dolphin. I resume taking her to lunch, movies, to my sculpture exhibit at a store in Lanikai.

Though I rarely surf with anyone other than family, it's easier not to make plans, just to go with the before-dawn patrol, it's delightful to surf with Reena occasionally when she's home, her string bikini defining her strong, dark little body. She graduates in a year from Colorado State University, the top veterinary college, will move home to Robin, who is glad not to keep flying back there, so far from the surf, to visit her.

But the big, bad news is in March 2008, when Aloha Airlines goes bankrupt. Suddenly, without warning, everyone is out of a job, even pensions. Tyler was about to be promoted to captain and now it's all over, for everyone. He goes through months of searching for another airline, considering Santa Barbara as an option, and the prospect saddens me. In the meantime, I love being with this active baby, already walking at eight months, running at nine. He isn't mellow, resists the car seat, backpack, stroller, he won't be confined; Kawela is not easy, but has so much personality I adore him and hold him as much as he'll let me before wiggling away. So I'm crushed when Ty's news is that he's gotten a job flying with Virgin Blue. In New Zealand.

They're happy about their upcoming adventure. I play with Kawela several times a week now, in the shallows at Kāhala Beach, in our pool, milking every moment with him before they move away. The timing isn't great, but we have plans to shoot the white water again, this time on the Colorado River, which we've hoped to do for years. So we're included with twenty Outrigger Canoe Club friends, are excited to charge the rapids on inflatable rafts. (A nice sendoff for me is an article in our newspaper with photos of Kilia and me from a few months prior, of us surfing together. It was like a follow-up of another article and photos of us a few years before, playing volleyball together, a mother-daughter twist.)

I weep farewell to Ki, Ty and BabyBoy as Robert and I take off for Santa Barbara for a few weeks before the river. It is an extraordinary adventure, all of us hiking, laughing and hanging on for the white-knuckle, bucking, ripping descent on the Colorado. We are all sea-soned water people, expect it to be easy, tame, and it's not at all, which is a huge, fun surprise. Even the buff, strong surfers and paddlers are occasionally challenged, including Robert, as a few have been thrown, and we laugh often at night over libations, each with an anecdote, though we've already laughed through much of the day.

The kicker is a storm in the distance one day, behind us, we hear the thunder, love the lightning as we paddle and pull in for the night a few hours after lunch. That night we tuck into our sleeping bags at dark, the only night we don't put up our tent. Until it pours. Oops, this was not forecast this far south and no way in hell we can set up the tent now, in the dark and the driving rain. We are all squealing, groan-ing, giggling, but dear Robert grabs tarps for us, wraps one around me like a burrito, so I fall asleep, snug and dry. The next morn I'm the first one up, as usual, sipping coffee, when I see a shoe rush down the river, then a paddle, then an empty boat. I report it quickly to our guides, as it doesn't seem to augur well. Later we discover the paddlers were stranded on a cliff during the storm, had to be helicoptered out. Turns out it was intense as far as storms go and that we were lucky to be much further down the river.

CHAPTER THIRTY-THREE

ABOUT THIS TIME COMES THE MOST HORRIFIC NEWS. Don't remember how my younger sister divulged it, but apparently she was sexually abused as a child by Daddy. I recoil from this repugnant information, cannot get my mind around it. Don't want to, and in fact initially don't really believe it. Not that Clark was incapable of the heinous act. He'd always been a perv, but does that make him a pedophile? Incestuous?

Apparently the revelation came to her, not long ago, through a sudden memory while having spiritual bodywork. I decide not to let myself dwell on it, don't want to imagine it, but I let it into my heart, feel a swelling of compassion and understanding for her. No wonder she's had health issues. I am so sorry.

Oh, my God. The realization of this travesty settles around me. I need to accept it happened, though it feels like my heart slammed shut regarding Dad. Which, of course, means it will only hurt me. Not forgiving someone only hurts yourself, as a closed heart truly blocks your energy.

I believe that at some level a partner senses when their mate is having sex elsewhere, that everything is energy, therefore the energy dynamic changes between them. If one were to become wholly conscious of their subconscious, they'd have to acknowledge it. And yet, how painfully difficult that would be on so many levels. It seems Mummy could not allow this introspection for her own reasons.

How horrible to be him, to live with himself all those years.

CHAPTER THIRTY-FOUR

I AM GOING TO VISIT BABYBOY, my daughter and son-in-law in New Zealand in September, which is their spring. They've rented an attractive big cabin with adjoining studio in the hills above Titirangi, a mile or so from the ocean. My excitement dwindles in this cool rain forest, and I struggle to remain cheerful, helping Ki. Ty is often gone for the day flying to Sydney, etc., then has to leave for several days, and the weather in the spring is not conducive to outside activities, like strolling Kawela to the beach. In fact, when the mist and chill clears, he's still unhappy in a stroller, backpack, car seat, and lets us know it. Kilia is frustrated in a foreign country with a baby and with Ty often gone, though she's found wonderful friends, even has a meeting place at a community day care where young mothers accompany their babies. Kilia and I pack up and drive to Piha, a beautiful but windswept camp spot on the ocean with Kawela, but it's even chillier there.

Kilia and I fight, don't remember what triggered it other than our own frustration in difficult circumstances, and I'm glad to leave (after two weeks) when Ty returns from studying for whatever pilot course in Brisbane. Robert and I fly again to Noozy in early December, their summer, and it's much more fun to have both our men there. And Ki is happier to get out more while we play with chatty BabyBoy, and this time the five of us camp at Piha. But it's still chilly, rainy and somehow I get bitten by what we later guess is a spider. It begins as a tiny dot, becomes gradually swollen and angry, infected, and we have it looked at by Kilia's naturopathic friend, who administers natural cures. It changes nothing, gets worse, and we go to a conventional doctor fast before we depart. She gives me antibiotics, says we should not travel, which we ignore, I'm wheeled into the airport to fly out the next day. I feel down leaving Kawela (and the kids), but the focus is on my swollen, infected leg.

Robert insists we get a second opinion the minute we get home. He looks up a doctor in the phone book. He finds an "infectious disease expert," which I scoff at, why would I need that title, someone of that ilk? And yet, we are so grateful she sees us immediately, says I need to go to hospital that second, it is probably MRSA, a dangerous staph, I could lose my leg. Really?! Hadn't heard of MRSA, but she describes how deadly it is becoming, how resistant to antibiotics we were all becoming, since they are pumped into our animals, our food. I stay three days, a drip going nonstop, which I also came home with.

I realize I dodged a bullet, exclaim to Robert over and over how much I appreciate what he did. As well as how fortunate that he chose that particular doctor out of the phone book. I can't surf for a few weeks, or play volleyball, but am thrilled when I can resume.

The tragic news of Jett Travolta's death is reported. It is stunningly sad and we are heartsick for Kelly, John and Ella. He had apparently had seizures in the past few years, which we knew, and they'd had him on drugs to help control them. They had always been devoted to Jett, it has to be shattering for them. And must have left an enormous hole in their lives. I cannot imagine how they will heal. Linda goes back to the funeral at their Florida home, I send a sculpture of a mother and babe to Kelly.

We continue basking in Olela's love at dinners in her home, which often include Gaylord and Carol, Patsy when she's not on Kaua'i, and Olela's charming brother Butter and his mate.

Robert and I return to Noozy a third time in February 2009, early fall for them, and, though it's beautiful, it's still dank and chilly occasionally, but we are delighted to be outside on many pretty, sunny days. Kawela is even chattier at a year and a half and mellow when he can run around, Ki is much happier, and the morning after we arrive she announces we must leave for Piha right away, the surf is up and it's good conditions. Robert and Tyler will take Kawela to the gym, which they've gotten in the habit of doing, so Ki and I pile their two surfboards (unused until now) in the car with snacks, and we hele on out. It's a gorgeous drive in the sun, and when we come around the bend and look over the cliff to Piha, we squeal with joy at the perfect lines of glassy waves below. It's one of the highlights of my life, the two of us paddling out to this heretofore hideously windy, wild freezing surf, which I couldn't have imagined to look like this.

The waves are a few feet overhead, there's few guys out, and we catch one after another, giggling. Because Ki calls out "Ma, don't you want to come over here closer," etc., the guys hear this, ask where we're from and, when they realize we're Hawaiian, mother and daughter, they are so cute, gracious and tell us to go for every wave. Never have we had such an uncompetitive, easy session of two hours in perfect eight-foot faces.

We take advantage of Ty's benefits to fly to Oz at a huge discount, dash off to Annie Abel-Smith's daughter and son-in-law's huge property outside of Melbourne for a few days with the three of them. We bounce around in their Jeep, checking out koala bears through miles of eucalyptus trees, go to a classic country fair complete with gigantic snakes before heading to Bondi Beach where we've booked an apartment. My dear friend Jane is there visiting her kids, so we share hilarious meals, drinks and laughter. I'd never been to Bondi, so I'm eager to borrow a board from Robin's friend here, which he's arranged, and have a few fun sessions at the famous beach. Nothing as good as Piha, though.

So what a happy surprise to return to Noozy and hear that the surf at Piha is up again, that Ki and I must go the next day for another fabulous session. The next ten days are fun-filled with Kawela while Ki and Ty have a few dates, Robert plays tennis with Ki, we go to beaches, New Zealand's fabulous parks, even to Waiheke Island on the ferry for a few nights to an oceanfront rental. Yet when we depart in the rain I confide to Robert that I will have to see them again when they come back home, I'm not keen on another long flight to the chilly rain forests of New Zealand. Thankfully they decide they've had enough (who knows what their winter will be like in a few months?) and Tyler quits piloting for Virgin Blue to return home.

Sky (Jimmy and Stephanie's daughter) and her husband, Brett, have tiny imp Malia, and their second daughter is due to be born this year in Pacific Palisades. We get to see them annually when they come for Thanksgiving, as Sky organizes our whole family to potlucks at homes Brett's rented on the North Shore. A lovely passing on of the tradition Jimmy started for us all years ago, though he does not join us at these events, unfortunately, perhaps since both his first and second wife are always with us. Also, he is rather antisocial.

One day I discover that Robert has sold my motorcycle without telling me, has replaced the 600cc Honda Shadow, 500 pounds for a 250cc Honda Rebel weighing almost half that at 320 pounds. I am indignant he took it upon himself and as I test-drive it I'm annoyed. "It feels like a fucking tuna can, Robert. It's pitiful, so light and junk, I can't believe you did that." But then after a few weeks I realize it was probably a good move, begrudgingly thank him for it, as I know it's all I really need for the short jaunts I ride now.

We go on our first "cruise" (though 140 people on a river boat on the Danube isn't what you think of when you hear the word), in October 2010 for two weeks from Amsterdam to Budapest. Fabulous, amazing meals and eighteen of our Punahou classmates make for a special, fantastic holiday. Each day we'd pull into a town or city and we could walk through Vienna (where we returned for an evening concert), Salzburg, etc. or bike along the Danube for hours, learning, laughing, eating and drinking. The following fall, 2011, just Robert and I go on a tiny cruise boat of fifty passengers for two weeks from Athens to Croatia, with divine food and stunning beauty. I weep when we pull into Montenegro at dawn, one of the most tranquil, tiny ports, flanked by steep cliffs that we later hike. A highlight is the astounding discovery in Split, Croatia of sculptor Ivan Mastrovich, who also wrote and was architect of his home on the sea for his bigger-than-life bronzes. Such a gift, so talented I am awed, standing next to each piece gazing at the persona and emotion he captured. He'd been discovered whittling wood as a sheepherder and sent to study under

Rodin. In '12 we celebrate our fortieth anniversary on the *crème de la crème* of small cruise lines, 200 people from Monte Carlo to Saint Tropez, down the Italian islands of Corsica, Sicily, etc. and up the boot of Italy to the Amalfi coast, ending in Rome. I could live that way for months of the year, eating the extravagant buffets of the most gourmet, sumptuous food I've ever had in my life and stopping in beautiful villages for spontaneous adventures, though Robert felt too pampered and decadent sometimes.

Robert's stoked to arrange another family canoe race, paddling with his sons and grandson. I had planned a surprise birthday for his seventieth, but instead he surprises us by getting sick and we cancel it. He has never been fond of celebrating his birthdays, unlike me, so no big deal.

Todd, a stern yet friendly disciplinarian VP at Kapa'a High, and Anne (who also works in a health clinic, has done bookkeeping, catering) have the busiest, fullest calendar, while continuing to be excellent parents. Their three sons excel at soccer, tennis,volleyball and surfing, get high marks in school and they're becoming such good musicians they've started their own little band. (Which all began when Kai was teensy and Robert had him plucking his guitar, then finally gave him one.) The son of their music teacher joins them doing "gigs" for birthdays, charities, even weddings on Kaua'i. Kai plays electric guitar, Wy plays bass guitar and Noa plays drums, while they all sing. They are so cute they have their own little 'groupies' of little girls watching them.

A temporary fence goes up to protect precocious BabyBoy from our little pool, yet we take him in often to swim with floaties on his arms, until he learns to swim in the shallows at Kāhala Beach by the time he's two. I am stoked to have him several times a week as he cracks me up; when he'd been talking about getting his own lawnmower for Christmas for months, but at the moment he is bratty, and I warn him Santa knows when he's naughty or nice, and he says, "Oh, oh, no' mo' lawn mowah!" And at three: when I laugh at a story he is telling to himself, he says, "No! Ignore me!" Or when I say we're joining someone nearby he says, "No, I don't want to go over there, I might growl at them." Or "No, Chu Chu, I'm *not* Lambie Lam, I'm Kawela." So I ask if I can call him "Lambie Lam" when we're at home and he says, "No, but you can call me Scrumptious."

I have to make up stories to keep my moppet still long enough to hold him, nibble his downy arms and neck. And at four I teach him a new word. Robert's not only deaf in one ear, he has started tuning me and others out occasionally, and when he doesn't hear Kawela, I tell BabyBoy to call him a deaf "mofo," which is a quaint, favorite word of mine, meaning mothafucka. So the first time he says, "Umbi, you are a deaf mofo," Robert chokes laughing, knowing he doesn't understand the word, yet, but . . .

Tyler works a year at Hawaiian Electric as an engineer, before becoming a self-employed handyman, while approaching senior pilots to help him get a job flying for Hawaiian Airlines. (I told him he should take in the photo of me with other HAL flight attendants forty-five years ago, as surely my stellar nine-month stint would impress them.) Finally he got the job, which we knew was inevitable, since he was known to be a crack pilot. Kiwi cleans houses and once again begins studying for her master's as a family therapist, having quit this path twice, when Ty chose to move from Santa Barbara to Florida for flight school, then again when Aloha Airlines went belly-up and they moved to New Zealand. (She'd announced to me my first trip to Noozy to see Kawela that he was an only child, and tears stung my eyes as I held my tongue.)

Reena returns after graduating to be a veterinarian, to all of our joy, thus we begin seeing more of her parents. Sharad and Aparna Shaw, both physicians, though Sharad is recently retired and has learned to surf, is learning to ride my motorcycle and play a guitar. A charming, unusual man, and probably the only Indian on the planet to take up these pursuits after retiring from being an emergency physician. It is out of character for most men to be so enterprising at that age, much less a thoroughly Indian man, and I attribute it partly to living in exotic Hawai'i all these years.

We adore Aparna as well, watch Robin being so proper and courteous to his accomplished future in-laws, and are tickled with the news that they will buy Reena and Robin another house. Most youths cannot imagine owning their own home in Hawai'i, yet how blessed that Robin, almost forty, and Reena not yet thirty, get to own a second home on the south shore. Wow. Robin's always been enterprising, he hasn't ever paid mortgage on his North Shore home, as he's rented out the big house and lived only in the adjoining apartment. So now they find a house in 'Āina Haina, will add on an apartment to live in, and immediately rent out the big house. They have a big pool, are on a stream and eventually put in a gazebo above it, where we perch with wine and beer, feeling like we're in the country as we gaze up the stream at the ducks, banana trees, mountains. Robin begins stand-up surfing, with a paddle, getting ready to compete in this new sport as he shapes boards for himself and others.

But the excitement in late summer 2010 is Robin and Reena's wedding. In their inimitable fashion, Reena and Robin buy a wedding dress, veil, plastic bouquet and tuxedo from Goodwill for a song (the only expense being the fresh maile lei around Robin's neck) and a photographer captures them jumping off the lava-rock cliff into Waimea Bay, grinning, with the famous surf spot in the background. This "wedding photo" is in the newspaper, but equally charming is the close-up photo of them emerging from the ocean, intact and beautiful, as if they'd indeed just married.

Ki and Ty have a lovely curry dinner (Hawaiian style) in their backyard at Waimānalo for all of the Indian family and ours. Fragrant plumeria waft over the warm evening, the stunning backdrop of the Ko'olau, the lit torches and two families joined by love. Two days later the small wedding is on the south shore at a beachside park near Niu Valley. Robert will marry them, everyone's in high spirits. Reena and her family and attendants are dressed in colorful saris adorned with flowers, Robin's in white with a bright sash and scarf, and they will dash out front to surf right after the ceremony with siblings and pals. Robert brings tears to our eyes with his simple elegance, I tear up looking at this precious lady Robin has attracted, breathe in their beauty, the sparkling ocean and brilliant blue sky behind them.

The reception with wonderful Indian food follows that evening at Sharad and Aparna's cliffside home, and the music is a surprise: Kai, Wyatt and Noa playing a variety of songs that bring tears to our eyes.

I have been seeing two Sunny Buddys weekly the past four years now that my little pal has a friend who's become her boyfriend. It's more fun now, as he laughs often, is extremely friendly and gets a kick out of my sense of humor. When I am going to deliver her home after our lunch and movie, I tease that I cannot stop when I pull over as the traffic is too heavy on Kalaniana'ole Highway, so when I slow down she will have to jump out, maybe do a tuck and roll. He thinks that's hilarious, so her brief anxiety is allayed when I start commanding for her to "be ready, I can't slow down more than twenty mph, don't forget to tuck and roll." They are in their forties, but childlike, just like me.

Robert has been mentored by an ex-'Iolani student in surfboard and canoe repair, and after a year he begins a thriving hobby/business that he operates out of our garage, as well as out of the Hui Nalu Canoe Club. It's wonderful how adept he's become learning a new craft, endearing how enthralled he is, often showing his handiwork to me as though he's Michelangelo.

Robert is still approached often by ex-students declaring he was the best teacher they'd had, and now the kids of ex-students as well.

We celebrate Olela's ninety-fourth birthday before leaving in the fall for ancient parts of Provence again. It's a long trip for just a few weeks for us, but feel intoxicated nevertheless, and we're a bit reluctant to be away from home longer. When Olela dies in December, it feels like the end of an era, we know we'll miss that precious, unique, quirky lady. And we are glad then that we came home sooner.

Sky and Brett have another angelic towhead, Mehana, who challenges their older sister, Malia, to be the center of attention.

Adorable baby Benjamin is born to the Travoltas. Kell has him when she is almost fifty years old, a miracle, really, and one they richly deserve. We are all elated for them and get to meet the precious urchin while they're on Kauaʻi, with Todd and Anne and their boys. (Arriving at their rented home we realize it's in front of the surf spot where Bethany Hamilton had her arm chewed off by a shark while surfing. Which, in itself, is amazing, since she has gone on to surf brilliantly with one arm, better than I surf with two, I realized as I watched at Hanalei surfing next to her recently.)

CHAPTER THIRTY-FIVE

IT IS NOW SUMMER 2013 and I am sixty-nine years old. A few friends have asked over the years if I'm still writing. I reply, no, I have nothing else to say. So when asked recently why don't I write a memoir, I'm still unsure I have anything to say. Is it interesting to the public when I ramble on about my classes, adventures, about our kids? The writing rule is there has to be pain, suffering or trauma to overcome in a book to engage the reader, which I am grateful not to have had thus far. But it hasn't been all sunshine either.

Our eldest son, Rob, has continued self-medicating the past few years, don't really know how long, maybe as far back as the realization his marriage was troubled. Or longer. It turns out Judi's complaints were more on target than we knew. When someone cries wolf too often, it tends to be treated like "white noise" and ignored. I've loved Judi, but began tuning her out eventually. Instead of getting marriage counseling, perhaps Rob did, too, as he'd been drinking way too much, yet none of the rest of us could tell. He was more powerful and fit than Robert and yet his "hollow" leg was full. He was addicted, and though we all realized it was problematic, it was easy to see how we hadn't known it to be true. He was still a fine, busy chiropractor, as several contented clients have told us, still paddling, surfing, working out daily, still doing a huge share of domestic duties, plus being a hands-on dad. He also always seemed robust and happy, as well as engaging with all his stories.

So after he left Judi four or five years ago, they separated a few more times. I was conflicted when he came to stay with us again, not wanting to enable him nor be involved, so when he didn't make the time to find his own place, I insisted he do so after two weeks. Lucky to stay in available apartments for another year and a half, he found the right place for himself a few months ago, then began divorce proceedings. And hopefully he's committed to healing himself. He knows I love him unconditionally, from a distance, will no longer listen to his denial or lies. And it really is not my *kuleana* (business, responsibility).

I definitely feel Robert enabled him as a youth (as he did the others, though, somehow, they weren't affected negatively), which can be crippling emotionally as maturity is stifled later, and we saw Rob enabling his daughters and wife. (Ryan had summer jobs in high school, just as his dad Rob and brothers did.) Though Judi worked occasionally in fashion or in Rob's clinic, we wondered why he didn't insist she work full time years ago as debts accrued. The girls weren't often idle, as both did babysitting, Hana made crafts, but they didn't get actual jobs and were quite dependent on their parents.

Beautiful Hana lived through the deception of a troubled marriage and an alcoholic father. Though she'd been a powerful, sponsored surfer rivaling the best in her age group in Hawai'i, she had pulled out of competitive surfing recently as she was no longer enthused. Sadly, she became severely anorexic in a matter of months. Robert and I had, months prior to this, voiced it'd be best she go away to college, be on her own, become independent. And lately she'd been working at a full-time job, yet felt no inclination to leave. I guess it was natural for an eighteen-year-old to hover nearby while her parents floundered. So it was a conundrum, we held our tongues, but now, when she was alarmingly thin (and would not get therapy), she seemed fed up with the scene, so left for work and school in California. This scared hell out of me, knowing the dangers of being so anorexic. I felt she should go to a clinic. But that didn't happen and, after almost two years, Hana is thankfully getting healthier. Ryan has graduated as an engineer, has a fabulous, salaried job working on the UCLA campus. Hailey just graduated from La Pietra with good grades (and is still a darling Walt Disney character), sponsored as a top stand-up paddler, a different sport from stand-up surfing, as it's racing on flat water.

Todd is still a masterful vice principal at Kapa'a High, has limited time to surf or play volleyball when he's not parenting, driving his three sons to several games a day, or homemaking. Anne has begun her own business as the Kauaʻi Concierge, and they blend careers and children beautifully. Kai excels as a sophomore at Kapaʻa High, is quietly focused on his sports and their band, which is becoming sought after. Wyatt is outgoing, read a thousand-page book (*Shantaram*) while finishing his last quarter in the ninth grade, is a jock as well, and a serious music afficionado. Noa is a lighthearted child who laughs constantly, also amazing at sports, school, and the drums. They live a healthy, outdoor lifestyle in the country, are the epitome of a loving family. They are such an extraordinary family, the children are so oft-admired, that Robin's comment, "When Reena and I have a baby, we want Anne and Todd to raise it," is a typical observation.

Robin has had exciting success as a top competitor on the Stand Up World Tour of stand-up paddlesurfing the past three years, to the envy of friends and siblings. Traveling every three or four months to Brazil, Tahiti, the Caribbean, France, California and elsewhere, as well as Sunset Beach on Oʻahu and the Big Island, he is sponsored and sells his boards shaped just for the sport. And though he missed a ranking of No. 1 in the world by half a point at Sunset the first year behind a twenty-year-old when he was forty, now, at forty-three, he's remained No. 2, on and off, for the three years the World Tour has existed. It seems apparent it'll be a while before my son and daughter-in-law conceive, as he loves his career and Reena loves hers. Occasionally she'll join him on a surf jaunt if she desires, but usually she's content at home working and with her pals.

For years I would say that Reena would rather have puppies than babies, caring greatly for animals and not being drawn to babies at all (just as Mia wasn't when she got hāpai, having had a popular dog store in Ketchum as well as five dogs in her home at all times in Santa Barbara and, when she called in tears, I talked her through it, reassuring her it would change when the babies were born to her and Matt, which it certainly has). So, after six years of dating, almost three of marriage, Reena and Robin are finally off to Africa for their honeymoon in March, tied into his next contest in Brazil.

Now, to our joy and amazement, they call from Africa to say they are hāpai. Again I shriek at this surprise, which is due the end of this year. And they are having a girl, the first for us after four grandsons. I can hardly wait.

Kilia has recently gotten her master's in marriage and family therapy, which is fulfilling for her and makes us proud that she persevered, knowing she will make an excellent therapist. Another healer in the family. Tyler has begun his third year as a HAL pilot, and they've had free trips to surf in Oz, Tahiti, back to Vermont, and elsewhere, one of the perks. Kawela is fun and as active as ever, so is harder to keep up with. If I know he's coming under my watch that afternoon, I have to curtail my three-hour session surfing in order to have the energy to keep up. Or if I have an exciting, tough match playing volleyball the other three days of the week with Kilia and other younger wāhine, I ask Umbi for help.

I lost interest in sculpting almost two years ago. The inspiration and desire had ebbed. Which actually saddened me, as I missed the creativity. My sculptures are in four or five stores still, but I was never as productive before that month in Pietrasanta or since. I am extremely low-tech, hate computers, and when I sculpted in my upstairs studio and Robert might come up to go online next to me, I would actually feel sorry for him. And yet here I am, on my computer the past six months, writing this. One door closes, another opens.

I have massages weekly, knowing it moves any stuck energy in the body and keeps me supple, and I do yoga less than I should to keep me limber. I can't remember when I got sick last, maybe seven or eight years ago I had the flu. I play volleyball three times a week and surf the other mornings before dawn, when there's less wind and surfers. And I feel I am better than I've ever been now, in both sports.

Paddling out at 5 a.m. on a malia morning recently way before dawn, under a silver disc of a full moon, a quiet joy blooms and billows through me; I am one with the ocean. (Not the same way when, years back, I sometimes felt so much one with the waves, I almost seem incapable of separating myself in order to stand and ride them. Not so all-encompassing.) Silver illumines the ocean now as I check out the landmarks to decide if I'm in the lineup as nobody else is out yet. A shape emerges and though the moonlight edges every ripple, I'm surprised how little I can discern the height and depth of the wave as I paddle for it; it's bigger than it seemed and I'm taking a faster drop than expected as I swoop down a face before it breaks. The rush is magic. A bit spooky though, being out here alone for too long, and I'm glad to see another surfer as I paddle back out, making the odds fifty percent better. I cannot imagine life without this scene, and know I must stay as agile and strong as I am now at almost seventy. Why not?

Last year was our fiftieth reunion at Punahou. A fun week, though I see local classmates like Patsy, Jackie, Wendy, Terry, Honeybun, Paddy, Hilary, Annie, Laura and others with regularity, as we've had mini reunions on our own over the years at Hāna, Maui, Hanalei and Mālaekahana. All of us babes are vigorous, healthy and, of course, fitter than most of the guys. (Not as easy to hug, laugh, vent feelings for men as it is for us.) I've always been big on venting, spewing out the frustration and anger, and Robert has gotten good at that, too. Hopefully that helps break the cycle of cancer in his family.

Robert is still powerful, fit and handsome, but lost his hair years ago. He could care less, but I am shallow enough to want more of it on his head, take a bit from that studly chest, and so when he comes home with his head shaved, as he prefers it now, I am dismayed. "Well, you'll have to put a bag on your head when we make love," I say to his laughter.

Child and Family Services has progressed, with new rules about the kids "aging out" of the system. After eighteen years old, they will continue to be helped financially, a crucial aspect at that point in their lives.

I still believe one hundred percent in the value of my class, still hope somehow perhaps Oprah will get her hands on this book, arrange it so I could teach it to teachers. As basic and simple as the premise of love and fear is, nowhere is it taught! And, of course, though it's a simple premise, it is not easy to learn as one ages, so it would be assimilated easier by children, to learn that they are choosing fear when acting or feeling negatively. Certainly I am still learning from it, as I forget or choose not to be loving. I know that I chose to be me, but I strive to choose to be a calmer, more loving me. But I still answer when asked, "How are you?" with one word: happy! (which I feel I've been most of my life).

It truly amazes me how society accepts fear in so many venues. Religions separate and divide us from each other and God with fear, and I think most religions are fear-based. Wars are completely waged on fear, which is, of course, what power, control and greed come from. Politics is riddled with fear, even Obama has been sucked in. Health care and its terms are fear-based. ("Fighting" cancer, instead of loving oneself into health and healing.) The media (including movies) are driven by fear to attract an audience. Even schools are often based on fear, the grading concept being an indicator of failing or not; the way authority isn't challenged. New technology is spawning fear by allowing children (as well as adults) to be so connected they are disconnecting from each other.

It is heartening though to hear again about the "Indigo Children" (who I first heard about fourteen years ago in Cancun, at a spiritual workshop) now numbering more than a million, who are so astonishingly psychic, and another group of children who apparently are unable to get sick, and that their consciousness is transmitting mind to mind, like the hundredth monkey phenomenon, even changing their DNA in the process.

"The field of epigenetics refers to the science that studies how the development, functioning and evolution of biological systems are influenced by forces operating outside the DNA sequence, including intracellular, environmental and energetic influences."

The Institute of HeartMath deems integral elements of the model for who we are and what we can be are the thoughts, feelings and intentions we have every day. After two decades of studies, HeartMath researches say other factors such as the appreciation and love we have for someone or the anger and anxiety we feel also influence and alter the outcomes of each individual's DNA blueprint.

Stem-cell biologist Bruce Lipton, Ph.D., says the distinction between genetic determinism and epigenetics is important.

"The difference between these two is significant because this fundamental belief called genetic determinism literally means that our lives, which are defined as our physical, physiological and motional behavioral traits are controlled by the genetic code," Lipton said. "This kind of belief system provides a visual picture of people being victims. If the genes control our life function, then our lives are being controlled by things outside of our ability to change them. This leads to victimization that the illnesses and diseases that run in families are propagated through the passing of genes associated with these attributes. Laboratory evidence shows this is not true."

This is evidence, for me, of not only genetics not ruling us, but also how illness and dis-ease does not just "happen" to us, we are creating ourselves, moment to moment.

After forty-two years, Robert and I are still deeply in love. He is my best friend. He's more Hawaiian than I am, in the truest essence of the word, so giving and generous of spirit. I'd always heard marriage is work and never believed it, but since he has retired and is contentedly immersed in his craft, he is acting like the boy he stopped being too soon in his youth, when he became the big, strong, responsible college guy and new father at twenty-one. I'm glad for him, except he forgets and becomes unconscious of simple things as my mate, like looking right into my eyes and tuning out what I'm saying. I'm not always a chatterbox, preferring long periods of silence, doing my own thing, leaving before he wakes up to surf before dawn and so forth. So I ask the "brain surgeon" or "rocket scientist" or whatever intense job he's focused on at that moment, to stop rushing into his next project, stay in the moment, be more conscious. And it's not just me he's tuning out. I watch him with our kids, friends, and he'd never have done this when he was working as a teacher, so I blame retirement. He's trying, as he hates it when I get angry, and I know I need to learn patience through this. Realize it's teaching me also to stay in the now, as I don't like the harridan I can be with him.

If he wasn't so kind, smart, funny, patient, earnest, sexy and good-looking, I might become a lesbian in the next few years, move to Italy, or become mute in our marriage. I am even wondering if I should take a refresher course in sign language for the deaf mofo.

Meanwhile, I just surfed one of the epic waves of my life in the recent south swell here on O'ahu, charging left on a nine- to ten-foot, glassy face for what felt like minutes, reminding me of the high a few years back when I surfed during the tsunami warning while everyone was evacuating, so only a few guys were out, the conditions were perfect, and the waves were three or four feet overhead.

Talk about love and beauty!

Good from Far, Far from Good

ABOUT THE AUTHOR

Chula still surfs and plays volleyball daily in beautiful Hawai'i, in the same home where she's lived for forty-two years with her husband, Robert, and the termites. She has her four grown children and seven grandchildren nearby, and is happily anticipating the eighth by the end of the year, right before she turns seventy. She counts her blessings and is open to teaching her class to teachers—passing the torch!

Good from Far, Far from Good